MARGARETE SEIDENSPINNER
Volkswirtschaft: Übersetzungsübungen
Fachsprache Englisch

Cornelsen
& OXFORD

studium kompakt Fachsprache Englisch

Volkswirtschaft: Übersetzungsübungen

Die Hochschulreihe studium kompakt Fachsprache Englisch wurde von den Verfasserinnen und Verfassern in Zusammenarbeit mit der Verlagsredaktion entwickelt.

Verfasserin:	Prof. Dr. Margarete Seidenspinner
Verlagsredaktion:	Dr. Blanca-Maria Rudhart
Layout:	Gisela Hoffmann
Technische Umsetzung:	Sabine Theuring
Umschlagsgestaltung:	Bauer + Möhring grafikdesign, Berlin

Die Deutsche Bibliothek – CIP-Einheitsaufnahme:
Seidenspinner, Margarete:
studium kompakt Fachsprache Englisch:
Volkswirtschaft: Übersetzungsübungen/Margarete Seidenspinner. –
  1. Aufl. – Berlin: Cornelsen & Oxford University Press GmbH & Co., 2002
  ISBN 3-8109-3120-9

 http://www.cornelsen-teachweb.de

1. Auflage
5   4   3   2   1   Die letzten Ziffern bezeichnen Zahl
06 05 04 03 02 und Jahr des Druckes.

© 2002 Cornelsen & Oxford University Press GmbH & Co., Berlin
Das Werk und seine Teile sind urheberrechtlich geschützt.
Jede Verwertung in anderen als den gesetzlich zugelassenen Fällen
bedarf deshalb der vorherigen schriftlichen Einwilligung des Verlages.

Gesamtherstellung: Druckerei zu Altenburg

Bestellnummer 31209

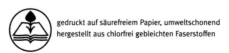

Contents

Introduction   5

I   Unemployment in Germany   9
I.1   Text: Die Bekämpfung der Arbeitslosigkeit
I.2   Sample translation
I.3   Exercises

II   The East German Labour Market   33
II.1   Text: Der ostdeutsche Arbeitsmarkt nach dem „Transformationsschock"
II.2   Sample translation
II.3   Exercises

III   Supply and Demand   51
III.1   Text: Der Verlauf von Angebots- und Nachfragekurven
III.2   Sample translation
III.3   Exercises

IV   Price Determinants   71
IV.1   Text: Die Entwicklung der Energiepreise
IV.2   Sample translation
IV.3   Exercises

V   Business Cycles   85
V.1   Text: „Pro" und „contra" Konjunkturprogramm: Muss der Staat helfen?
V.2   Sample translation
V.3   Exercises

VI   The European Union   105
VI.1   Text: Der lange Weg zu einer gemeinsamen europäischen Währung
VI.2   Sample translation
VI.3   Exercises

VII	**The Dollar and the Euro**	119
VII.1	Text: Technische Analysen	
VII.2	Sample translation	
VII.3	Exercises	
VIII	**The Federal Reserve System**	135
VIII.1	Text: Die Zentralbank der Vereinigten Staaten	
VIII.2	Sample translation	
VIII.3	Exercises	
IX	**A New Economic World Order**	153
IX.1	Text: Die politische Aufgabe des IWF	
IX.2	Sample translation	
IX.3	Exercises	
X	**The World Debt Crisis**	171
X.1	Text: Schuldenerlass für die Ärmsten der Armen	
X.2	Sample translation	
X.3	Exercises	
	Appendix	189
	Key	
	Glossary	
	Reference & Further Reading	
	Index	

Preface

Modern languages and economic theory have a number of features in common. Both represent intricate systems in themselves and strive to come to terms with complex environments. 'Structural economy', for instance, is an inherent principle of natural languages, a principle which, at times, seems to be at cross purposes with the infinite semantic creativity, another innate quality of languages, which has enriched ordinary and specific language usage.

Contemporary English has engendered terms which graphically depict the idiosyncracies of our 'digital' age. Thus, it has come up with the 'telecommuter' who works from the seclusion of his 'electronic cottage' or leads a life 'in the fast lane'. It has presented us with the blunt images of 'ecocide' and 'money laundering'. Politicians, journalists and economists are inclined to resort to euphemisms and will speak of 'lay-offs' and 'displacements' rather than of 'dismissals'. On the other hand, there is just as much that divides the economist from the linguist. Economists are used to working with precise, narrowly defined terms that are deeply rooted in academic traditions. They deduce and make forecasts on the basis of assumptions that may not extend to the everyday pragmatism of natural languages which thrive on idiomatic diversity, multi-layered implications and figurative ornament.

This volume therefore attempts to meet a tall order by converting the contents and structures of one specific area into another one, a task that regularly defies the translator's best efforts. There are numerous examples where a commonly used term in one language proves to be inconvertible as the target language offers no equivalent because its own economic background does not require it. This is the case, for instance, with the historically grown remuneration systems in Germany and the UK: there are no 'minimum wages' in Germany just as there is no *Tarifautonomie* in Anglo-Saxon economies.

Natural languages are characterised by polysemy and multiple functionality which makes the task of mastering them all the more challenging. Bearing this in mind, the current volume *Volkswirtschaft: Übersetzungsübungen*, like its predecessor *Betriebswirtschaft: Übersetzungsübungen*, seeks to increase the language awareness of the economist as well as the ESP-proficiency of the language student

It comprises ten chapters, each divided into three distinct parts
- firstly, the original text which focuses on subjects of current interest, such as the World Debt Crisis, the role of the Federal Reserve System or unemployment,
- secondly, comprehensive notes which highlight ESP-areas and common linguistic errors,
- and thirdly, exercises that have been designed to encourage the application of English language patterns and to enhance idiomatic usage.

Some of the exercises focus extensively on the interpretation and presentation of graphs, diagrams and models as these are an economist's staple diet and in many cases a source of linguistic errors. The volume investigates ESP-terminology within the context from which it originates. It has been guided by pragmatism rather than doctrine, attempting to offer methods rather than methodology. It is mainly intended
- for students of interdisciplinary university courses that combine economic, intercultural and language modules,
- for professional people aiming to improve their competence in the above-mentioned areas,
- for teachers of economics who deliver their lectures in English.

It is suitable for autonomous learning and self-tuition and for any person who takes an interest in the profundities of Economics as well as the linguistic pitfalls involved in cross-cultural communication.

Margarete Seidenspinner

Authors

Prof. Dr. Margarete Seidenspinner (M.B.A.), who was in overall charge of this project, has obtained degrees in Educational Studies, American Language and Literature as well as Business Studies from German and British universities. She has taught at London University and the University of the Witwatersrand in Johannesburg and currently holds a tenure at the Fachhochschule Heilbronn where she reads Intercultural Studies and International Management.

Prof. Dr. Renate Neubäumer, is a 'dyed in the wool' economist who lectures in Economics at the Akademie der Arbeit in der Universität Frankfurt am Main. She has published numerous works on Economics and has meticulously revised the subject-related contents of this volume as well as some of the texts for the translations.

Paul Cooper, B.A. (hons) is one of the Managing Directors of KCC Language Consulting GmbH, Mannheim, a company that advises well-known global corporations on linguistic and intercultural issues.

I Unemployment in Germany

I.1	**Text: Die Bekämpfung der Arbeitslosigkeit**	10
I.2	**Sample translation**	12
I.2.1	Notes on the translation	
I.3	**Exercises**	29
I.3.1	Employment and pay	
I.3.2	Collective agreements and new forms of employment	
I.3.3	Redundancies and dismissals	

1.1 Text: Die Bekämpfung der Arbeitslosigkeit

I Unemployment in Germany

Im Jahr 2000 waren in der Bundesrepublik 3,9 Mio. Menschen ohne Arbeit. Die Anzahl der offenen Stellen betrug 514.000, sodass – wenn man berücksichtigt, dass nur etwa jede zweite offene Stelle beim Arbeitsamt gemeldet wird – auf jeden freien Arbeitsplatz etwa vier Bewerber kamen. Während weitgehend Einigkeit darüber besteht, dass gegen die hohe Arbeitslosigkeit etwas getan werden muss, ist stark umstritten, welche Maßnahmen zur Bekämpfung der Unterbeschäftigung geeignet sind.

- So fordert die Mehrheit der „Fünf Weisen" des „Sachverständigenrates zur Begutachtung der gesamtwirtschaftlichen Entwicklung" eine Fortsetzung der moderaten Lohnpolitik: „Die realen Lohnsteigerungen (müssen) hinter der Produktivitätszunahme zurück-

(The Guardian, 29 April 2000, p. 3)

Has early retirement been pensioned off?

bleiben. Nur dann besteht die Aussicht, dass Arbeitslosigkeit in Beschäftigung umgewandelt wird".[1] Dagegen befürwortet ein Mitglied des Rates eine inflations- und verteilungsneutrale Lohnpolitik. Realeinkommen sollten nicht schwächer – und auch nicht stärker – steigen, als es der Produktivitätsfortschritt vorgibt; andernfalls würde eine zu schwache Kaufkraft die Nachfrage nach Konsumgütern und somit deren Absatzmöglichkeiten beeinträchtigen.

- Zudem tritt der Sachverständigenrat für eine deutlichere Differenzierung der Lohnstruktur ein, d. h., die Arbeitseinkommen sollten insbesondere zwischen Unternehmen derselben Branche mit unterschiedlicher Gewinnsituation, zwischen Regionen mit unterschiedlich hohen Arbeitslosenquoten und zwischen Arbeitnehmerinnen und Arbeitnehmern mit niedriger und hoher beruflicher Qualifikation stärker differieren. Außerdem sollte es niedrigere Einstiegslöhne für (Langzeit-) Arbeitslose geben.
- Vor allem aber verlangt eine Reihe von Wirtschaftswissenschaftlern eine Deregulierung des deutschen Arbeitsmarktes, die den Betrieben mehr Spielraum bei der Einstellung, dem Einsatz und der Kündigung von Arbeitnehmern lässt. Insbesondere Leiharbeit und befristete Beschäftigung sollten ausgebaut und starre gesetzliche Kündigungsschutzregelungen gelockert werden. Die Tarifparteien sollten sich über eine stärkere Flexibilisierung der Wochen- und Jahresarbeitszeit einigen.
- Andere Arbeitsmarktökonomen sehen die Ausweitung der Teilzeitbeschäftigung – nicht nur für Frauen, sondern auch für Männer – als einen Ansatzpunkt für mehr Arbeitsplätze: dies hat die Bundesregierung mit der Verabschiedung eines gesetzlichen Anspruchs auf Teilzeitarbeit aufgegriffen.
- Schließlich setzen sich die Gewerkschaften für den Abbau der hohen Überstundenzahl ein. Sie sehen dies auch als Solidaritätsbeitrag der (abhängig) Beschäftigten gegenüber den Arbeitslosen. Allerdings wären von einer Reduzierung der bezahlten Überstunden meist nur Facharbeiter und mittelqualifizierte Angestellte betroffen, denn einfache Arbeiter/innen und Angestellte machen selten Überstunden, und höher qualifizierten Angestellten werden die Überstunden nicht extra entgolten.

(Renate Neubäumer)

---

[1] Jahresgutachten des Sachverständigenrates zur Begutachtung der gesamtwirtschaftlichen Entwicklung 2001/02, Ziffer 399.

I.2 Sample translation

Combating[1] **unemployment**

In the year 2000, 3.9 million people **were out of work**[2] in the Federal Republic of Germany, whereas **the number of jobs to be filled**[3] **amounted to**[4] 514,000: **that is to say**[5] there were four applicants **for each job opening**[6] **if it is taken into account**[7] that **roughly only one out of two vacancies**[8] **is reported to**[9] the employment exchange[10].

Although there is a general consensus about the fact[11] that something has to be done about **the high unemployment figure**[12], the measures considered appropriate to fight underemployment **are fiercely disputed**[13].

- **Thus**[14], the majority of the five 'wise men' **of the 'German Council of Economic Experts'**[15] demand that a moderate **pay policy**[16] be pursued[17]: 'The increases in real pay[18] must take second place to productivity gains[19]. Only this can be expected to transform unemployment into employment.' **In contrast to this**[20], one member of the Council of Experts **advocates**[21] **a pay policy which is neutral in terms of inflation and income distribution**[22]. Real incomes **should neither adopt a slower nor a quicker pace than the one set by the growth in productivity**[23], otherwise **too low a**[24] **purchasing power**[25] would **weaken**[26] the demand for **consumer goods**[27] and, **consequently**[28], their **sales potential**[29].

- In addition, the Council of Experts **supports**[30] a **greater**[31] differentiation **in pay patterns**[32]; in other words, **earned incomes**[33] ought to differ more substantially between corporations **belonging to the same industrial sector but to different profit brackets**[34], between regions **that have**[35] different unemployment rates and between employees with higher or lower qualifications. Moreover, there ought to be lower **starting wages**[36] for the (long-term) unemployed.

- However, a number of **economists**[37] demand, first and foremost, that the German labour market be deregulated[38] **as this would give companies more leeway**[39] with regard to **recruitment, utilization**[40] **and dismissal**[41] of employees. **Loan employment**[42] and limited employment contracts, in particular, **should be extended**[43] and **rigid**[44] legal **employment protection regulations**[45] should be relaxed[46]. **The parties involved in collective bargaining**[47] ought to **agree to greater flexibility regarding weekly and annual working hours**[48].

- Other labour market economists see **a larger degree of**[49] part time employment – not only for women but also for men – **as a first step towards the creation of more jobs**[50]; and **the Federal Government has taken up this suggestion**[51] by making legal provision for the right to pursue part-time employment[52].

- **Last but not least**[53], **the trades unions are committed to reducing the high number of overtime hours**[54]. They also consider this to be an act of solidarity on the part of **wage and salary earners**[55] towards the unemployed. However, a reduction of paid overtime would, **for the most part**[56], affect **skilled workers**[57] and semi-qualified **salaried employees**[58], as **ordinary workers**[59] and white-collar workers hardly ever work overtime and the more highly qualified employees **are not awarded extra overtime pay**[60].

2.1 Notes on the translation

[1] *die Bekämpfung:* combating; tackling; fighting

[2] *waren ... ohne Arbeit:* were out of work; were unemployed; were without employment

Further relevant collocations with 'unemployment'
to avert: *abwenden*
to stave off/to keep ... at bay: *fernhalten*
to contain: *eindämmen*
to check: *aufhalten*
to keep in check: *unter Kontrolle halten*

[3] *die Anzahl der offenen Stellen:* the number of jobs to be filled; the number of vacancies/vacant positions

Alternative translation
the positions to be filled numbered/totalled ...

> 'Number' is a highly idiomatic noun and verb. The noun can be abbreviated as No. or, especially in US documents, as #.
> 'Number' generally signifies
> - an amount of units
> - a sum of units; a total
> - a large quantity; a group; a collection
> - a numeral type
> - one item of a numbered series
> - a single part of a programme; a piece of music
> - an issue of a magazine
> - a grammatical form indicating singular or plural

← Please note

Some usage examples
The number of students *(Anzahl an Studierenden)* in the final year is currently sixty.
'Three' is a cardinal number *(Kardinalzahl)*; 'third' an ordinal number *(Ordnungszahl)*.

'7', '11', and '13' are prime numbers *(Primzahlen)*.
A 'compound number' *(zusammengesetzte Zahhl)* is a quantity expressed in two or more units or denominations, e.g. 5ft 8in; 2 kg, 30 min.
The project had to be completed for a number of *(eine Reihe von)* reasons.
A large number *(Großteil)* of the world's population is illiterate.
What is your ID number *(Personalausweisnummer)*?
This number *(Ausgabe)* of the New York Times was sold out within hours.
Can you remember the licence number of the car *(Autokennzeichen)*?
Please put the following words in their plural number *(Plural)*.
You must have got the wrong number. *Sie haben sich sicher verwählt.*

Idiomatic/colloquial usage
He's got himself 'a cushy little number' in this company. *Er schiebt eine ruhige Kugel in dieser Firma.*
Your days are numbered. *Deine Tage sind gezählt.*
'Number cruncher' *(Zahlendrescher)* is a moniker for financial analysts, accountants, researchers and pollsters, etc. who perform complex calculations and sometimes tend to exaggerate the importance of numerical data.

Please note →

> 'Number' and 'figure' are not synonymous. The basic difference between these two terms can be illustrated thus:
> A Politicians are worried about the high number of *(hohe Anzahl an)* unemployed people.
> B 10 million is a relatively high unemployment figure *(Arbeitslosenzahl)*.
> Message A focuses on the 'people' without work, whereas B refers to the numerical quantity of 10 million.
>
> ### 'Figure' signifies essentially
> - a symbol for a number: e.g. 1, 2, 3, 4
> - a value, an amount, an estimate given in figures
> - a shape or form
> - a character or personality

Usage examples
Last month's sales figures *(Verkaufserlös/Verkaufszahlen)* exceeded the target by 20 per cent/percent [US].

In terms of managerial salaries, € 500,000 is a relatively moderate figure *(Summe/Betrag)*.
This young lady 'has got a good head for figures' *(kann gut mit Zahlen umgehen)*.
His figure *(Wertangabe/verlangter Preis)* for that house is very high.
'Cubes' *(Würfel)* and 'spheres' *(Kugeln)* are geometrical figures *(Figuren)*.
The cloud had the figure *(Gestalt)* of a dragon.
Karl Marx is a well-known figure *(Persönlichkeit)* in politics and economics.
Hamlet is the most enigmatic figure *(Charakter)* in Shakespeare.
She is the figure *(Ebenbild)* of perfection.
Science books use figures *(Abbildungen)* for explanation purposes.
figure-skating: *Eiskunstlaufen*

⁴ *betrug:* amounted to; totalled

> The intransitive verb 'to amount to' *(sich belaufen auf, betragen)* can be rephrased as 'to come to', 'to total' and 'to add up to'.

← Please note

Example
The damages paid out after the blizzard amounted to/totalled *(beliefen sich insgesamt auf)* three million pounds (£3m).

> Do not confuse 'to amount to' *(sich belaufen auf; betragen)* with 'to account for' *(ausmachen; betragen)* cf. V.2.1 Notes on the translation, item ⁵⁴.

← Please note

⁵ *sodass:* that is to say; in other words; that means
⁶ *auf jeden freien Arbeitsplatz:* for each job opening; for each job/position to be filled; for each vacancy

> *Arbeitsplatz* is a polysemous noun. Literally it means 'place of work'/'workplace' but mostly it is a metonym for 'job'.
> These two lexical items form separate semantic entities. In the above case, it is the 'jobs' which are lost, not the 'places' where people work.

← Please note

⁷ *wenn man berücksichtigt:* if it is taken into account; if due consideration is given to the fact (that)
⁸ *nur etwa jede zweite offene Stelle:* roughly only one out of two vacancies; approximately only every other/second vacancy

⁹ *gemeldet wird:* is reported to; is made known to; is registered with

¹⁰ b*eim Arbeitsamt:* the employment exchange; the labor exchange [US]; the (local) employment agency/job centre/employment office

¹¹ *während weitgehend Einigkeit darüber besteht:* although there is a general consensus about the fact; whereas there is broad agreement with regard to

Please note →

> Depending on the context, the prepositions connected to 'agreement' vary; and so does the translation of this noun into German.

Examples
In some countries, there seems to be no agreement about/as to shop opening hours. *In manchen Ländern scheint es keine Einigung/keinen Konsens zu den Ladenöffnungszeiten zu geben.*
The agreement between the two contracting parties was signed last week. *Die Vereinbarung zwischen den beiden Vertragsparteien wurde letzte Woche unterzeichnet.*
We would welcome your agreement to the proposal made by our company. *Wir würden Ihre Zustimmung zu dem Vorschlag unseres Unternehmens begrüßen.*
The agreement reached on the last item was minuted. *Die zum letzten Punkt erzielte Übereinkunft wurde protokolliert.*
For further usage examples and details on the collocations of 'agreement' and 'agree' see: J. Bauer, M. Seidenspinner, *Betriebswirtschaft: Übersetzungsübungen, studium kompakt Fachsprache Englisch*, Cornelsen & Oxford, Berlin, 2001, p. 59

¹² *die hohe Arbeitslosigkeit:* the high unemployment figure; the high level of unemployment; high unemployment

¹³ *ist stark umstritten, welche Maßnahmen ... geeignet sind:* the measures considered appropriate ... are fiercely disputed; the measures perceived as suitable ... are severely disputed

¹⁴ *so:* thus; hence; therefore

An alternative translation would be
'The majority of the 'five wise men', for instance, ... demand that ...

Please note →

> 'So' – in English (and in German) – can figure as an adverb, an apposition, a conjunction or an interjection. The most frequently used synonyms of 'so' are 'thus', 'therefore', 'hence', 'in this way' and 'accordingly'.

Usage examples
Products so/thus diversified attract more buyers. Products diversified in this way attract more buyers. *Produkte, die so/auf diese Weise diversifiziert wurden, bringen mehr Kunden.*
Thus/hence, the majority of the 'five wise men' ... demand ... *Also/dem entsprechend/dem gemäß verlangt die Mehrheit der "Fünf Weisen"* ...
By behaving in this manner, he raised a lot of eyebrows. *Indem er sich so/auf diese Art und Weise verhielt, erregte er einigen Anstoß.*
The adverb 'so' signifies 'to such a degree' and 'very':
He spoke so fast... *Er redete derart schnell* ...
You are so (very) kind. *Sie sind wirklich (sehr) freundlich.*
His clients were so/very shocked! *Die Kunden waren echt schockiert.*
The connectors 'so' and 'therefore' join a clause expressing a result to the main sentence:
The case was lost, so/therefore we gave it up. *Der Fall war verloren, also gaben wir ihn auf.*
He wanted to act, and so/therefore he did. *Er wollte handeln und tat es auch.*
The library is closed. So/that is why you cannot take out any books on loan. *Die Bibliothek ist geschlossen. Deshalb/also kannst du keine Bücher ausleihen.*
The conjunction 'so that' points out an intended consequence:
They lowered the interest rates so that/in order that loans would be cheaper. *Sie senkten die Zinssätze, um die Kredite billiger zu machen.*
'And so ... do/does' draw a parallel:
Most students dislike statistics and so do ours. *Die meisten Studierenden – auch unsere – haben eine Abneigung gegen Statistik.*
As an interjection 'so' covers a number of semantic varieties:
So/Well! You failed the test again! *Du hast die Prüfung also wieder nicht bestanden!*
The customer is unhappy. So!/So what! *Der Kunde ist nicht glücklich. Na und!*

[15] *des Sachverständigenrates zur Begutachtung der gesamtwirtschaftlichen Entwicklung:* of the German Council of Economic Experts

> The 'German Council of Economic Experts' *(Sachverständigenrat)* is an independent five-member body which has advised the German Government and Parliament on economic policy since 1963. It assesses the overall economic development in the Federal Republic and assists 'economic policy makers' *(wirtschaftspolitische Entscheidungsträger)* as well as the general public in arriving at 'informed judgments' *(fundierte Beurteilungen)* on economic matters. It analyses the economic situation and its likely development and investigates means of ensuring price stability, a high level of employment, the 'external balance' *(außenwirtschaftliches Gleichgewicht)* as well as efficient economic growth. In line with its legal mandate, the Council publishes an annual report as well as 'ad hoc reports' *(Sondergutachten)* which address particular economic issues. The members of the Council of Experts are nominated by the government and appointed by the President to serve five-year terms.

[16] *Lohnpolitik:* pay policy; compensation policy [US]/remuneration policy

Please note →

> In British English, compensation usually means 'damages', i.e. 'payment to make up for damage or a loss *(Schadenersatz/Schmerzensgeld)*.
> The generic term *Lohn* covers a variety of 'remunerations' *(Vergütungen/Entlohnungen)* but more specifically and traditionally, it signifies 'wages' (i.e. pay checks that are figured by the hour or by the week).

> 'Wages' *(Lohn/Verdienst)* are the price paid for work and the main form of 'earned incomes' *(Arbeitseinkommen; Einkünfte aus nichtselbständiger und selbständiger Arbeit)*. They may be classified as 'money wages' *(Nominallohn)*, i.e. the actual amount of money a worker receives from an employer, and 'real wages' *(Reallohn)*, i.e. the amount of goods and services money wages can buy. Real wages are 'wages [that have been] corrected for price increases' *(um Preissteigerungen bereinigt)*. Employers have spent an increasing percentage of their 'actual' *(tatsächliche)* labour cost on 'fringe benefits' and 'perks' *(zusätzliche Arbeitgeberleistungen)* rather than on the 'take-home pay' or 'net pay' *(Nettoverdienst)* of their employees.

In the UK and the US 'perks' (e.g. productivity bonuses, improved working conditions, more holidays) are usually offered in return for lower wages. 'Fringe benefits', e.g. 'interest-free loans' *(Arbeitgeberdarlehen)*, 'company cars' *(Geschäftswagen)*, 'company flats' *(Firmenwohnungen)* and company contributions to 'workplace pension schemes' *(Betriebsrenten)* or to private medical and dental insurance, and 'paid sick leave' *(Lohnfortzahlung im Krankheitsfall)* also count as 'substitutes for wages' *(Lohnersatz)* rather than 'pay-check contributions' *(Lohnzulagen)*.

'National security contributions' *(Sozialversicherungsbeiträge)* in the UK are charged as a percentage of an individual's income and spent by the government on social security and pensions. They are not identical with the German *Lohnnebenkosten* ('non-wage costs' also 'incidental labour costs') which are essentially 'social security contributions' *(Sozialversicherungsbeiträge)* on the part of the employers, for instance to state pension funds and to the legally compulsory 'unemployment and health insurance' *(Arbeitslosen- und Krankenversicherung)* schemes.

In Germany, wage bargaining between corporate management and unions is 'autonomous' and protected by law to an extent where external interference with 'collective bargaining' *(Tarifverhandlungen)* is prohibited. There is no legally required 'minimum wage' *(Mindestlohn)* as companies are only entitled to pay less than the collectively agreed 'basic wages' *(Tariflöhne)* in those cases where neither the management are members of an employers' association nor the employees of a union.

[17] *(fordert) ... eine Fortsetzung:* [demand that the moderate pay policy] be pursued; ... should be continued

Note that the third person singular form of the verb that follows *die Mehrzahl der/eine ganze Reihe von* changes to the third person plural in English.

← Please note

Examples
A large number of courses are offered by our university.
A wide range of products are sold at the local markets.

In formal English, verbs that denote proposals, requests and similar speech acts may be followed by a subjunctive verb form.

← Please note

However, in everyday usage the auxiliary 'should' is usually inserted in front of the second verb.

Example
The Council demanded that moderate pay policies (should) be formulated.
The HR Manager proposed that the applicant (should) be invited for an interview.

[18] *die realen Lohnsteigerungen:* the increases in real pay; the rise in real compensation [US]

Please note →

Note that 'real' *(Real-)* has to be connected to 'pay' in the English sentence. A 'real pay increase' would signify *eine echte Lohnerhöhung*.

[19] *müssen hinter der Produktivitätszunahme zurückbleiben:* must take second place to productivity gains; need to give way to productivity increases/productivity growth

[20] *dagegen:* in contrast to this; by contrast; unlike his colleagues; contrary to his colleagues

Please note →

'By contrast' and 'in contrast to/unlike his colleagues' are best placed at the beginning of the sentence or clause.

[21] *befürwortet:* advocates; argues in favour of; comes out in favour of

Please note →

'To advocate' closely corresponds with the meaning of *plädieren*. It signifies 'to speak or write in favour of', 'to recommend publicly' (e.g. a policy or belief), 'to support', 'to urge'.

See also *sich einsetzen für* (note [54]) and *eintreten für* (note [30]) below.

Example
The Minister advocates building more kindergartens. *Die Ministerin befürwortet/tritt ein für/plädiert für den Bau von mehr Kindergärten.*

[22] *eine inflations- und verteilungsneutrale:* a pay policy which is neutral in terms of inflation and income distribution; a remuneration policy that is neutral with respect/regard to inflation and income distribution

If pay policy is neutral in terms of income distribution, salaries and wages rise by the same degree as corporate incomes and equity. In other words, the two groups of income earners benefit equally from the growing national income.

²³ *sollten nicht schwächer – und auch nicht stärker – steigen, als es der Produktivitätsfortschritt vorgibt:* should neither adopt a quicker nor a slower pace than the one set by the growth in productivity; should neither rise more quickly nor more slowly than indicated by the growth/increase in productivity

> The 'growth in (labour) productivity' is a major influence on real wages growth over time. When more goods and services are produced without an increase in 'labour input' (*Arbeitseinsatz*, i.e. the number of labour hours invested), this may result in higher real wages or in lower sales prices.
> 'Productivity gains' are measured by the workers' average 'output' (*Ausbringung/Produktionsmenge*) in relation to 'labour input'.

²⁴ *eine zu schwache:* too low a; too weak a; an overly weak
²⁵ *Kaufkraft:* purchasing power; buying power; spending power

> 'Purchasing power' is the extent to which a monetary unit can buy goods and services. It is directly linked to the retail index and is used to compare the wealth of an average individual over a given period of time.

²⁶ *beeinträchtigen:* weaken; slow; impede; negatively affect/impact on
²⁷ *Konsumgütern:* consumer goods; consumption goods

> 'Consumer goods' consist of:
> - 'Consumer durables' (*Gebrauchsgüter, dauerhafte Güter*), also called 'durable (consumer) goods' or 'hard goods', have a relatively long lifetime, such as cars, washing machines or computers.
> - 'Consumer nondurables' (*Verbrauchsgüter*), also called 'nondurable (consumer) goods' or 'disposables' have a relatively short lifetime, such as food, perishable goods (*leicht verderbliche Waren*) or newspapers.

²⁸ *somit:* consequently; as a result; as a consequence; thereby

> 'Thereby' (*somit, hiermit, hierdurch*) may be considered to be dated; it is, however, quite common in academic texts, contracts and legal documents.

← Please note

²⁹ *Absatzmöglichkeiten:* sales potential; potential markets

●●●●●●

For further translations of *Absatz-* in composite nouns cf. II.2.1 Notes on the translation, item [19].

[30] *tritt [der Sachverständigenrat] für ... ein:* supports; recommends; promotes

See also *befürworten* (cf. note [21]) and *sich einsetzen für* (cf. note [54]) in this chapter.

[31] *deutlichere:* greater; more distinct; sharper

Relevant usage examples

Please note →

> 'Distinct' and 'distinctive' can be synonymous. However, in certain contexts, there are subtle differences between them.

Examples

Nurses wear 'distinctive' *([von einander] verschiedene/unterschiedliche)* uniforms.

The difference between 't' and 'd' is clearly distinctive *(deutlich erkennbar/ausgeprägt)* in English because this sound alone distinguishes 'hat' from 'had'.

We heard two distinct *(deutlich verschiedene)* sounds.

He spoke very distinctly/clearly *(deutlich)*.

[32] *der Lohnstruktur:* in pay patterns; in remuneration patterns; in the pay structure

[33] *die Arbeitseinkommen:* earned incomes

Related term

nicht verdientes Einkommen/Nicht-Arbeitseinkommen: unearned income

> This includes interest, dividends and government 'transfer payments' *(Transfereinkommen)*.

[34] *derselben Branche mit unterschiedlicher Gewinnsituation:* belonging to the same industrial sector but to different profit brackets; operating in the same business sector/sector of industry but achieving different profits

Please note →

> 'Branch' may be considered a false friend, as it does not, by itself, translate *Branche*.
> A 'branch' is an office or shop that is part of a large organisation, especially in retailing or banking *(Niederlassung, Filiale, Zweigstelle, Geschäftsstelle)*.

[35] *mit:* that have; with

[36] *Einstiegslöhne:* starting wages; initial wages; entry wages

[37] *Wirtschaftswissenschaftlern:* economists; economic scientists

> In an Anglo-Saxon context, the academic subject of 'Economics' or 'Economic Sciences' *(Volkswirtschaftslehre; Wirtschaftswissenschaft)* is neither synonymous with 'Business Administration' *(Betriebswirtschaftslehre)* nor with (the less frequent related term) 'Business Economics'.
> Please note that, unlike the Anglo-Saxon usage, German academic tradition includes 'Economics' *(Volkswirtschaftslehre)* and 'Business Administration' *(Betriebswirtschaftslehre)* in *Wirtschaftswissenschaften*.

← Please note

38 *eine Deregulierung des deutschen Arbeitsmarktes:* that the German labour market be deregulated

> 'Deregulation' or 'liberalisation' removes existing government impediments on a country's economic activities. It is generally considered as an approach to overcome overly restrictive regulations and, thereby, to help companies to benefit from a greater variety of business opportunities. It stimulates competition, for instance, by allowing a greater degree of 'privatisation' in previously state-run services.

39 *die den Betrieben mehr Spielraum ... lässt:* as this would give companies more leeway

> Literally speaking, 'leeway' *(Abdrift)* is the sideways drift of a ship or aircraft to 'leeward' *(in das Lee, in den Windschatten)*. In figurative language, it denotes 'additional space for manoeuvring', i.e. *Spielraum*.

← Please note

Example
The company admitted that they had very little leeway *(nur wenig Spielraum)* with regard to/regarding pricing.

40 *Einsatz:* utilization; job allocation

> 'Employment' is a potential translation for *Einsatz/Verwendung* but, in this sentence, it would create an awkward juxtaposition with 'employees'.
> 'Input' (as in 'labour input') is equally out of the question since it refers to the quantity of labour employed and not to allocation of specific tasks.

← Please note

41 *Kündigung:* dismissal

Please note →

'Dismissal' translates *Entlassung* and *Kündigung*. In the above text, it is advisable, for pragmatic reasons, to resort to 'dismissal' rather than using the somewhat cumbersome expression 'serving a notice of termination' *(eine Kündigung aussprechen)*.

Translation examples of *kündigen* and *Kündigung*
die Kündigung einreichen: to submit/to hand in one's notice; to tend one's resignation
jemanden kündigen: to serve (an employee) notice of termination/of dismissal
die Kündigung erhalten: to receive notice of one's dismissal
sozial nicht verträgliche Entlassungen/Kündigungen: socially objectionable redundancies/socially unacceptable dismissals
sozial verträgliche Entlassungen/Kündigungen: socially acceptable/non-objectionable redundancies/dismissals

Further translations
Ihm wurde fristlos gekündigt/er wurde fristlos entlassen. His employment contract was terminated without notice./He was dismissed without notice.
Der Arbeitsvertrag wurde fristgerecht gekündigt. The employment contract was terminated with due notice.

Please note →

The noun 'notice' is semantically multi-layered and comprises a variety of implications, the most common of which are included below.

Usage examples
This interesting piece of evidence must have escaped your notice/attention. *Dieser interessante Beweis muss Ihrer Aufmerksamkeit entgangen sein.*
We were given notice/notified/given notification that the consignment had been shipped. *Uns wurde mitgeteilt, dass die Lieferung versandt (worden) war.*
We saw the announcement/notice/bulletin of this month's special events. *Wir haben die Mitteilungen zu den Sonderveranstaltungen dieses Monats gesehen.*
The latest edition of this work received a favourable notice/review. *Die letzte Ausgabe dieses Werkes wurde positiv rezensiert.*

[42] *Leiharbeit:* loan employment

German labour law distinguishes between 'limited employment contracts' *(befristeten Beschäftigungsverhältnissen)* and 'temporary employment' *(Zeitarbeit)* in the sense of 'loan employment' *(Leiharbeit)*.

In colloquial English, 'temporary jobs in offices', especially in the context of 'vacation replacements' *(Urlaubsvertretungen)*, are often referred to as 'temping' *(Jobben)*.

← Please note

Examples
Many students 'temp' *(jobben)* as secretaries during term breaks. When Clara worked as a 'temp' *(Aushilfe)* in the construction industry, she 'stood in for'/'deputized for' *(hat vertreten)* the manager's secretary who was on 'maternity leave' *(Mutterschaftsurlaub)*.

43 *sollten ausgebaut werden:* should be extended; ought to be developed
44 *starre:* rigid; strict; inflexible; restrictive
45 *Kündigungsschutzregelungen:* employment protection regulations

There is no direct translation for *Kündigungsschutzgesetz (KSchG)* which finds its rough equivalent in the UK 'Employment Protection Act' *(Beschäftigungsschutzgesetz)*.
'Employment (Protection) Acts' warrant the rights of an employee to be protected from 'wrongful dismissal' *(unbegründete Entlassung)* and make legal provision for the various forms of 'redundancy compensations' *(Abfindungen aufgrund betriebsbedingter Kündigung)* in cases where employees are dismissed for any reason other than a breach of the employment contract. Moreover, they regulate the 'arbitration' *(Schieds-)*, 'mediation' *(Vermittlungs-)* and 'conciliation procedures' *(Schlichtungsverfahren)* used in industrial disputes.
In the case of 'senior corporate officers' *(leitende Mitarbeiter)*, a typical compensation is 'severance pay' *(Trennungsentschädigung)* which is often called a 'golden handshake' *(goldener Handschlag;* also *versilberter Abschied)*.
'Redundancies' are generally due to 'business or operational reasons' and are therefore *betriebsbedingt* per se. In other words, workers 'are made redundant' when there is a decline in the need for labour. People who lose their jobs under such circumstances are also known as 'displaced workers' *(freigesetzte Arbeitskräfte)*.

Please note →

> *Beschäftigungsschutz* should not be confused with *Arbeitsschutz*, i.e. the 'health and safety regulations' which ensure the welfare, safety and health of people at work and limit the hazards involved in their occupations.

[46] *sollten gelockert werden:* should be relaxed; ought to be slackened/loosened
Usage examples of 'slacken (off)':
Don't slacken your efforts until your project is completed. *Lass (in deinen Anstrengungen) nicht nach, bevor dein Projekt fertig ist.* The skiing business begins to slacken off in spring. *Das Skigeschäft fängt im Frühjahr an nachzulassen.*

[47] *Tarifparteien:* the parties involved in collective bargaining; the parties conducting/who conduct collective pay negotiations

> The, mostly British, term 'collective bargaining' *(Tarifverhandlungen)* is used whenever the official representatives of the labour force – usually the trades unions officials – conduct negotiations with the employers about pay increases and/or labour practices and work conditions. Cf. note [16] above.

[48] *sich über eine stärkere Flexibilisierung der Wochen- und Jahresarbeitszeit einigen:* agree to greater flexibility regarding weekly and annual working hours; agree to more flexibility with regard to/with respect to weekly and annual working time

> 'Flexible work scheduling'/'flexible working hours' *(flexible Arbeitszeit)*, also known as 'flexitime' or 'flextime' *(Gleitzeit)*, began in West Germany in 1967 and spread to other countries during the 1970's. Flexitime workers choose their own daily work hours, within specified limits, as long as they work the required number of hours per week. Most flexitime systems require employees to be present during 'core time' *(Kernzeit)*.

[49] *mehr:* a larger degree of; a larger extent of; a higher amount of
[50] *als einen Ansatzpunkt für mehr Arbeitsplätze:* as a first step towards the creation of more jobs; as a starting point in the creation of more jobs
[51] *dies hat die Bundesregierung ... aufgegriffen:* the Federal Government has taken up this suggestion; the Federal Government has followed up this proposal; the Federal Government has adopted this approach

⁵² *mit der Verabschiedung eines gesetzlichen Anspruchs auf Teilzeitarbeit:* by making legal provision for the right to pursue part-time employment; by legally establishing the right to pursue part-time employment
⁵³ *schließlich:* last but not least; finally
⁵⁴ *setzen sich die Gewerkschaften für den Abbau der hohen Überstundenzahl ein:* the trades unions are committed to reducing the high number of overtime hours; the unions advocate
See also *sich einsetzen* with *plädieren für* (note ²¹) and *eintreten für* (note ³⁹).

> 'To commit' is grammatically and semantically complicated. In the above translation, it expresses 'commitment' (cf. II.2.1 Notes on the translation, item ⁶²) but it also covers the following semantic nuances:

← Please note

Examples
The crime was committed/perpetrated in broad daylight. *Das Verbrechen wurde am helllichten Tag begangen.*
The judge committed the thief to prison. *Die Richterin verurteilte den Dieb zu einer Gefängnisstrafe.*
He did not want to commit himself./He was strictly non-committal. *Er wollte keinerlei Verpflichtung(en) eingehen. Er hielt sich vollkommen bedeckt.*
The aid worker was committed to helping the street children of Africa. *Der Entwicklungshelfer engagierte sich/setzte sich ein, um den afrikanischen Straßenkindern zu helfen.*
The haulage company committed itself to delivering the urgently needed components on time. *Das Transportunternehmen verpflichtete sich, die dringend benötigten Teile pünktlich zu liefern.*

> Note the gerund form in the translation and in the two latter examples.

← Please note

⁵⁵ *(abhängig) Beschäftigten:* wage and salary earners; people in paid/remunerative employment
For the *Erwerbstätige* cf. II.2.1 Notes on the translation, item ⁴⁵.
⁵⁶ *meist nur:* for the most part; mostly
⁵⁷ *Facharbeiter:* skilled workers; specially trained/qualified wage earners

> - 'Skilled workers' *(gelernte Arbeitskräfte; Facharbeitskräfte)* receive qualified 'occupational training' *(praktische Berufs-*

● ● ● ● ● ●

ausbildung) and obtain their 'vocational qualifications' *(berufliche Abschlüsse)* in a particular job at their workplace. In addition, they are offered a 'job-related' *(einschlägige)* 'theoretical grounding' *(theoretische Grundausbildung)* at their local vocational or technical college.
- 'Semi-skilled workers' *(angelernte Arbeitskräfte)* are trained on the job; they have acquired fundamental and general capabilities but cannot be employed for specialized work.
- 'Unskilled workers' *(ungelernte Arbeiteskräfte)* have received no vocational training. They perform simple manual or physical jobs.

For details on vocational training and related terms cf. II.2.1 Notes on the translation, item [59].

[58] *Angestellte:* salaried employees; non-manual employees; white-collar workers; employees; staff

[59] *einfache Arbeiter:* ordinary workers; manual/blue-collar workers; simple workers/labourers

Please note →

Apart from its more familiar synonyms, which are 'usual', 'customary', 'every day'; the adjective 'ordinary' may, in particular, connote 'inferior', 'common' or 'mediocre'.
This is a semantic feature it shares with the adjective 'common'. Although 'common' mostly signifies 'shared by all', 'universal', 'united', 'joint' and 'familiar', it also connotes 'of humble birth', 'coarse' and 'vulgar'.
'Simple' has different semantic implications again. It can mean 'elementary', 'easy to do' but also 'naive', 'unsophisticated', 'artless' and 'stupid'.

Usage examples

His behaviour was ordinary *(gewöhnlich/ordinär)* and tiresome.
Our success is due to the common/joint effort *(gemeinsame Anstrengung)* of our staff.
He was perceived as a common liar *(gemeiner Lügner).*
All we need is a simple majority *(einfache Mehrheit).*
He was the 'Simple Simon' *(Dümmling)* of his peer group.
He led a simple/ordinary life *(einfaches/genügsames Leben).*
Your plan requires more than a simple *(simple)* explanation.

[60] *werden die Überstunden nicht extra entgolten:* are not awarded extra overtime pay; do not receive (any) additional overtime award; are not paid extra for overtime work

Corel Library

3.1 Employment and pay

Find translations of the terms below which are all related to 'employment' and 'pay'. Make use of the Notes on the translation and of dictionaries where necessary.

I.3 Exercises

Example
Reallohn   real pay/real compensation/real wages

1. Arbeitgeber   —
2. Arbeitnehmer/innen   —
3. Arbeitseinkommen   —
4. arbeitslos   —
5. Aushilfskraft   —
6. Beschäftigte/r   —
7. Beschäftigung   —
8. Beschäftigungspolitik   —
9. Beschäftigungsverhältnis —
10. Einstiegsgehalt   —
11. erwerbsfähig   —
12. erwerbslos   —
13. Erwerbsquote   —
14. Geldlohn   —
15. Leiharbeit   —

Exercises

16 Lohnarbeit —
17 Lohnerhöhung —
18 Lohnpolitik —
19 Lohnstruktur —
20 Mindestlohn —
21 Monatslohn —
22 Naturallohn —
23 Nettoverdienst —
24 Nominallohn —
25 Spitzenlohn/-gehalt —
26 Tariflohn —

3.2 Collective agreements and new forms of employment

Fill in the gaps by choosing the appropriate English equivalent of the German terms in (brackets). Use words and phrases from the Sample translation and the Notes. Note that there may be more than one option.

1 __ __ (Gleitzeitarbeiter) choose their own daily work hours in addition to the __ __ (Kernzeiten) during which they have to be present.

2 In the traditional trades and industries, the liberalisation process has __ /__ (beseitigt) restrictive __ __/__ __ (Arbeitsregulierungen) and opened up a broader range of __ __ (Geschäftsmöglichkeiten).

3 The Government has finally made legal provision for the right to __ __ __ (einer Teilzeitbeschäftigung nachzugehen).

4 An increasing number of companies rely on __ __ (Zeitarbeitskräfte) to __ __ __/__ __ (vertreten) their regular staff during the vacation periods.

5 __ __ or __ (zusätzliche Arbeitgeberleistungen) are not identical with the German __ __ __/__ __ __ (Lohnnebenkosten).

6 In the British __ __ (Dienstleistungsbranchen), __ __ __ (tarifliche Lohnvereinbarungen) are also negotiated by the trades unions.

7 The parties involved in the __ __ __/__ __ (Tarifverhandlungen) finally agreed on the new pay scale for __ __ (Zeitarbeit).

8 German labour law distinguishes between __ __ __ (befristeten Beschäftigungsverhältnissen) and __ __ (Leiharbeit)

3.3 Redundancies and dismissals

Exercises

Translate the sentences below using a bilingual dictionary and the terms provided in the **Notes** to this chapter.

1. Betriebsbedingte Entlassungen und Freisetzungen von Arbeitskräften sind immer dann unvermeidlich, wenn der Arbeitsbedarf in einem traditionellen Industriezweig zurückgeht.
2. Viele betriebsbedingten Entlassungen sind auf Produktivitätssteigerungen zurückzuführen.
3. Die Kündigung wurde nicht rechtzeitig ausgesprochen und ist deshalb ungültig.
4. 200 Beschäftigte wurden entlassen, weil die Nachfrage im Kerngeschäft des Unternehmens weiter zurückgegangen ist.
5. Dieser langjährige Mitarbeiter wurde zwei Jahre vor Erreichen der gesetzlichen Altersgrenze entlassen.
6. Nach über 40 Dienstjahren stand ihm eine beachtliche Abfindung zu.
7. Beschäftigungsschutzgesetze regulieren auch Schlichtungs- und Vermittlungsverfahren zwischen Arbeitgebern und Arbeitnehmern.
8. Üblicherweise kündigt man (sein Beschäftigungsverhältnis) mindestens einen Monat, bevor man seinen Arbeitsplatz aufgibt.
9. Auch der Arbeitgeber kann einer/einem Beschäftigten kündigen.
10. Das Unternehmen wollte keine Gründe für die Entlassung der beiden Facharbeiter angeben.

II The East German Labour Market

II.1 **Text: Der ostdeutsche Arbeitsmarkt nach dem „Transformationsschock"** 34

II.2 **Sample translation** 37
II.2.1 Notes on the translation

II.3 **Exercises** 48
II.3.1 Labour and work
II.3.2 Employment and unemployment
II.3.3 Expectations, recommendations and requests

II.1 Text: Der ostdeutsche Arbeitsmarkt nach dem "Transformationsschock"

(Bundesanstalt für Arbeit: Amtliche Nachrichten, 2000)

II The East German Labour Market

Bereits zu Beginn des Jahres 1990 war zu erwarten, dass die Wirtschafts-, Währungs- und Sozialunion der DDR mit der Bundesrepublik Deutschland zu einem radikalen Wandel am ostdeutschen Arbeitsmarkt führen würde. So prognostizierten das Münchner „ifo-Institut" und das Ost Berliner „Institut für angewandte Wirtschaftsforschung", dass durch den „Transformationsschock" etwa 2,8 Mio. Arbeitsplätze wegfallen würden. Zum einen würde durch den Systemwechsel die „verdeckte Arbeitslosigkeit" aufgedeckt, eine Form von Arbeitslosigkeit, die insbesondere auf Planungs- und Organisationsmängel, wie z.B. Ausfallzeiten wegen verspäteter Materiallieferungen und defekter Produktionsanlagen, sowie auf den ineffizienten Einsatz von Arbeitskräften zurückzuführen sei. Beispielsweise sei der Personalbestand häufig an saisonalen und durch Exportaufträge verursachten Produktionsspitzen ausgerichtet. Zum anderen würde die Arbeitsnachfrage durch den Übergang zu westlichen Produktions- und Absatzbedingungen deutlich zurückgehen.

Allerdings war auch mit einem niedrigeren Arbeitsangebot zu rechnen, denn aufgrund der umfassenden Veränderung der politischen, sozialen und wirtschaftlichen Rahmenbedingungen war ein deutlicher Rückgang der Erwerbsquoten von drei spezifischen Bevölkerungsgruppen zu erwarten, und zwar bei

- Jugendlichen und jungen Erwachsenen: Ihre Erwerbsbeteiligung würde zurückgehen, weil künftig mehr Jugendliche sich für eine höhere Schulbildung und ein Studium entscheiden würden und weil von einer Verlängerung der Studienzeiten auszugehen sei.

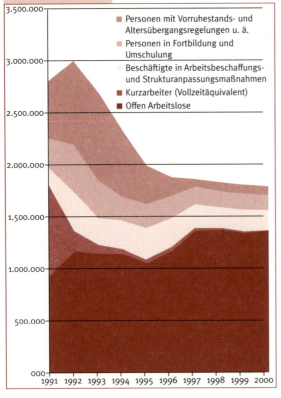

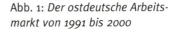

Abb. 1: *Der ostdeutsche Arbeitsmarkt von 1991 bis 2000*

- verheirateten Frauen: Für sie würde sich eine Berufstätigkeit nach der Wiedervereinigung finanziell weniger auszahlen, weil das westdeutsche Steuer- und Sozialversicherungssystem die „Alleinverdiener-Ehe" begünstigt. Auch würde es für Frauen schwieriger, einer Erwerbsarbeit nachzugehen, weil es keine so umfassende Kinderbetreuung mehr gäbe.
- älteren Arbeitnehmern: Ihnen würden sich mehr Möglichkeiten eröffnen, vor Erreichung des offiziellen Rentenalters aus dem Erwerbsleben auszuscheiden, sodass sich ihre Erwerbsquote der weit niedrigeren in der früheren Bundesrepublik annähern würde.

Insgesamt wurde zu Beginn des Transformationsprozesses damit gerechnet, dass ohne wirtschaftspolitische Gegenmaßnahmen die Zahl der Arbeitslosen in der ehemaligen DDR die Zwei-Millionen-Grenze überschreiten würde.

Die Arbeitsmarktpolitik musste zunächst dem Problem begegnen, dass neue Stellen bei weitem nicht so schnell geschaffen werden konnten, wie Arbeitsplätze durch den Transformationsprozess verloren gingen. Die Erwerbstätigenzahl sank 1993 von schätzungsweise 9 $^1/_2$ Mio. zu Zeiten der DDR auf 6,2 Mio. Dementsprechend waren die „Instrumente der ersten Stunde" auf Arbeitsmarktentlastung zur Vermeidung offener Arbeitslosigkeit gerichtet. Durch Kurzarbeit wurde die Arbeitsnachfrage in den ersten beiden Jahren weniger stark abgebaut. Hinzu kam die Vorruhestands- bzw. die Altersübergangsregelung, die sich 1993 mit 850.000 Beteiligten in vollem Umfang auswirkte. Insgesamt verhinderte dies, dass die Zahl der offen Arbeitslosen über 1,2 Mio. stieg, d.h. die Arbeitsmarktpolitik hatte ihre „Feuerwehrfunktion" erfüllt.

Die Arbeitsmarktpolitik hat weiterhin die Funktion, eine „Brücke" zu regulärer Beschäftigung zu bauen, indem sie die (Um-)Qualifizierung von Arbeitnehmern für neue Stellen fördert. Dies kann zum einen durch Fortbildungs- und Umschulungsmaßnahmen geschehen, zum anderen durch Lohnkostenzuschüsse, die für Unternehmen Anreize schaffen, nicht adäquat ausgebildete Mitarbeiter einzustellen und „on the job" zu qualifizieren. Dabei darf allerdings nicht übersehen werden, dass eine erfolgreiche Reintegration der arbeitssuchenden Teilnehmer an diesen Maßnahmen nicht nur von der Qualität ihrer Qualifikation (und ihrem Engagement) abhängt, sondern auch von der Arbeitsmarktsituation. Deshalb bedarf es flankierender wirtschaftspolitischer Maßnahmen, um die Schaffung neuer Arbeitsplätze zu fördern.

(Renate Neubäumer)

II.2 Sample translation

The East German labour market[1] in the wake of[2] the 'transformation shock'

As far back as the early days of 1990[3], the economic, monetary and **social union** between the GDR and the Federal Republic of Germany **was expected**[4] to transform the East German labour market in a radical way[5].

Corel Library

The Munich "ifo-Institute" and the East Berlin "Institute for Applied Economic Research", **for instance**[6] predicted that the 'transformation shock' **would result in the loss of about 2.8 million jobs**[7]. Firstly, **by changing to a different system**[8], **'disguised unemployment'**[9] would be **revealed**[10]. This type of unemployment is **mainly**[11] **brought about by**[12] **planning and organisational deficiencies**[13], such as **outage times**[14] caused by delayed **deliveries of materials**[15] and **defective production plant**[16], as well as by the inefficient employment of workers. The number of persons employed, for instance, **was often geared towards**[17] production peaks deriving from seasonal demand and export orders. Secondly, **switching to**[18] Western production and **marketing conditions**[19] would markedly reduce the **demand for labour**[20].

On the other hand, **it was equally likely that there would be less manpower available**[21] as the **wide-ranging**[22] changes in the political, social and economic **framework**[23] were expected to result in significantly lower **employment rates**[24] among at least three specific groups of the population, **namely**[25]

- adolescents and young adults. Their **participation in the job market**[26] would decline because, in future, more young adults **would decide in favour of secondary as well as higher education**[27] and because **university courses would presumably take longer to complete**[28];

- married women. After reunification, **pursuing a job**[29] would **be less lucrative**[30] for them as the West German taxation and social security system **benefits**[31] 'single-income marriages'. Moreover, **the pursuit of gainful employment**[32] would become more difficult for women **as the comprehensive child care comparable to that provided in the GDR would cease to exist**[33].
- elderly[34] employees. **They would benefit from a wider range of opportunities**[35] **to retire from working life**[36] before reaching the official retirement age; **hence the employment rate of this group would approach**[37] that of the former Federal Republic, **which was much lower**[38].

At the beginning of the transformation process, **it was estimated**[39] that the number of unemployed people in the former GDR **would exceed**[40], in total, the two-million mark **unless economic policies were put in place to counter this development**[41].

First of all[42], **labour market policies**[43] had **to tackle the problem**[44] **that creating new job openings took a lot longer than shedding jobs**[45] during the transformation process. The **number of people in gainful employment**[46] **fell**[47] from an estimated 9.5m during GDR times to 6.2m in 1993. **Accordingly**[48], **the instruments employed during the foundation phase**[49] were are aimed at easing the pressure on the labour market in order to avoid open unemployment. **By introducing short time work**[50], the demand for labour was more slowly reduced in the first two years. In addition, there were **the early retirement or transitional retirement schemes**[51] whose full impact was felt in 1993 with 850,000 people participating in them. In total, **this prevented the open unemployment figure from rising above 1.2 million**[52]; **in other words**[53], the employment policies **had succeeded in providing the necessary stopgap measures**[54].

Furthermore, labour market policies have the task **to provide 'back-to-work' incentives**[55] **by encouraging occupational (re)training for new vocations**[56]. On the one hand, this may be achieved **by continuing education and retraining schemes**[57], and, on the other hand, **by labour cost subsidies**[58] **which offer incentives to employers**[59] **to take on undertrained staff**[60] in order to qualify them 'on the job'. One should, however, not overlook the fact that the successful reintegration **of those job seekers who participate in**[61] these schemes not only depends on the quality of their qualification (and on their **commitment**[62]) but also on the particular situation in the labour market. This is why the creation of new jobs requires supportive political and economic measures.

● ● ● ● ● ● **2.1 Notes on the translation**

¹ *Arbeitsmarkt:* labour market; job market; employment market

> In an economic context, 'labour' *(Arbeit/Arbeiter)* is a collective noun that has several distinctive meanings:
> - manual work; toil; exertion, effort *(Arbeit)*
> - the total number of workers available which makes up the 'labour force' or 'workforce' *(Arbeitskräfte)* of a country
> - workers as a group *(Arbeiterschaft)*
> - organisations representing the workers
> - one of the 'factors of production' *(Produktionsfaktoren))*, i.e. the resources of an economy utilized to produce goods and services. In classical economic theory, these factors have been defined as 'labour', 'land' and 'capital', but modern economists have extended this definition to include 'human capital' *(Humankapital)*, i.e. the qualifications, skills and expertise that contribute to a worker's productivity, 'environment' and 'technological progress'.

Please note →

> One single manual worker is referred to as 'blue-collar worker', and in certain sectors (construction, farming) as 'labourer'.

Usage examples

He was a hard-working agricultural labourer/farm hand *(Landarbeiter)*.

The building site workers were well paid for their labour *(anstrengende Arbeit)*.

cheap-labour/low-wage countries: *Billiglohnländer*

² *nach:* in the wake of; after; in the aftermath of

Please note →

> The alternatives given here are not synonymous:
> 'Aftermath' refers to the consequence of something that has been detrimental or destructive *(Nachwehen)*.
> The 'wake' *(Kielwasser; Spur)*, in its literal sense, is the 'track left by a moving vessel or plane'; in figurative speech, it denotes something that follows behind.

Examples

It took Europe many years to recover from the aftermath of World War II. *Europa brauchte Jahre, um sich von den Folgen des 2. Weltkrieges zu erholen.*

Floods often follow in the wake of tornadoes. *Oft folgen Überschwemmungen den Wirbelstürmen auf dem Fuss.*

[3] *bereits zu Beginn des Jahres 1990:* as far back as the early days of 1990; as early as the beginning of 1990
For detailed explanations on the usage of the multifunctional adverbs *schon, erst* and *nur* see: J. Bauer & M. Seidenspinner, *Betriebswirtschaft: Übersetzungsübungen, studium kompakt Fachsprache Englisch*, Cornelsen & Oxford, Berlin, 2001; pp. 75-76.

[4] *war zu erwarten, dass die Wirtschafts-, Währungs- und Sozialunion:* the economic, monetary and social union was expected to
Cf. below: 3.3 Expectations, recommendations and requests for details on the translation of impersonal expressions such as: *es ist zu erwarten/es steht zu erwarten/man erwartet, dass …*

[5] *zu einem radikalen Wandel am ostdeutschen Arbeitsmarkt führen würde:* to transform the East German labour market in a radical way; to change the East German labour market radically; to lead to a radical transformation of the East German labour market

[6] *so:* for instance, for example
Cf. I.2.1 Notes on the translation, item [14].

[7] *etwa 2,8 Mio Arbeitsplätze wegfallen würden:* would result in the loss of about 2.8 million jobs; would make approximately/roughly 2.8m people redundant; would cost about 2.8m jobs

[8] *durch den Systemwechsel:* by changing to a different system; by changing systems; due to the change in systems; due to the transition to a different system

← Please note

> If the verb *wechseln* is translated, it is essential to put the connected accusative noun in its plural form ore use 'change to'.
> *Ich möchte gerne die Universität wechseln* is translated as:
> I would like to change universities./I would like to change to another university.
> I would like to change the (this) university means: *Ich würde gerne die(se) Universität ändern.*

Further usage example
All our parts will have to be changed to *(umgestellt … auf)* American standards.

[9] *verdeckte Arbeitslosigkeit:* disguised unemployment; concealed unemployment; hidden unemployment

> 'Disguised unemployment' characterizes a situation in which the workforce are, technically speaking, in employment, but in which their productivity is negligible or close to zero.

Such a situation can arise as a result of cultural or political practices and restrictive labour representation such as the former 'permanent employment policies' *(dauerhafte Beschäftigungspolitik)* of Japanese companies, 'peak-oriented staffing' *(an Produktionsspitzen ausgerichteter Personalbestand)* or 'overstaffing' *(Überbesetzung)*.

'Cyclical unemployment' *(konjunkturelle Arbeitslosigkeit)* is 'demand-deficient unemployment' *(Arbeitslosigkeit aufgrund fehlender Nachfrage)* that occurs as a result of decreasing 'aggregate demand' *(gesamtwirtschaftliche Nachfrage)* and general business activity during economic recessions.

'Structural unemployment' *(strukturelle Arbeitslosigkeit)* is a long-term phenomenon due to changing demand patterns, to the decline of certain industries or to structural weaknesses in national economies as they occur, for instance, in the wake of natural and man-made disasters.

'Seasonal unemployment' *(saisonale Arbeitslosigkeit)* arises in industries such as agriculture, construction and tourism.

Related terms
Arbeitslosengeld: unemployment benefit/unemployment pay
Arbeitslosenhilfe: unemployment aid
Berufsunfähigkeitsrente: occupational invalidity pension
Sozialhilfe: public assistance (benefit); social security pay

[10] *aufgedeckt:* revealed; uncovered; disclosed; laid bare
[11] *insbesondere:* mainly; primarily
[12] *auf ... zurückzuführen sei:* is ... brought about by; is ... caused by; results from/derives from
[13] *Planungs- und Organisationsmängel:* planning and organisational deficiencies; flawed planning and organisation
Cf. item [16] below.
[14] *Ausfallzeiten:* downtimes; outage times; lost working hours
[15] *Materiallieferungen:* deliveries of materials

Please note →

Material – when it denotes 'the substance or the articles necessary for building or creating something' – is generally translated as 'materials'.

Examples
Baumaterial: building materials.
Lehrmaterial: teaching materials.
Schreibmaterial: writing materials.

> As an adjective, 'material' signifies 'physical' or 'worldly' as well as (figuratively) 'substantial' or 'essential':

← Please note

Examples
Unrelenting effort was a material factor in her outstanding attainment. *Ausdauer und harte Arbeit trugen wesentlich zu ihrem überragenden Ergebnis bei.*
He was a material witness to this case. *Er war ein unentbehrlicher Zeuge in diesem Verfahren.*

[16] *defekter Produktionsanlagen:* defective production plant; faulty production facilities

> 'Faults' *(Fehler)* are 'deficiencies' inherent in materials, equipment, processes and – last but not least – human beings.

← Please note

Usage examples
design faults/fault in design: *Konstruktionsfehler*
We all have our faults. *Wir alle haben unsere Fehler.*
It's not our fault. *Wir sind nicht daran schuld.*

> 'Defect' and 'defective' indicate a 'lack of perfection' in e.g. materials or equipment. Please note that 'defect' is a noun; the German adjective *defekt* has to be rendered as 'defective'.

← Please note

Usage examples
production defect: *Produktionsfehler*
zero defect production: *Produktion mit einer Fehlerquote von Null*
These components are all defective. *Diese Teile sind alle schadhaft.*
The lift is out of order. *Der Fahrstuhl ist defekt.*

[17] *sei häufig an ... ausgerichtet:* was often geared towards; was frequently oriented towards
[18] *den Übergang zu:* switching to; changing to; the adoption of
[19] *Absatzbedingungen:* marketing conditions; sales conditions

> There is no one-word translation for *Absatz* which is an inclusive term for the process by which goods and services are moved from the suppliers or providers to the end users. This process involves sales, distribution and marketing activities.

← Please note

Further usage examples
Absatzpolitik: sales/distribution policy
Absatzpotential: sales potential/market potential
Absatzprognose: sales projection

●●●●●● *Absatzrisiko:* merchandising risk
Absatzrückgang: drop/decrease in sales
Absatzschwierigkeiten: difficulties in marketing the product
Absatzzahlen: sales figures/market data
Absatzziel: sales target

[20] *Arbeitsnachfrage:* demand for labour; demand for manpower; labour demand
Arbeitsnachfrage is synonymous with *Arbeitskräftenachfrage*.

[21] *war auch mit einem niedrigeren Arbeitsangebot zu rechnen:* it was equally likely that there would be less manpower available; it was also assumed/believed that there would be a lower level of labour supply/manpower supply/less labour available
Arbeitsangebot is synonymous with *Arbeitskräfteangebot*.

[22] *umfassenden:* wide-ranging; comprehensive; also: sweeping

[23] *Rahmenbedingungen:* framework; overall/general conditions

[24] *Erwerbsquoten:* employment rates; level of employment; level of labour participation

[25] *und zwar bei:* namely; in particular

[26] *Erwerbsbeteiligung:* their participation in the job market; their labour participation

[27] *sich für eine höhere Schulbildung und ein Studium entscheiden würden:* would decide in favour of secondary as well as higher education; would choose secondary as well as university education; would opt for secondary as well as a post-secondary education [US]

> In Germany, formal education is divided into several stages which correspond (roughly) to the following educational levels in the UK and the US.
> - *vorschulische Ausbildung:* pre-elementary/pre-school education
> - *Grund(schul)ausbildung/Primarstufe:* elementary education [US] primary education [GB]; junior school
> - *Sekundarstufe:* secondary level/secondary education; secondary school
>   *Sekundarstufe I:* (formerly: middle school); junior high school [US]; upper elementary level; (lower) secondary level
>   *Sekundarstufe II:* senior high school [US]; (upper) secondary level; lower and upper sixth form [GB]
> - *tertiäre Bildungseinrichtung/höhere Fachschule:* tertiary college. In GB, this is an institution that includes the

> secondary school's sixth form (2 years) and vocational training.
> - *Hochschulausbildung:* post-secondary education [US]; higher education; university education
> 'Institutions of higher education'/'institutions of higher learning' *(Hochschuleinrichtungen)* provide a wide selection of three or four-year liberal arts and career programmes as well as post-graduate courses.
> For vocational training cf. note [56] below.

[28] *von einer Verlängerung der Studienzeiten auszugehen sei:* university courses would presumably take longer to complete; post-secondary/university education could be assumed to take longer

[29] *eine Berufstätigkeit:* pursuing a job; pursuing an occupation

[30] *würde sich ... weniger auszahlen:* would be less lucrative; would be less remunerative

[31] *begünstigt:* benefits; favours; is more advantageous for

[32] *einer Erwerbsarbeit nachzugehen:* the pursuit of gainful employment; taking up remunerative employment

[33] *es keine so umfassende Kinderbetreuung mehr gäbe:* as comprehensive child care comparable to that provided in the GDR would cease to exist; as comprehensive childcare would cease to exist; as the comprehensive childcare that was available in the GDR would no longer exist

> In this context, the qualifying apposite *so* implies a comparison which signifies 'comparable to that existing in the GDR'.
> The meaning condensed in this 'implied comparative' has to be explained and added to the translation in order to convey the full implications of the German sentence.
> A more pragmatic approach would be to ignore *so* altogether as it does not carry a semantic message on its own.

← Please note

[34] *ältere:* elderly; older; senior

> 'Older' and 'elder' represent 'implied' or 'indirect comparatives' which refer to a member of a group who is 'of greater age'; in our case an employee who is close to retirement age.
> Likewise, 'senior' denotes 'older' while at the same time implying 'of higher rank' or 'longer in service'. 'Senior employee' could, therefore, be misunderstood in the above context.

← Please note

● ● ● ● ●   Examples
a senior citizen: *ein Rentner*
a senior officer; a senior manager: *eine Führungskraft*
the senior year [US]: the final-year students: *der Diplomjahrgang*

[35] *Ihnen würden sich mehr Möglichkeiten eröffnen:* they would benefit from a wider range of opportunities; they would be able to take advantage of a greater number of opportunities

[36] *aus dem Erwerbsleben auszuscheiden:* to retire from working life; to opt for retirement from their working life

Please note →

> The idiomatic verb 'to pension' connotes *ausrangieren/ausmustern*.

Related expressions
Rentner: Old age pensioner, OAP [not 'politically correct']; pensioner; senior citizen
in Rente gehen: to retire from work (on a pension)
betriebliche Altersversorgung: workplace pension scheme/company pension scheme
Berufsunfähigkeitsrente: disability pension

[37] *sodass sich ihre Erwerbsquote ... annähern würde:* hence the employment rate of this group would approach; so that the employment rate of elderly/senior employees would be closer to

Please note →

> The German text uses *ihre* to avoid repeating 'senior employees' for reasons of style. However, this kind of repetition — for the sake of clarity — would not be considered to be stylistically deficient in English texts.

[38] *der weit niedrigeren:* which was much lower; which was a lot/considerably lower

[39] *wurde damit gerechnet:* it was estimated

Alternative translation
The number of unemployed people in the former GDR was expected to exceed ...

[40] *überschreiten würde:* would exceed; top; move past; break through

[41] *ohne wirtschaftspolitische Gegenmaßnahmen:* unless economic policies were put in place to counter this development; unless economic policies were established to offset/counterbalance this development; unless economic countermeasures were taken

> *'Politik'* can signify the following
> - 'Policy': a countable noun referring to a plan of action pursued by a government, a party or an individual; the plural 'policies' includes individual measures or strategies
> - 'Politics': a non-countable abstract denoting the art and the science of directing and administering a state or community. Moreover, it is a subject that can be studied at schools and insititutions of higher education.
> - 'Politicking' are political activities that are primarily aimed at 'catching votes' and at expanding existing power bases.

← Please note

Examples
All three electricity providers pursue their own environmental policies *(Umweltpolitik)*.
She has recently obtained a university degree in Politics *(Politologie)*.
What kind of economic policy *(Wirtschaftspolitik)* could the southeast Asian countries have adopted to prevent the crisis?

[42] *zunächst:* first of all; at the outset; at the beginning

> Related expressions
> Whereas 'at the outset' and temporal adverbial expressions, 'first of all' signifies 'before everything else' *(zuallererst)* and 'of the highest priority' *(vorrangig)*.
> 'At first' means 'originally' *(zuerst/ursprünglich)*.

← Please note

Usage examples
Product development must, first and foremost *(an erster Stelle/vorrangig)*, analyse customer needs.
At first, the government believed that they might be able to find a 'quick fix' for the unexpected rise in unemployment but eventually they realized that they would need more time to succeed.

[43] *Arbeitsmarktpolitik:* labour market policies; manpower policies

> A singular usage of 'policy' would be possible here, too.

← Please note

[44] *dem Problem begegnen:* to tackle the problem; to address the problem; to counter/to confront the problem; to face the problem

[45] *dass neue Stellen bei weitem nicht so schnell geschaffen werden konnten, wie Arbeitsplätze ... verloren gingen:* that creating new job openings took a lot longer than shedding jobs; new jobs were created a lot more slowly than people were being made redundant

[46] *Erwerbstätigenzahl:* the number of people in gainful employment; the number of people gainfully employed

> *Erwerbstätige* are all persons in employment. They may be on a company's payroll or self-employed, work full-time or part-time, receive payment in kind or no pay check at all [as may be the case with relatives working in family-owned businesses].

[47] *sank:* fell; dropped; decreased
[48] *dementsprechend:* accordingly; in line with this
[49] *die Instrumente der ersten Stunde:* the instruments employed during the foundation years; the tools which were initially employed/utilized
[50] *durch Kurzarbeit:* by introducing short-time work/shorter working hours
[51] *die Vorruhestands- bzw. durch die Altersübergangsregelung:* the early retirement or transitional retirement schemes

Please note →

> 'Scheme' *(Maßnahme/Regelung/Programm/Plan)* implies more than a simple plan of action. Generally, it denotes a carefully devised and laid out programme or a concrete measure to be taken.
> Examples
> The engineers developed a scheme to cut down on reduplicated work effort.
> They were not impressed by the revised colour scheme for the shopfloor.

[52] *verhinderte dies, dass die Zahl der offen Arbeitslosen über 1,2 Mio. stieg:* this prevented the open unemployment figure from rising above 1.2 million
Cf. I.2.1 Notes on the translation, item [3].
[53] *d.h.:* in other words; that is to say; i.e
[54] *hatte ihre „Feuerwehrfunktion" erfüllt:* had managed to provide the necessary stopgap measures; had successfully provided emergency solutions
[55] *eine „Brücke" zu regulärer Beschäftigung zu bauen:* to provide back-to-work incentives; to lead people back into regular employment

> In the UK, one way of reducing unemployment is the 'welfare-to-work' initiative established in 1999 as a public-private partnership. It includes a series of 'new deals' for young and

> long-term unemployed people, for people with a disability and 'lone parents' *(Alleinerziehende)*. The scheme has helped to finance (re)training aimed at providing recognized qualifications, child care and individual career guidance.

[56] *indem sie die (Um-)Qualifizierung ... für neue Berufe fördert:* by encouraging occupational (re)training for new vocations; by supporting vocational (re)training for new jobs/occupations/careers

> In the UK and the US, 'occupational/vocational training' *(Berufsausbildung)* can be pursued at a number of technical and vocational institutions and professional schools.
> Community and junior colleges [US] as well as university colleges [GB], for instance, offer two-year programmes in both general and advanced vocational (or career) training. After completing a two-year course at a community/junior or technical college, a student receives an associate's degree (A.A.). At British universities, two-year programmes lead to a 'Higher National Diploma' (HND).
> Related terms
> *berufspraktische Ausbildung:* on-the-job training
> *betriebliche Ausbildung:* in-company training
> *Berufsschule:* vocational/occupational/technical college; occupational high school
> *höhere Berufsschule:* advanced vocational/technical college; tertiary college
> *technische Fachschule:* technical (high) school
> *Sonderschulausbildung/Spezialausbildung:* special education (These schools provide appropriate learning opportunities for disabled or especially gifted pupils).
> *Erwachsenenbildung:* adult education; continued adult education
> *duale Ausbildung:* sandwich course
> *anwendungsorientierte Ausbildung:* vocationally-oriented training/education

[57] *durch Fortbildungs- und Umschulungsmaßnahmen:* by continuing education and vocational retraining schemes; by means of continuing occupational training and retraining

[58] *durch Lohnkostenzuschüsse:* by labour cost subsidies; by payload subsidies

●●●●●● ⁵⁹ *die für die Unternehmen Anreize schaffen:* which offer incentives to employers: which induce the employers to ...; which are inducements for the employers

⁶⁰ *nicht adäquat ausgebildete Mitarbeiter einzustellen:* to take on undertrained staff; to recruit/employ inadequately trained staff

Please note →

> Note that the pronouns and verbs following 'staff' must be put in the plural.

⁶¹ *der arbeitsuchenden Teilnehmer an:* of those job seekers who participate in; of those job seekers who take part in/attend

⁶² *Engagement:* commitment; degree of involvement

Please note →

> The English 'engagement' translates a variety of meanings but not the *Engagement* in the sense of *sich engagieren, sich einsetzen.*

Usage examples of 'engagement'
The couple's secret engagement *(Verlobung)* was finally communicated to their parents.
John was always on time for his engagements/appointments *(Termine).*
The director extended the actor's engagement *(Theatervertrag, Engagement)* by five weeks.
They were unable to meet their financial engagements/obligations *(Verpflichtungen).*
For usage examples of 'to commit' cf. I.2.1 Notes on the translation, item ⁵⁴.

II.3. Exercises

3.1 Labour and work

Find translations of the terms below which are all related to 'labour' and 'work'. Make use of the Notes on the translation and of dictionaries where necessary.
Example
organisierte Arbeiterschaft   organized labour
1 angelernte Arbgeiter   __
2 Arbeiterschaft   __
3 Arbeitsangebot   __
4 Arbeitsmarkt   __
5 Arbeitsmarktpolitik   __
6 Arbeitsnachfrage   __
7 Arbeitsplatz   __

8 Arbeitsstunden —
9 Arbeitszeit —
10 Ausfallzeiten —
11 Berufstätigkeit —
12 Berufsunfähigkeit —
13 Erwerbsleben —
14 Erwerbstätigkeit —
15 Facharbeiter —
16 Kurzarbeit —
17 Mindesterwerbsalter —
18 offene Stellen —
19 Überstunden —
20 ungelernte Arbeiter —

Exercises

Corel Library

3.2 Employment and unemployment

Complete the text below by choosing the appropriate English equivalent of the German terms in (brackets). Use words and phrases from the Sample translation and the Notes. Note that there may be more than one option.

1 The production facilities were transferred to a country where __ __ / __ __ (billige Arbeitskräfte) was available.
2 Most __ (erwerbsfähige) persons between 16 and 64 __ (suchen) or __ (ausüben) __ __ (Erwerbstätigkeit).
3 __ __ (Schaffung neuer Stellen) is a long-term undertaking whereas __ __ (Arbeitslosengeld) is a __ __ (kurzfirstige Massnahme) to reduce the dependency of the __ __ (Arbeitssuchenden) on social security payments.
4 The 'welfare-to-work' programmes established by the Blair government are mainly aimed __ __ (erleichtern) the return of the __ __ (Langzeitarbeitslose) to __ __ (reguläre Beschäftigung).
5 They also include supportive __ (Rückkehr ins Berufsleben) measures for __ __ (Alleinerziehende) and people suffering froma disability.
6 __ __ (Überbrückungsmaßnahmen) are aimed at __ __ (die Arbeitslosigkeit einzudämmen).
7 During economic recessions, __ __ / __ __ __ (die Erwerbsquoten) tend to fall and the number of __ __ (freigesetzte Arbeitskräfte) rises.

The East German Labour Market 49

Exercises

8 Countering __ __ *(strukturelle Arbeitslosigkeit)* means offering extensive __ __ *(Umschulungs-)* programmes for __ *(betriebsbedingt arbeitslose)* workers and financial __ / __ *(Anreize)* to assist the growth of new industries.

9 __ __ *(konjunkturelle Arbeitslosigkeit)* occurs as a result of decreasing __ __ *(gesamtwirtschaftliche Nachfrage)*.

10 The __ __ *(Personalbestand)* in the construction sector is subject to seasonal demand.

3.3 Expectations, recommendations and requests

With certain verbs, impersonal German constructions preceded by the pronoun *es* or the pro-form *man* are 'personalized' when they are translated into English. In the above example, *man* is replaced by the dative object of the same sentence. It would be incorrect to link the main sentence and the subordinate clause by resorting to the connector 'that'.

Example
Man erwartet von Managern, dass sie ihren Worten Taten folgen lassen.
Managers are expected to practise what they preach.
Now apply the same principle to the following sentences.

1 Man erwartet von unseren Mitarbeitern, dass sie die operativen Prozesse kontinuierlich verbessern
2 Es wurde von unseren Facharbeitern verlangt, an der Umschulung teilzunehmen.
3 Es war notwendig, dass ein Teil unserer Beschäftigten vorzeitg in den Ruhestand ging.
4 Es war nicht beabsichtigt, diese Arbeitsplätze zu gefährden.
5 Es sollte gar nicht vorkommen, dass solche Probleme auftreten.
6 Man hat uns empfohlen, einen Arbeitsmarktexperten zu Rate zu ziehen.
7 Es wurde ihnen geraten, wegen der erwarteten konjunkturellen Erholung keine weiteren betriebsbedingten Kündigungen mehr auszusprechen.
8 Es stand zu erwarten, dass dieses Verfahren nicht zum Erfolg führen würde.
9 Man nahm an, dass er seine Kündigung einreichen würde.
10 Man hält den neuen Abteilungsleiter für ausgesprochen arbeitnehmerfreundlich.

III Supply and Demand

III.1 **Text: Der Verlauf von Angebots- und Nachfragekurven**   52

III.2 **Sample translation**   54
III.2.1   Notes on the translation

III.3 **Exercises**   64
III.3.1   Interpreting linear curves
III.3.2   Graphs, diagrams and charts
III.3.3   Prepositional objects

III.1 Text: Der Verlauf von Angebots- und Nachfragekurven

III Supply and Demand

Angebots- und Nachfragekurven stellen eine mikroökonomische Betrachtung des Marktes für ein bestimmtes Gut dar. Der Preis dieses Gutes spielt eine zentrale Rolle dafür, welche Menge die Verkäufer (in den meisten Fällen die Unternehmen) innerhalb eines Zeitabschnitts anbieten und welche Menge dieses Gutes die Käufer (in der Regel die Haushalte) nachfragen.

Der Zusammenhang zwischen Preis und pro Zeiteinheit angebotener Menge wird mit einer *Angebotskurve* abgebildet. Um diese Kurve zu erstellen, werden zunächst auf der Ordinate verschiedene Preise (oder Werte der unabhängigen Variablen) und auf der Abszisse verschiedene Werte der abhängigen Variablen abgetragen und danach die verschiedenen Preis-Mengen-Kombinationen (oder Wertekombinationen) in das Koordinatensystem eingezeichnet.

Die meisten Angebotskurven für Güter und Dienstleistungen haben einen steigenden Verlauf. Die Steigung der Angebotskurve vermittelt einen Eindruck, wie stark die Anbieter mit ihrer Menge auf Erhöhungen der Produktpreise reagieren. So signalisiert ein senkrechter Verlauf der Angebotskurve, dass die Anbieter auch bei stark steigendem Marktpreis ihr Angebot nicht ausweiten werden. Man spricht dann von einem „starren" oder „preisunelastischen Angebot", eine Bezeichnung, die auf ein nicht vermehrbares Gut, wie beispielsweise die Grundstücke in der Innenstadt von Frankfurt am Main, zutrifft.

Ein Maß für die Stärke der Reaktion der Anbieter auf eine Preisänderung (bei einem bestimmten Ausgangspreis) ist die *Preiselastizität des Angebots*; sie gibt an, um wie viel Prozent sich die angebotene Menge ändert, wenn der Preis um ein Prozent steigt oder fällt. Bei einem waagerechten Verlauf der Angebotskurve hat die Angebotselastizität den Wert „unendlich". Das Angebot ist dann „unendlich elastisch", d. h. bereits eine marginale Preiserhöhung verursacht eine extreme Ausweitung der angebotenen Menge.

Analog dazu wird die *Nachfragekurve* in das Diagramm eingezeichnet. Sie hat in der Regel eine negative Steigung, denn wenn das Gut teurer wird, sinkt die nachgefragte Menge. Aus dem Schnittpunkt von Angebots- und Nachfragekurve ergibt sich der Gleichgewichtspreis, d. h. der Preis, bei dem angebotene und nachgefragte Menge übereinstimmen.

Ein Maß für die Stärke der Reaktion der Käufer auf Preissteigerungen eines bestimmten Produkts ist die *Preiselastizität der Nachfrage*. Wenn eine Preisänderung zu einer überproportionalen Änderung der

Nachfrage führt, gilt die Nachfrage als „elastisch" und der nach der Formel berechnete absolute Wert der Elastizität ist größer als Eins. Analog dazu ist die Nachfrage „unelastisch", wenn die Änderung der Nachfrage unterproportional ist. Der Elastizitätswert ist dann kleiner als Eins. Wenn die Gesamtnachfrage proportional auf eine Preisänderung reagiert, dann ist der Elastizitätswert der Nachfrage gleich Eins. Bei Angebots- und Nachfragekurven wird immer die Ceteris-paribus-Bedingung unterstellt, der zufolge alle Einflussgrößen der angebotenen und nachgefragten Menge – außer dem Preis – unverändert bleiben. Ändert sich beispielsweise bei der Nachfragekurve eine dieser C.-p.-gesetzten Größen, wie die Präferenzen der Nachfrager oder ihr *verfügbares Einkommen*, so ergibt sich eine andere Nachfragefunktion, und die zugehörige Nachfragekurve dreht oder verschiebt sich.

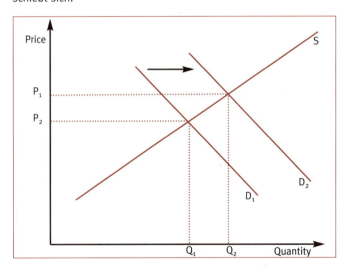

Figure 1: *A shift in the demand curve*

Verschiebt sich die Nachfragekurve wie in Abbildung 1 von D_1 nach D_2, führt dies, bei Beibehaltung des bisherigen Gleichgewichtspreises P_1, zu einem Nachfrageüberschuss. Das bedeutet, dass nicht mehr alle Nachfragenden das von ihnen gewünschte Gut zum Gleichgewichtspreis erhalten und einige „leer" aus gehen. Folglich wird der Preis solange steigen, bis, bei einem neuen Gleichgewichtspreis P_2, angebotene und nachgefragte Menge wieder übereinstimmen.
(Renate Neubäumer)

III.2 Sample translation

The shape of[1] **supply and demand curves**[2]

Supply and demand curves **represent a microeconomic view**[3] of a market for a **specific good**[4]. The **price**[5] of this good **plays a decisive part in determining**[6] **which quantities will be provided by the sellers**[7] (who, in the majority of the cases, are companies) and which quantities of this good **will be purchased**[8] by the **buyers**[9] (represented, as a rule, by households) within a given period of time.

The relationship between the price of a product and the quantity supplied **per time period**[10] is **depicted**[11] in a *supply curve*. **This curve is plotted**[12] **by first marking different prices**[13] (or values of the independent variable) on the **y-axis**[14] and by indicating different values of the dependent variable on the **x-axis**[15]. The different price-quantity relations (or combinations of values) are then plotted on the **graph**[16]. Most supply curves for goods and services **slope upwards**[17]. The **gradient**[18] of the supply curve **reflects the degree of responsiveness of the quantity supplied by the sellers**[19] to changes in the product price. A straight-line vertical supply curve[20] indicates, for example, that the **suppliers**[21] **will not increase the quantity of the products they provide even if the market price increases substantially**[22]. This is referred to as 'inflexible supply' or 'price-inelastic supply', a term which applies to a **nonproducible asset**[23] such as **real estate**[24] in the city centre of Frankfurt am Main.

Price-elasticity of supply[25] **is a measure of the degree of responsiveness of the suppliers**[26] to a price change (**relating to a specifically determined initial price**[27]). It indicates **to what degree**[28] **the quantity supplied responds to**[29] a price increase or price decrease of one per cent. **If the supply curve is a straight horizontal line**[30], supply elasticity approaches an 'infinite' value. In such a case, supply is **'perfectly elastic'**[31], in other words, **even a marginal price increase**[32] **generates**[33] **an excess**[34] of the quantity offered.

Similarly[35], the *demand curve* is plotted in the graph. It usually **slopes downward**[36], for if the price of the good is raised, demand usually declines. **It interacts with the supply curve to determine**[37] **the equilibrium market price**[38], i.e. the price at which the quantity of the demanded good is **equal to**[39] the quantity supplied.

Price-elasticity of demand[40] measures the degree of responsiveness of the buyers to price changes of a given product. If a price change results **in a more than proportionate**[41] change in demand, demand is said to be **'elastic'**[42], and the **elasticity statistic**[43] calculated as an absolute value according to the formula will be **greater than one**[44]. Similarly, if the change in demand is **less than proportionate**[45], demand

is **'inelastic'**[46] and the elasticity quotient will be **less than**[47] one. If total consumer demand develops proportionally in response to a price change, elasticity of demand equals **unity**[48].
Supply and demand curves **are always based on the ceteris paribus assumption**[49] according to which all factors affecting the quantity of supply and the quantity of demand – with the exception of the price – **remain equal**[50].
If any of the ceteris paribus variables affecting, for instance, the demand curve change, such as consumer preferences or **their disposable income**[51], and hence *the purchasing power* of the buyers, **this results in**[52] a different demand function **which causes the corresponding curve to rotate or to shift**[53].
A shift in the demand curve from D_1 to D_2, as shown in Figure 1, results in a surplus of demand, **if the current equilibrium price P_1, is maintained**[54]. Not all consumers can purchase the good they desire at the equilibrium price and some come away 'empty-handed'. **Consequently**[55], the price will rise **to a point where** – at a new market equilibrium P_2 – supply will once again match demand.

2.1 Notes on the translation

[1] *der Verlauf von:* the typical shape of; the shape of

← Please note

> *Verlauf* has no direct equivalent in English. Most economics textbooks use 'shape' or 'slope' in similar contexts. Sometimes, it might be advisable to employ the gerund forms of the verbs that collocate with 'curve'.
> Example
> 'plotting'/'drawing' demand and supply curves
> Alternatively, one could consider not to translating *Verlauf* at all as 'shape' is semantically covered by 'curve', and this makes the English sentence somewhat clumsy.
> It would be incorrect to resort to 'course' or 'form'.

Examples for the usage of 'course', and 'form'
in the course of the meeting: *während des Treffens*
in the course of history: *im Lauf der Geschichte*
a form of/manner of expression: *eine Ausdrucksweise*
This can take the form of a letter. *Das kann in Briefform geschehen.*

[2] *Angebots- und Nachfragekurven:* supply and demand curves

For the relevant verb-noun collocations of 'demand' cf. IV.2.1 Notes on the translation, item [6].

> This is the interaction between 'supply', i.e. the goods and services flowing into a market, and 'demand', i.e. the consumers' (and other economic entities such as the factors of production, currencies and shares) willingness to purchase these goods if they have the means to do so.
>
> The different forms of 'demand' and 'supply'
> - 'Realised demand' *(realisierte Nachfrage)* is another expression for 'amount bought' *(gekaufte Menge)*, 'actual demand' or 'ex post demand' *(ex-post-Nachfrage)*.
> - Correspondingly, 'realised supply' *(realisiertes Angebot)* is known as 'amount supplied', 'actual supply' or 'ex-post supply'.
> - 'Intended demand' or 'planned demand' *(geplante Nachfrage)* are synonymous with 'ex ante demand' *(ex-ante-Nachfrage)*.
> - 'Intended supply' or 'planned supply' *(geplantes Angebot)* are the same as 'ex ante supply'.
> - 'Aggregate demand' *(gesamtwirtschaftliche Nachfrage)* is the sum of demands for all the goods and services within an economy.

[3] *stellen eine mikroökonomische Betrachtung ... dar:* represent a microeconomic view; offer a microeconomic perspective

[4] *bestimmtes Gut:* specific good; specific commodity

> 'Goods' *(Güter)* is a largely polysemous generic term for everything people associate with positive values, including assets such as personal property, income, leisure and security.
> In economic theory, 'goods' comprise a number of commodities, services and utilities:
> - 'Final goods' *(Endprodukte)* are 'consumer goods' (cf. I.2.1 Notes on the translation, item[27])
> - 'Intermediate goods' *(Zwischenerzeugnisse/Vorprodukte)* or 'producer goods' *(Produktionsgüter)* include 'primary products' or 'primaries' *(Rohstoffe)*, 'capital goods' *(Investitionsgüter)* and 'semi-finished goods' *(Halbfabrikate)*.
> 'Good' can be synonymous with 'commodity' *(Ware)* and 'freight' *(Fracht)* i.e. articles exchanged or shipped for commercial purposes. However, more specifically, 'commodities'

> (Handelsgüter) are materials traded in the 'commodity exchange' (Warenbörse).

Usage examples
goods train: *Güterzug*
They were not able to deliver the goods. *Sie konnten nicht halten, was sie versprochen hatten.*

5   *Preise:* prices
    For the different types of prices and usage details cf. IV.2.1 Notes on the translation, item °°.
6   *spielt eine zentrale Rolle dafür:* plays a decisive part in determining; plays a crucial/central/essential role in determining

> *Dafür* is an ancillary structure which, in the German text, replaces a prepositional accusative, namely *für das Festlegen der Preise*. This accusative must be fully translated in order to convey the precise sense of the German sentence.

← Please note

7   *welche Menge die Verkäufer ... anbieten:* which quantities will be provided by the sellers; which amount will be supplied by the sellers
8   *nachgefragt:* purchased; demanded; obtained
9   *Käufer:* buyers

> 'Buyer' also signifies *Einkäufer*. In the above context, however, it is synonymous with 'consumers' or 'users' of a product.

← Please note

10 *pro Zeitabschnitt:* per time period; over a period of time
11 *wird mit der Angebotskurve abgebildet:* is depicted in the supply curve; is shown/illustrated/demonstrated in the supply curve
    The above verbs are all semantically related, and therefore translate *abbilden*, but each includes unique aspects:
    • to depict: to represent by drawing, painting; to portray
    • to illustrate: to clarify/to explain by using analogies and examples
    • to demonstrate: to show; to manifest, to prove
12 *um diese Kurve zu erstellen:* this curve is plotted; this curve is drawn

> 'Plot' as a noun and verb are highly polysemous including a number of idiomatic usages.
> In natural science, 'to plot' is
> • to determine the location of a point by means of its coordinates *(einen Punkt bestimmen)*

← Please note

Supply and Demand   57

- to mark a point on a graph to indicate a position *(einen Punkt einzeichnen)*
- to draw a curve by connecting the points marked out on the graph *(eine Kurve erstellen)*
- to represent (an equation or function) by means of a curve drawn on a graph *(eine Funktion abbilden)*
- to make a map, a diagram or a chart of a route *(geographisch abbilden)*

Usage as a noun
The two pupils made a plot (secret plan) to cheat in the exam.
All settlers were given a plot of land to set up their farms.

Usage as a verb
The flight of the balloon was drawn/plotted on a chart.
The nurse plotted the patient's temperature over several days.
The new road was plotted on the map. The boys plotted/schemed/conspired to have their revenge.
The land was plotted out/divided into house lots.
The story was plotted/devised in a realistic fashion.

[13] *werden zunächst ... verschiedene Preise abgetragen:* by first marking different prices; by first indicating/plotting/entering different prices

[14] *Ordinate:* y-axis; ordinate; vertical axis
[15] *Abszisse:* x-axis; abscissa; horizontal axis
[16] *Koordinatensystem:* graph; set of axes

Please note →

Note that 'axes' is pronounced [æksiːz].
- 'Graph' is a multifunctional semantic unit. In linguistics, it denotes any written sign or symbol (cf. Glossary), in mathematics, it is short for 'graphic formula'. The verb 'to graph' signifies 'to draw a line or diagram representing some degree of change, an equation or function'.

Example
Let's draw/plot a graph to show the exchange rate fluctuations *(Wechselkursschwankungen)* of the dollar against the yen in the last ten years.
It is this semantic foundation that underlies the meaning of the noun which, as a rule, makes reference to a 'mathematical curve' *(Kurve im mathematischen Sinne)* or other 'diagrams' *(Diagramme)* representing the relation(s) of the variables in an 'equation' *(Gleichung)* or 'function' *(Funktion)*. This type of

curve usually forms an integral part of a 'set of axes' *(Koordinatensystem)*. They also plot chronological developments.
- Likewise, the meaning of 'diagram' manifests itself in the semantic implications of the verb. 'To diagram' means literally 'to mark out by lines' and, consequently, the noun denotes, first and foremost, an outline, a plan or sketch used for illustration, explanation and to point out essential information on the specific features and/or function of the item drawn. In mathematics, 'diagrams' represent drawn geometrical figures such as cubes, globes, pyramids or cones; in engineering, they refer to mechanical drawings, e.g. a cross section of a machine 'drawn to scale' *(nach Maßstab gezeichnet)*, an architectural or a technical plan.

Examples
He drew a diagram/sketch to show the visitor how to get to his office.
The engineers presented a diagram/drawing showing a cross section of the new turbine.
The architect diagrammed/drew the floor plan to indicate how he would divide the office space.

Although 'diagram' – being the more comprehensive term – may also denote 'graph', it would be incorrect to refer to the above presentations as 'graphs'.
Note also that 'diagram' – unlike 'programme'/'program' – has only one written form.
- 'To chart' represents yet another semantic variation of the afore-mentioned expressions. The verb signifies 'to make a map', 'to plot a course', to make a detailed list' or 'breakdown' *(detailierte Aufstellung)*. In line with this, a chart can be a map used for navigation, an outline map on which weather information is plotted or any sheet offering graphical, tabular or diagrammatical information.

← Please note

Examples
The navigator charted the course of the ship.
The weather chart shows where temperatures dropped below zero last night.
American history books tend to include a chart of the Presidents of the United States.

• • • • • •

> Types of graphs and/or diagrams:
> - 'Line diagrams' (also: 'line curves'; 'curves'; 'lines') can be dotted, ragged (cf. VII.1 Technische Analysen), straight, descending, ascending or sloping upwards and downwards.
> - 'Pie charts' are 'circular diagrams' *(Tortendiagramme, Kreisdiagramme)* that are divided into sectors. Individual sectors can be 'exploded' *(herausgeschoben/versetzt)* in order to highlight individual elements.
> - 'Scatter diagrams' *(Streuungsdiagramme)* indicate the specific nature of the relationship between two variables. They may, for instance, highlight areas of concentration, i.e. 'clusters' *(Cluster; Klumpen)*, and other distribution patterns *(Verteilungsmuster)*.
> - 'Bar charts' (also: 'bar graphs'; 'bar diagrams') display 'vertical bars' *(Säulen)* or 'horizontal bars' *(Balken)* to make comparisons.
> - 'Histograms' *(Klassenhäufigkeitstabellen/Histogramme)* are representations of a 'frequency distribution' *(Häufigkeitsverteilung)* by means of rectangles whose widths represent 'class intervals' *(Klassenbreiten)* and whose vertical areas are proportional to the corresponding frequencies.

[17] *haben einen steigenden Verlauf:* slope upwards; are positive curves; are upward sloping; are positively sloped; have a positive gradient

[18] *Steigung:* gradient; inclination

[19] *vermittelt einen Eindruck, wie stark die Anbieter mit ihrer Menge ... reagieren:* reflects the degree of responsiveness of the quantity supplied by the sellers

A closer translation would be
The slope of the supply curve reflects to what extent/degree the quantity supplied by the sellers reacts to/responds to changes in the product price.

[20] *ein senkrechter Verlauf der Angebotskurve:* a straight-line vertical supply curve; a vertical supply curve

[21] *Anbieter:* suppliers; sellers

Please note →

> 'Supplier' also signifies *Zulieferer, Lieferant*.

[22] *auch bei stark steigendem Marktpreis ihr Angebot nicht ausweiten werden:* will not increase the amount of the products they

offer even if the market price goes up considerably; will not increase the quantity of the products they provide/supply even if the market price rises markedly/substantially

> The accusative object *ihr Angebot* has to be paraphrased before it is translated. In English, it is not 'their offer' that is increased but 'the amount of goods the sellers supply' to the market.

← Please note

²³ *nicht vermehrbare Güter:* nonproducible asset; nonproducible (productive) good
²⁴ *Grundstücke:* real estate; property; landholdings
²⁵ *Preiselastizität des Angebotes:* price-elasticity of supply
²⁶ *ein Maß für die Stärke der Reaktion der Anbieter ist:* is a measure of the degree of responsiveness; is a measure of how the suppliers respond to/react to; measures to degree of responsiveness of the suppliers

> It would be incorrect to say 'a measure for'.

← Please note

²⁷ *bei einem bestimmten Ausgangspreis:* relating to a specifically determined initial price
²⁸ *um wie viel Prozent:* to what degree; by how many per cent
²⁹ *sich die angebotene Menge ändert:* the quantity supplied responds to; the quantity supplied reacts to
³⁰ *bei einem waagerechten Verlauf der Angebotskurve:* if the supply curve is a straight horizontal line; if the supply curve shows up/is shaped like a horizontal line; if the supply curve plots/constitutes/forms a horizontal line
For further details on the translation of *Verlauf* cf. note ¹ above.
³¹ *unendlich elastisch:* perfectly elastic; infinitely elastic; completely/totally elastic

> The opposite is 'completely inelastic' or 'zero elastic'.

← Please note

³² *bereits eine marginale Preiserhöhung:* even a marginal price increase; even a slight price increase

← Please note

> The quantifying appositions *bereits*, *schon*, *selbst*, *sogar* (which could all have been employed in the German sentence), are usually translated as 'even': However, if the quantities they specify are measurable or countable, these appositions may have to be rendered in a more precise way, for instance, as 'even as little as'.

> For details on the usage of similar quantifiers see: J. Bauer & M. Seidenspinner, *Betriebswirtschaft: Übersetzungsübungen, studium kompakt, Fachsprache Englisch*, Cornelsen & Oxford, Berlin, 2001; p. 172.

[33] *verursacht:* generates, produces; causes; occasions; results in
[34] *eine extreme Ausweitung:* an excess of; an extreme extension of; a disproportionate increase in
[35] *analog dazu:* similarly; in an analoguous fashion; likewise
[36] *hat ... eine negative Steigung:* slopes downward; is a negative curve; has a negative gradient; is negatively sloped; is downward sloping
[37] *aus dem Schnittpunkt der Angebots- und der Nachfragekurve ergibt sich:* it interacts with the supply curve to determine; the point where the supply curve and the demand curve intersect determines; the point of intersection between the supply curve and the demand curve determines; the point where the supply curve cuts the demand curve
[38] *der Gleichgewichtspreis:* the equilibrium market price; the market clearing equilibrium; the market-clearing price

> An 'equilibrium price' is the only price which is consistent with the market plans of both households and companies.
> Mathematically, we can summarize the different conditions that bring about an equilibrium or a disequilibrium as:
> - if intended supply > (is greater than) intended demand, the price will fall (disequilibrium condition)
> - if intended supply < (is less than) intended demand, the price will rise (disequilibrium condition)
> - if intended supply = (equals/is equal to) intended demand, the price will remain constant
> - realised supply _ (is identical with) realised demand at all prices (identity)

[39] *übereinstimmen:* is equal to; exactly matches
[40] *Preiselastizität der Nachfrage:* price elasticity of demand:
Price elasticity of demand is calculated as:

$$PED = \frac{\text{percentage change in quantity demanded}}{\text{percentage change in price}}$$

$$PED = \frac{\text{\% change in quantity demanded}}{\text{\% change in price}}$$

> The latter example reads as: 'PED equals the percentage change in the quantity demanded over/divided by the percentage change in price.'

← Please note

41 *zu einer überproportionalen:* in a more than proportionate; in a disproportionately high
42 *elastisch:* elastic

> If total consumer expenditure increases in response to a price fall, demand is 'relatively elastic' *(relativ elastisch).*

> However, it would be misleading to refer to the whole of a flat demand curve as 'elastic' or to the whole of a steep one as 'inelastic' since elasticity generally varies from point to point along the curve.

← Please note

43 *Elastizitätswert:* elasticity statistic; elasticity quotient
44 *größer als Eins:* greater than 1; > 1; over one

> In mathematics, it would be incorrect to say 'bigger than'.

← Please note

45 *unterproportional:* less than proportionate; disproportionately low
46 *unelastisch:* inelastic

> If total consumer expenditure decreases in response to a price fall, demand is 'relatively inelastic' *(relativ unelastisch).*

47 *kleiner als eins:* less than one; < 1; below one

> It would be inaccurate to say 'smaller than' one.

← Please note

48 *Eins:* unity

> In mathematics, 'unity' denotes
> - the numeral one
> - a quantity assuming the value of 1

49 *wird immer die Ceteris-paribus-Bedingung unterstellt:* are always based on the ceteris paribus assumption; are always constructed on/founded on the assumption of 'all other values being equal'

> Demand functions are based on the ceteris paribus assumption which is Latin for 'all things being equal'. It is thereby assumed that all the determinants of demand – with the exception of the price – are held constant.

← Please note

In economic shorthand, this shows up as: Q = f(P)
Ceteris paribus assumptions are relevant when forecasts are deduced from theoretical models.

[50] *unverändert bleiben:* remain equal; are kept constant
[51] *ihr verfügbares Einkommen:* their disposable income; the disposable income of the buyers

> The supply and demand principle is based on the assumption that suppliers and consumers act rationally. Companies seek to maximise their profits and households the total 'utility' *(Nutzen)* of the products they purchase. However, consumers face a whole series of 'constraints' *(Zwänge/Nebenbedingungen) such as* their limited disposable incomes.

[52] *so ergibt sich:* this results in; this produces; this creates; this occasions
[53] *und die zugehörige Nachfragekurve dreht oder verschiebt sich:* which causes the corresponding curve to rotate or to shift; which will bring about a shift or a rotation in the respective demand curve
[54] *bei Beibehaltung des bisherigen Gleichgewichtspreises P1:* if the current equilibrium price P1 is maintained
Cf. also III.3.3 Prepositional objects.
[55] *folglich:* consequently, as a result

III.3 Exercises

3.1 Interpreting linear curves

An error frequently committed in presentations describing trends is that the person giving the presentation confuses the vocabulary required to characterize the curve and that needed to describe the trend shown in the curve.

Instead of saying that 'the prices have nosedived', students are sometimes tempted to say that 'the curve has nosedived' *(die Kurve ist abgestürtzt)* or 'the curve is falling down' *(die Kurve fällt hin)*. It is equally incorrect to say that 'the price forms a trough' when it is the curve which forms a trough.

Curves can
- be drawn/be plotted in/on graph: *in ein Diagramm eingezeichnet werden*
- form/be shaped like a line: *wie eine Gerade verlaufen*
- slope upwards: *steigend verlaufen*

- slope downwards: *fallend verlaufen*
- shift rightward/leftward: *sich nach rechts/nach links verschieben*
- form a kneepoint: *senkrecht abfallen*
- form a trough: *eine Wanne/ein Tal bilden*
- level off; form a Plateau: *auslaufen; ein Plateau bilden*
- run in parallel: *parallel zueinander verlaufen*
- intersect/cut one another: *sich schneiden*
- interact: *miteinander in Beziehung treten*
- merge: *ineinander aufgehen; sich verbinden*
- converge: *zusammentreffen; aufeinander zulaufen*
- cross the origin/be drawn through point 0: *durch den Nullpunkt verlaufen*

Line curves can be

....	dotted: *gepunktet*
----------	interrupted/dashed: *gestrichelt/unterbrochen*
—·—·—·—	dashed and dotted/dash dot lines: *Punkt-Strich-Linien; gepunktet und gestrichelt*
───────	coloured: *farbig*
~~	undulating: *gewellt*
ＶＶＶＶＶＶＶ	serrated: *gezackt*
O---O---O---O	marked by circles: *mit Kreisen markiert*
■---■---■---■	marked by squares: *mit Quadraten gekennzeichnet*
◆---◆---◆---◆	marked by diamonds: *mit Rauten durchsetzt*
△---△---△---△	marked by triangles: *mit Dreiecken gekennzeichnet*

Let's revise some of the terminology used in the text. Look at **Figure 1** before you complete this exercise.

1 __ __ or curves in a __ __/__ *(graphische Darstellung)* can be __ *(flach)*, __ *(steil)* or a combination of both.
2 Ascending curves have a __ __ *(positiven Verlauf)* or __ __ *(verlaufen steigend)*; descending ones have a __ __ *(negativen Verlauf)* or __ __ *(verlaufen fallend)*.
3 A __ __ *(Gerade)* is a curve with a constant __/__ *(Steigung)*.
4 Curves may __ __ __ *(parallel verlaufen)*, __ *(sich drehen)*, __ __ *(sich nach oben verschieben)*, __ __ *(sich nach unten verschieben)*, __ __ *(sich nach links verschieben)* or __ __ *(sich nach rechts verschieben)*.
5 Curves may __/__/__ *(schneiden)* the __/__ *(x-Achse)*, the __/__ *(y-Achse)* or the __ __ __/__ __ *(Achsenkreuz/Nullpunkt)*

Exercises

6 The __ *(tiefste)* point on a curve is its __ or __, the highest its __ or __ *(Spitze)*.

7 Figure 2 shows a typical __ / __ *(Verlauf)* of the demand curve.

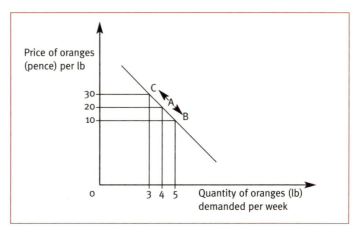

(B. Harrison, R. Nutter: *GCSE Economics*, Addison Wesley Longman, 1997, p. 62

Figure 2: *Demand curve based on the data provided in Table 1*

Price per lb of oranges (£)	lbs of oranges demanded by households
0.30	3
0.20	4
0.10	5

Table 1: *Range of orange prices and quantities bought per week*

8 It __ / __ / __ *(gibt an)* the price of the commodity listed in Table 1 __ __ __ *(in Abhängigkeit von)* the quantity of demand.

9 The price is __ *(gemessen)* on the y-axis or __ axis, the quantity demanded on the x-axis or __ axis.

10 The three __ *(Punkte)*, where price __ *(sich schneidet mit)* quantity, namely A, B, and C, indicate the quantities of a product demanded by the households at three different prices.

11 __ *(Bei)* position B, for instance, the price __ __ *(beträgt)* 10 pence per lb of oranges and the quantity demanded is 5lbs; the __ *(Wert)* of sales is therefore 10p x 5 = 50 pence.

12 This __ *(Gleichung)* can be read as 'ten pence times five __ / __ __ __ *(ist gleich)* 50 pence.'

13 If the price at A rises from 15 p to a new __ *(Gleichgewichts-)* position of 20 pence per pound, we __ *(verschieben uns)* to

position C of the curve as this rise automatically __ *(erzeugt)* a change in the quantity of the __ *(Waren)* purchased.
14 This change in demand to C represents a __ __ __ *(Nachfragerückgang)* which is not quite identical with __ __ __ *(Nachfragekonzentration)*.
15 On the other hand, if the price falls __ *(um)* 5p to 10p, there is an __ *(Ausweitung)* of demand.

Exercises

Corel Library

3.2 Graphs, diagrams and charts

Complete the exercise below by choosing a suitable English equivalent of the German terms in (brackets). Use words and phrases from the **Notes on the translation** and your bilingual dictionaries. Note that there may be more than one option.
1 In English, the noun 'graph' stands for __ __.
2 In mathematics, this term __ __ *(nimmt Bezug)* to a curve or any other __ *(Diagramm)* representing the __ *(Beziehung)* of the variables in an __ *(Gleichung)* or function.

Supply and Demand 67

Exercises

3 The noun 'diagram' carries a large number of different meanings but, first and foremost, it denotes __ *(Zeichnungen)*, __ *(Skizzen)* and __ *(Übersichtszeichnungen/Umrissskizzen)* made for explanatory purposes.

4 In engineering and other scientific areas, diagrams are generally __ *(geometrische)* or __ *(mechanische)* drawings such as __ *(Querschnitte)* and __ *(Längsschnitte)* of technical equipment drawn to scale.

5 'Chart' refers to a __ __ *(graphische Darstellung)*, too, as well as expressing a number of independent meanings.

6 'To chart' signifies to __ *(aufzeichnen)* a course and to detail __ *(Informationen)* by __ *(anordnen)* it in lists, __ *(Aufstellungen)*, __ *(Tabellen)* or __ *(Diagrammen)*.

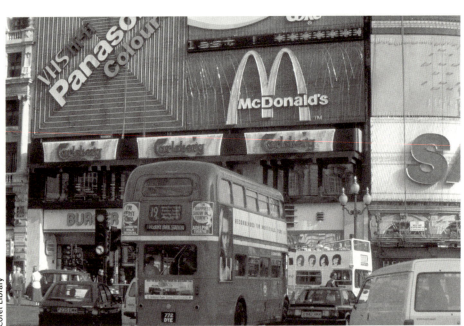

Corel Library

3.3 Prepositional objects   Exercises

With very few exceptions, 'by' is no direct equivalent of its homonymous German counterpart *bei*.
Bei may be rendered directly by resorting to a variety of prepositions or adverbial phrases:
bei dieser Gelegenheit: on this occasion
bei einem Grundpreis von: at a basic price of
bei unserem Glück: with our luck
beim Fenster: at the window
bei den Verhandlungen: in the course of the negotiations

Alternatively, the dative object formed with *bei* may be paraphrased as a subordinate clause, a relative clause, an infinitive or a gerund structure. Please pay attention to the fact that all tenses have to be aligned with the context in which the dative object is imbedded.

Examples
beim Errechnen der Gesamtsumme: when the total is calculated
bei dieser Betrachtungsweise: on adopting this perspective; when/if this perspective is adopted
bei Bezahlung mit Kreditkarten: if payment is made by

Translate the following sentences. Include the English expressions given in (brackets).
1   Bei dieser Kurve handelt es sich um eine Angebotskurve.
2   Stellen Sie beim Erstellen der Kurve sicher, dass alle Werte richtig eingetragen sind.
3   Bei diesem Verfahren ist Folgendes zu beachten.
4   Bei der Ceteris-paribus-Bedingung wird unterstellt, dass alle Einflussgrößen konstant bleiben.
5   Bei einem Preisanstieg um 5% sinkt vermutlich die Nachfrage.
6   Bei unserem ersten Versuch, das stark nachgefragte Modell zu erwerben, gingen wir leider leer aus.

IV Price Determinants

IV.1 **Text: Die Entwicklung der Energiepreise** 72

IV.2 **Sample translation** 73
IV.2.1 Notes on the translation

IV.3 **Exercises** 80
IV.3.1 Depicting price trends
IV.3.2 A fair market price?
IV.3.3 Putting on a price tag

IV. 1 Text: Die Entwicklung der Energiepreise

IV Price Determinants

Wären die Weltenergiemärkte wettbewerblich orientiert und frei von staatlicher Einflussnahme, würden sich die Preise nach der Grenzkostenregel entwickeln: d.h. die Kosten der teuersten Förderstätte, die gerade noch benötigt wird, um die bestehende Energienachfrage zu decken, würden den Preis bestimmen.

Die Energiequellen würden, etwas vereinfacht, streng in der Reihenfolge ihrer Bereitstellungskosten beansprucht. Wäre es so, lägen die Energiepreise deutlich niedriger und die Weltenergieversorgung würde wesentlich stärker durch Öl aus dem Nahen Osten dominiert.

Die Realität sieht jedoch ganz anders aus. Sowohl auf der Nachfrage- wie auf der Angebotsseite greifen die Staaten in den Markt ein. Beschränkung der Förderung, Behinderung von Importen und insbesondere hohe Steuern und Abgaben in Förder- wie Verbrauchsländern lassen den Wettbewerb als preisbildenden Faktor oft in den Hintergrund treten.

(„Chancen und Risiken der künftigen Weltenergieversorgung", Energiewirtschaftlicher Arbeitskreis der RWE AG, Mai 1998)

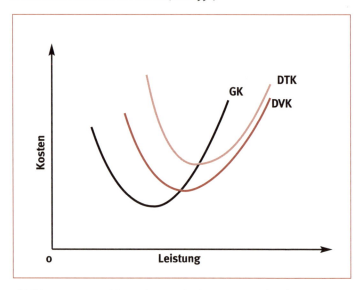

Abbildung 1: *Entwicklung der Durchschnittskosten (DTK), der variablen Durchschnittskosten (DVK) und der Grenzkosten (GK) bei ertragsgesetzlicher Kostenfunktion.*

Energy price trends

If the world's energy markets were **competitively oriented**[1] and free from **government intervention**[2], **prices**[3] would develop **in terms of the marginal cost rule**[4]: that is to say, the price would be determined according to the cost of the most expensive **production site**[5] **needed so as to just cover the demand for energy**[6].

Putting it simply[7], energy sources would be **utilized**[8] strictly according to their **procurement costs**[9]. **If this were the case**[10], energy prices would be **significantly lower**[11], and the world's energy supply **would be far more strongly dominated**[12] by oil **from the Middle East**[13]. In reality, however, things are quite different.

Governments intervene[14] in the market **on both the demand side and the supply side**[15]. **Limitations on production**[16], **import restrictions**[17] and, above all, high taxes and **duties**[18], in both the producing countries and the consumer countries all mean that **competition often becomes a less important price determinant**[19].

IV. 2 Sample translation

2.1 Notes on the translation

[1] *wettbewerblich orientiert:* competitvely oriented; truly/genuinely competitive

> 'Oriented' has a second form 'orientated' which is gaining ground in all varieties of English.

← Please note

Related expressions
unsere Konkurrenz: our competitors
konkurrenzfähigePreise: competitive prices
nicht wettbewerbsfähige Produkte: uncompetitive products
Wettbewerbsstrategien: competitive strategies
wettbewerbsintensiver Markt: highly competitive market
Cf. also note [19] below.

[2] *staatlicher Einflußnahme:* government intervention; any exertion of influence on the part of/by the state

> *Einflussnahme*, in the above context, implies an undesirable 'exertion of influence' on the part of the state. For this reason, 'interference' which signifies *Einmischung* could be used as an alternative translation.
> 'Government' is the most common translation for *staatlich*. 'Public' *(öffentlich)* usually signifies 'state-owned' or 'state-administered' thereby denoting the opposite of 'private'.

← Please note

| In American English, 'state', refers to the federal states. |

Examples
staatliche Subventionen: government subsidies
staatliche Unterstützung: government aid
staatliches Unternehmen: state-owned enterprise; state enterprise
staatliche Rente: state pension
staatlich verordnet: state-ordained; imposed by the state
Staatsausgaben: government spending (cf. V.2.1 Notes on the translation, item [20])
Staatsbetrieb: state-owned/government-owned enterprise
Staatseinnahmen: national revenues
Staatsverschuldung: national debt (cf. IX.2.1 Notes on the translation, item [38])

3   *Preise:* prices

> Economists distinguish between
> - 'nominal prices' *(Nominalpreise)* which are calculated on the basis of 'current prices' *(laufende Preise)*. They play an important role when the nominal GDP is valued. However, they make no allowance for the effects of inflation.
> - 'real prices' or 'money prices' *(reale Preise)* which are founded on 'constant prices' *(konstante Preise)*. They have been 'corrected for inflation' *(inflationsbereinigt)* and are used when the real GDP is valued.

Useful collocations
price booster: *Preistreiber*
price bracket/price range: *Preisklasse*
price bottom: *Preisuntergrenze*
price ceiling: *Preisobergrenze/oberste Preisgrenze*
price competition: *Preiswettbewerb*
price control: *Preiskontrolle; Preisregulierung*
price cutter: *Preisbrecher*
price cutting: *Unterbietung von Preisen*
price fixing/price rigging: *Preisabsprache; Preisfixierung*
price floor: *unterstes Preisniveau*
price leader/price maker: *Preisführer*
price limit: *Preisgrenze*
price margin: *Preisspanne*
price ring [GB]/price cartel: *Preiskartell; Preisfixer*

price tag: *Preisschild*
price taker: *Mengenanpasser*
price war: *Preiskampf*
cost price: *Selbstkostenpreis*
fair market price: *marktgerechter Preis*
rock-bottom price: *Tiefstpreis*
top price: *Höchstpreis*
unit price: *Stückpreis*
to price: *den Verkaufspreis festlegen/berechnen*
Cf. also IV.3.1 Depicting price trends.

[4] *nach der Grenzkostenregel:* in terms of the marginal cost rule; according to/in accordance with/in line with the marginal cost rule

> - 'Marginal cost' (MC) is the additional cost incurred by increasing the total output by one unit.
> - Average total cost (ATC) is the total unit cost divided by the number of units produced, i.e. the cost per average 'unit of output' *(Leistungseinheit)*. It can be split up into
> - average fixed cost (AFC) and
> - average variable cost (AVC).
>
> Figure 1 illustrates the relationship between marginal cost (MC), average total cost (ATC) and average variable cost (AVC) based on the 'principle of diminishing returns' *(Ertragsgesetz)*. The MC function is the first 'derivation' of the ATC function. It cuts the ATC curve and the AVC curve at their minima where MC and average costs are identical.
> Under conditions of perfect competition (cf. note [19] below), companies would be price takers and the marginal cost of a product would be identical with its market price.

[5] *Förderstätte:* production site; production location; site of production; place of production

> There is no English noun or compound which translates the specific meaning of *Förderung* in the German text above. 'Production' is the best alternative here.

← Please note

Usage examples
oil producing countries: *Erdöl produzierende Länder*
oil (production) platforms: *Förderinseln, Bohrinseln*
coal (producing) mines: *Kohlebergwerke*
Coal is no longer mined/extracted here: *Hier wird keine Kohle mehr gefördert/abgebaut.*

Scandinavia is an important timber producer: *Skandinavien ist ein wichtiger (Nutz-)Holzlieferant.*

⁶ *die gerade noch benötigt wird, um die Energienachfrage zu decken:* needed so as to just cover the demand for energy; required so as to just meet/satisfy energy demand

Typical collocations with 'demand' are
to create demand: *Nachfrage erzeugen*
to stimulate/encourage demand: *die Nachfrage anregen/fördern*
to revive/boost/step up demand: *die Nachfrage beleben/anheizen/erhöhen*
to control/regulate demand: *die Nachfrage steuern/regulieren*
to cater for/match/keep pace with/keep up with demand: *mit der Nachfrage Schritt halten*
to curb demand: *die Nachfrage dämpfen*
to outstrip demand: *die Nachfrage übertreffen*
to experience a poor/moderate growth in demand: *eine schwache/mäßige Zunahme der Nachfrage erleben*
to experience a soaring/stagnating/slackening demand: *eine rasante/stagnierende/nachlassende Nachfrage erleben*

⁷ *etwas vereinfacht:* putting it simply; roughly speaking; to express it in simple terms

Please note →

> Do not say 'simply put' or 'simply expressed'.

⁸ *beansprucht:* utilized; used; made use of
⁹ *Bereitstellungskosten:* procurement cost; cost of procurement; cost of supply; supply cost

Please note →

> Possible translations, in this context, for *bereitstellen* are 'procure' and 'supply'.

'To procure' means, generally speaking, 'to make available', 'to acquire or obtain [by care or effort]'; 'to secure': (*sich*) *verschaffen; beschaffen; sich sichern; besorgen.*

Examples
He procured a position in exports for his brother. *Er besorgte/verschaffte seinem Bruder eine Stelle im Export.*
He was unable to procure water for his car. *Er war nicht in der Lage, für sein Auto Wasser zu beschaffen.*
In 'materials management' *(Materialwirtschaft), Bereitstellungskosten* may be rendered as 'cost of maintaining the inventory/the (reserve) stock'.

In 'supply management' *(Versorgungsmanagement)*, the terms 'procurement' *(Beschaffung)* and 'purchase' *(Einkauf)* are employed.
Related examples
energy supply: *Energieversorgung*
food supply: *Nahrungsmittelversorgung*

¹⁰ *wäre es so:* if this were the case; if this were/was really true; if this were really so

¹¹ *deutlich niedriger:* significantly lower; considerably lower; markedly lower

> In combination with a comparative form (e.g. *deutlich teurer*, *deutlich mehr*) *deutlich* is always translated in the above way. Do not use 'clearly' or 'plainly' in this context.

← Please note

Compare the following examples:
clearly visible: *deutlich sichtbar*
plainly recognizable: *deutlich erkennbar*
distinctly pronounced: *deutlich ausgesprochen*

¹² *würde wesentlich stärker ... dominiert:* would be far more strongly dominated; would be much/a lot more strongly dominated

> *Wesentlich* here does not mean 'fundamentally' or 'essentially' but 'a lot' and has to be translated accordingly.

← Please note

Compare the following sentences:
The dollar was considerably stronger today *(erheblich/wesentlich stärker)*.
Her answer was fundamentally correct *(grundsätzlich richtig)*.

¹³ *aus dem Nahen Osten*: from the Middle East

> 'Middle East' is a loose definition for the area around the East Mediterranean and North Africa including Israel, Turkey, Egypt and the Arab Countries. This is equivalent to *Naher Osten/ Vorderer Orient*.
> The German *Mittlerer Osten*, by contrast, refers to a much larger region that stretches to Afghanistan and Northern India.

¹⁴ *greifen die Staaten ... ein:* governments intervene; national governments intervene; the state intervenes

¹⁵ *auf der Nachfrage- wie auf der Angebotsseite:* on both the demand side and the supply side; on the demand side as well as on the supply side

●●●●●●

Please note →

'Side' has to be repeated here for reasons of clarity. Hyphenated German compounds are usually translated as two full words.

[16] *Beschränkung der Förderung:* limitations on production; restrictions on production
Typical collocations with 'restrictions' are
impose restrictions: *Beschränkungen/Einschränkungen auferlegen*
bypass restrictions: *Beschränkungen umgehen*
overcome restrictions: *Beschränkungen überwinden*

Please note →

Note the idiomatic expression: 'to know one's own limitations': *seine eigenen Grenzen kennen*

[17] *Behinderung von Importen:* import restrictions; trade barriers

'Import restrictions' *(Importbeschränkungen)* limit the amount of imports into a country by a variety of techniques. These include voluntary export restraints but more often 'import quotas' *(Einfuhrkontingente)* and 'import duties' *(Einfuhrzölle;* cf. item [18]). They are imposed on a wide range of imports mostly in order to protect domestic industries from foreign competition and/or to reduce 'balance of payments deficits' (cf. V.2.1 Notes on the translation, item [25]).

[18] *Abgaben:* duties; levies

Abgaben is a collective noun for all compulsory payments to authorities. In the above context, it comprises
- 'Customs duties' *(Zölle;* also: 'import duties', 'tariffs', 'import levies' are 'ad valorem tariffs' *(Wertzolltarife).* They are levied as a percentage of the price of the import by the national customs.

The term 'tariff' has a second meaning: i.e. 'the (printed) list of the rates of customs duties'.

- 'Excise duties' *(Verbrauchssteuern)* are paid in addition to VAT. They are a single-stage tax not only levied on imported goods but also on certain home-produced commodities, most notably on oil and tobacco products and alcoholic beverages. Moreover, they are imposed on gambling.

Useful collocations
Zoll erheben: to levy customs duties
Zollabfertigung: customs clearance
zollpflichtig: liable to duty (as opposed to duty-free)
[19] *lassen den Wettbewerb als preisbildenden Faktor oft in den Hintergrund treten:* competition often becomes a less important price determinant; competition, more often than not, has to take second place in price determination; competition, frequently, has to take a back seat

> 'Competition' is, generally speaking, a situation in which anybody who wishes to buy or sell has a choice of possible suppliers and customers.
> - 'Perfect competition' or 'pure competition' *(vollkommener/ vollständiger Wettbewerb)* describes a market structure in which the following applies: a) there are a large number suppliers and buyers; b) all firms produce identical or homogeneous products; c) there is perfect market transparency; d) this market is infinitely quick to respond to change. All traders in this market act as pricetakers i.e. they buy and sell at a price they cannot influence.
> - The more common structure, however, is 'imperfect competition' *(unvolkommener Wettbewerb)* which is a collective name for
> - an 'imperfect polypoly' *(unvollkommenes Polypol)* if conditions b, c, or d are not met,
> - an 'oligopoly' *(Oligopol)*, where a few powerful suppliers are able to erect barriers against new entrants to their industry,
> - a 'monopoly' *(Monopol)* where only one corporation dominates the industry.

Related terms
gesunder Wettbewerb: healthy competition
unlauterer Wettbewerb: unfair competition

IV.3 Exercises

3.1 Depicting price trends

'Price' is a resourceful noun that is able to form a large variety of collocations.

In the passive voice 'prices' can 'be' *(werden)*
- determined: *bestimmt/festgesetzt/festgelegt/gebildet*
- maintained at a certain level: *beibehalten*
- kept stable: *stabil gehalten*
- raised/put up/increased: *heraufgesetzt/erhöht*
- driven up/pushed up/boosted: *in die Höhe getrieben*
- decreased/reduced/lowered: *gesenkt/reduziert*
- be cut/trimmed: *beschnitten/gestutzt*
- slashed: *drastisch reduziert*
- corrected/revised upward or downward: *nach oben oder unten korrigiert*

What can prices do?

They can
- stagnate: *stagnieren*
- hover around a certain figure/position: *sich um eine bestimmte Zahl/um einen bestimmten Punkt bewegen*
- to remain (stuck) at a certain level: *auf einem Niveau stehen bleiben/festsitzen*
- touch/reach a certain value: *einen bestimmten Wert erreichen*
- remain equal/constant, unchanged/steady: *stabil, konstant, unverändert bleiben*
- experience ups and downs/go up and down/fluctuate/experience ups and downs: *sich auf und ab bewegen/schwanken*
- move ahead of/anticipate a trend: *eine Entwicklung vorwegnehmen*
- lag behind a trend: *einer Entwicklung hinterherhinken*

- increase/go up/rise: *steigen/in die Höhe gehen*
- soar/shoot up/balloon/surge: *in die Höhe schießen/sich rasant entwickeln*
- double; triple; quadruple; multiply: *sich verdoppeln; sich verdreifachen; sich vervierfachen; um ein Vielfaches steigen*
- approach a figure: *sich einer Zahl annähern*
- to edge closer to a value: *sich langsam auf einen Wert zubewegen*
- be up by 3 percent on the previous day: *um 3% höher liegen als am Vortag*

Exercises

- rocket sky high: *in den Himmel schießen*
- double; triple; quadruple; multiply: *sich verdoppeln; sich verdreifachen; sich vervierfachen; um ein Vielfaches steigen*
- climb to a preliminary peak: *auf einen vorläufigen Spitzenwert klettern*
- reach a 6-month high: *einen Halbjahreshöchststand erreichen*
- peak: *einen Spitzenwert erreichen*
- touch their record high: *ihren (absoluten) Höchststand erreichen*
- break/exceed/move past the $ 100 barrier/line/mark: *die Hundertdollargrenze durchbrechen/hinter sich lassen*

- slide/slip downhill: *wegrutschen/abrutschen*
- decrease/drop/fall: *sinken/fallen*
- decline/weaken: *sich abschwächen/sich rückläufig entwickeln*
- slow sharply: *stark nachlassen*
- plummet/plunge/nosedive: *abstürzen, in den Keller gehen, purzeln*
- be down by 3 percent on the previous day: *gegenüber dem Vortag 3 % verlieren*
- plunge below their initial value: *hinter ihren Anfangswert zurückfallen*
- fall to a new low: *ein neues Tief erleben/erreichen*
- undercut/undershoot a level: *ein Niveau unterschreiten*
- reach/hit/be at/touch their all-time low: *ihren absoluten Tiefstand erreichen/erleben*
- hit the bottom: *am Boden liegen*

- recover/pick up again: *sich erholen*

The following exercise has been designed to facilitate the task of describing trends and fluctuations. Look at the graph embedded in the following text and complete the sentences. Use the expressions listed above as well as those offered in III.3.1 Interpreting linear curves and III. 3.2. Graphs, diagrams and charts.

1. The graph illustrates to what extent the fuel prices __/__ *(sich entwickelten/schwankten)* in the first term of 2001.
2. Moreover, it seeks to explain why the market price of petrol is currently __ __ *(unverhältnismäßig hoch)*.
3. The measure to __/__ *(bestimmen)* the exact degree of change is per cent.

Exercises

(Der Spiegel, Nr. 18 (2001), p.72)

Figure 2: *A fair Market Price?*

4 Three fuel prices are __/__/__ (gegenübergestellt) in the graph, namely
- the Rotterdam spot market price of petrol, which is plotted as a red line)
- the price for crude oil paid in Rotterdam (marked in black)
- the price of petrol charged at the filling stations (before petrol tax and VAT) which is indicated by this double line

5 In January 2001, all three prices were __ __/__ (gleich)

6 Let's __ __ (anschauen) the black line first: In the new year, the price for crude oil rose by 5 per cent and then __ __/__ __ (fiel dann zurück) to its previous level.

7 However, from then onwards, this oil price __ __/__ __ (stieg steil an), a trend which – notwithstanding minor __ (Schwankungen) – continued well into February where crude oil prices __/__ __ __ __ (erreichten ihren bislang höchsten Stand) at 17.5 per cent __ (über) their January level.

8 Owing to the __/__/__/__ __ (Rückgang) of demand, the crude oil price gradually __ (purzelte) to just 2 per cent under its January level thereby hitting the term's __ __/__ __ (absoluten Tiefstand).

9 In mid-April, it __ (kletterte) back to 12 per cent, but within a short period of time it had been pushed back to 8 per cent, a level which, showing a slight __/__ __ (Abwärtstrend), it __ (beibehielt) till the end of the month.

10 How does this __ (vergleichen) to the red line, which __/__ (aufzeichnet) the development of the spot market price for petrol paid in Rotterdam?

11 In January and February, the spot market price more or less followed the __ __ (vorgegebenen Trend) by the crude oil price.

12 However, owing to the vast amounts of petrol purchased by the US in January, the Rotterdam price developed independently __ (nach oben schießend) towards its first peak of 17.5 per cent which __/__ (übertraf) the crude oil value by as much as 8 per cent.

Exercises

13 Like the crude oil price, the Rotterdam price __/__ (erlebte) a further increase in February and, subsequently, a short-lived __/__ (Rückgang) that ground to an abrupt halt in March.
14 When petrol prices started going down in the second half of February, the US responded by virtually __ __ (leer kaufen) the Rotterdam spot market, and this __/__ (erzeugte) a __ __ (ständig breiter werdende) gap between the two price curves as the petrol price __ __ __ __/__ __ __ (getrieben wurde) to ever higher levels.
15 In April, it finally started to __ (in den Himmel steigen), quickly __/__ __ (sich zubewegend auf) a point where petrol cost 40% more than it had done four months previously.
16 The third price is the petrol station price before excise tax and VAT. In the first two weeks of January, this curve __ __ (verläuft parallel) to the crude oil curve.
17 But under the impact of US purchases, it began to __ __/__ (in die Höhe zu schießen) in January and to __/__ __/__ __ __ (sich zubewegen auf) the spot market price, completely __ (aufgehend in) with the development of the latter in April when the red line and the double line finally __ (zusammentrafen).

3.2 A fair market price?

Please put the verbs (given in brackets) into their correct tense. Pay attention to the <u>flag words</u> as well as to the publication date of the article and other contextual indicators, such as 'as a result'.
In one sentence, there is no flag word but reference is obviously made to the same recent develoment. In some cases, the passive voice has to be used.

1 US __ (drive) up prices
2 The US __ not __ (build) any oil refineries <u>for 25 years</u> and the stock levels of petrol are as low as they last __ (be) <u>40 years ago</u>.
3 This is why the Americans __ __ (look) for alternatives and __ __/__ __ (find) them in Europe where they __ __ (buy) up the market and __ __ (push) up the prices for the finished product.
4 <u>In January alone</u>, 140,000 barrels __ __ (ship; passive voice) to the US per day.
5 By contrast, <u>throughout the first quarter of 2000</u> a mere 50, 000 barrels __ __ (export; passive voice).
6 <u>As a result</u>, the petrol price __ __ (become) completely de-coupled from the crude oil prices.

Exercises

7 Whereas the price for crude oil __ (tumble) once more to 8 per cent in April, the petrol price which __ __ __ (paid; passive voice) at the Rotterdam spot market virtually __ (go) through the roof by climbing to its all-time high at 45 per cent .)

3.3 Putting on a price tag

Translate the sentences below using a bilingual dictionary and the terms provided in the **Notes** to this chapter and in the above exercises.

1 Der Gesamtpreis für diesen Computer beträgt/beläuft sich insgesamt auf $1000.
2 Berufsstress geht fast immer zu Lasten *(at the price)* der Gesundheit.
3 Für die Erhöhung unseres Marktanteiles in den mittleren Preisklassen *(medium-price brackets)* haben wir einen hohen Preis bezahlt.
4 Es wäre schwierig, spontan *(off the top of my head)* einen Preis für dieses Gemälde zu nennen.
5 Von der Galerie wurde ein Preis von 50.000 Pfund Sterling für das Bild festgesetzt.
6 Wollen Sie diese Informationen zu jedem Preis?
7 Dieses Modell ist unbezahlbar.
8 Das ist ein kostspieliges Vergnügen.
9 Der Begriff „Preisfixierung" bezeichnet eine illegale Absprache von Verkaufspreisen in einem Kartell.
10 Preisbrecher reduzieren ihre Preise drastisch, um ihre Konkurrenten zu unterbieten.
11 Das Preisniveau für Musikkassetten kam ins Rutschen, als die ersten CDs herauskamen.
12 Um Ihre Leistung zu beurteilen, müssen wir den Wert Ihres Beitrags beziffern *(put a price tag on your contribution)*.
13 Wir können nicht nur qualitätsmäßig sondern auch preislich mit dem Marktführer konkurrieren.

V Business Cycles

V.1 Text: „Pro" und „contra" Konjunkturprogramm:
Muss der Staat helfen?   86

V.2 **Sample translation**   88
V.2.1 Notes on the translation

V.3 **Exercises**   99
V.3.1 Economic cycles
V.3.2 Citing statements
V.3.3 Combating recession

V Business Cycles

V.1 Text: "Pro" und "contra" Konjunkturprogramm: Muss der Staat helfen?

Brauchen wir unterstützende Eingriffe der Politik, um die Wirtschaft wieder „auf Touren" zu bringen oder sind derartige Maßnahmen eher kontraproduktiv?

Dr. Alfred Boss, Leiter des Forschungsbereichs „Öffentliche Finanzen" beim „Kieler Institut für Weltwirtschaft", lehnt finanzpolitische Maßnahmen zur Anregung der Konjunktur rundweg ab und nennt dafür fünf Gründe:

- Es sei anzunehmen, dass sich die Konjunktur wegen der kräftigen Leitzinssenkungen auch ohne weitere fiskalpolitische Impulse im Frühjahr 2002 erholen werde.
- Es sei unsicher, ob Konjunkturprogramme tatsächlich positiv auf die Konjunktur wirken. Denn die dafür erforderliche Aufnahme zusätzlicher Kredite durch den Staat würde zu Zinssteigerungen führen, die wiederum Privatinvestitionen verdrängen könnten.
- Selbst wenn expansive finanzpolitische Maßnahmen vorübergehend die Nachfrage erhöhen würden, könnten sie eventuell erst „zur Unzeit" wirken, d. h. die Konjunktur erst dann ankurbeln, wenn sie bereits wieder „angesprungen" sei.

(John Sloman, *Economics*, Prentice Hall, 2000, p. 423)

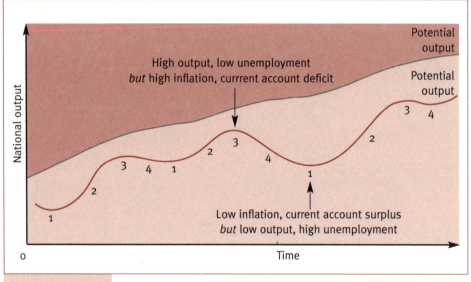

Figure 1: *The business cycle and the four macroeconomic objectives*

- Finanzpolitik mit der Absicht der Konjunktursteuerung führe auf lange Sicht zu steigenden staatlichen Defiziten. Die Erfahrungen der Vergangenheit lehrten, dass Politiker zwar während der Rezession die Staatsausgaben erhöhten oder die Steuern senkten, es aber im Aufschwung versäumten, defizitbegrenzende Maßnahmen vorzunehmen.
- Die zusätzliche Kreditaufnahme begünstige wegen des Zinsanstiegs im Inland den Nettokapitalzustrom aus dem Ausland und habe eine Aufwertung des Euro zur Folge, die wiederum die Ausweitung der Exporte bremsen würde. Allerdings sei dieser letztere Effekt gering, weil er sich auf alle Mitgliedsländer der EU verteile.

Dagegen setzt sich Bernd Mülhaupt, Referatsleiter bei der Hans-Böckler-Stiftung, für eine antizyklische Geld- und Fiskalpolitik ein. Er fordert zunächst von der Europäischen Zentralbank deutliche Zinssenkungen, denn Rezession sei die unmittelbare Gefahr, nicht Inflation. Allerdings sei eine expansive Geldpolitik alleine unwirksam. Den entscheidenden Anstoß müsse der Staat durch eine vorübergehende Ausweitung der Neuverschuldung geben. Dabei sei ein Vorziehen der Steuerreform nur die zweitbeste Lösung, weil bei der Verlagerung der Ausgabenentscheidungen auf den privaten Sektor die vom Staat eingesetzte „Konjunkturspritze" nicht in voller Höhe nachfragewirksam werde.

Stattdessen plädiert Mülhaupt für eine Ausweitung der öffentlichen Investitionstätigkeit, mit der gleichzeitig die Infrastruktur verbessert und Wachstumsimpulse gegeben werden könnten. Für ein solches Konjunkturprogramm sei der „Stabilitäts- und Wachstumspakt der EU" kein Hindernis, weil bei voller Ausschöpfung der Defizitquote von 3% des Bruttoinlandproduktes (BIP) noch eine zusätzliche Neuverschuldung von rund 20 Mrd. Euro zu lasse.

Den Einwand von Boss, das Programm könnte prozyklisch wirken und die Inflation anheizen, bezeichnet Mülhaupt als nicht stichhaltig, und dem Argument, höhere Staatsausgaben zur Stimulierung der Wirtschaft könnten private Investitionen verdrängen, hält er entgegen, dass es Jahre dauern werde, bis die Kapazitäten der deutschen Wirtschaft wieder ausgelastet seien. Nicht tragfähig sei auch der Hinweis auf die „Offenheit" der deutschen Volkswirtschaft bei einer Importquote von einem Drittel des BIP. Gleichwohl sei eine konzertierte Aktion der westeuropäischen Länder wünschenswert.

(R. Neubäumer: Zusammenfassung von „Muss der Staat helfen?" *in: Rheinischer Merkur*, 2. November 2001)

V. 2 Sample translation

The 'pros' and 'cons' of economic stimulation[1]: should the government lend a helping hand[2]?

Do we need **support policies**[3] **to rev up the economy**[4] or do such measures tend to be counterproductive?

Dr. Alfred Boss, **Head of the 'Public Finance' Research Section**[5] at the Kiel Institute of World Economics, **rejects financial policies aimed at stimulating economic growth out of hand**[6] for the following five reasons.

- Due to the substantial cuts in the key lending rates[7], **the economy can be expected to recover**[8] in the spring of 2002 even without additional financial stimuli.
- **It is doubtful whether**[9] pro-cyclical spending **will effectively have a positive impact on business cycles**[10] **as it necessitates additional borrowings on the part of the state**[11] and entails an increase in interest rates **which, in their turn, might 'crowd out' private investment**[12].
- Even if expansionary financial policies **were to boost demand**[13] **over the short term**[14], their impact might be **'out of synch'**[15]; in other words, **they might not crank up the economy until recovery has actually 'kicked in'**[16].
- Financial policy **aimed at regulating economic cycles**[17] results in increasing financial deficits for the state **over the long term**[18]. **The lessons to be learnt from the past are**[19] that, although politicians have tended to increase **government spending**[20] or **to cut**[21] taxes **during recessions**[22], they have failed **to take measures to limit budget deficits**[23] **during economic upturns**[24].
- Additional borrowings – due to the increase in domestic interest rates – would facilitate **inflows of net capital**[25] from abroad, **thereby causing an appreciation of the euro**[26], which – for its part – would slow the expansion of exports[27]. However, **the latter effect would be negligible**[28], as it would be spread across all EU member states[29].

By contrast, Bernd Mülhaupt, **Section Head**[30] at the Hans-Böckler-Foundation, **argues in favour of**[31] anti-cyclical monetary and **fiscal policies**[32]. He claims that it is recession – not inflation – **which poses an immediate threat**[33] and demands, **as a first step**[34], that the European Central Bank should substantially lower interest rates. However, an expansionary monetary policy **on its own**[35] would be **ineffective**[36]. **It is the state that must provide the crucial stimulus**[37] by temporarily expanding its short-term debt[38]. Bringing forward the tax reform has to take second place[39] for the following reason: **if the decisions on**

spending are left to the private sector[40], the 'financial injections' administered by the state[41] do not fully impact on demand[42].
As an alternative, Mülhaupt advocates **the expansion of public investment**[43], as this would improve infrastructure and, at the same time, stimulate growth.
The **'EU Stability and Growth Pact'**[44] **does not constitute an impediment to such economic stimuli**[45] because the current deficit rate of 3 per cent of the **gross domestic product (GDP)**[46], if it were to be fully utilized, **would allow for additional borrowings of roughly €20bn**[47].
Mülhaupt maintains that Boss's **objection**[48] as to the programme possibly having a pro-cyclical effect and **stoking-up**[49] inflation **is unsound**[50]. And **he counters the claim** that a higher level of government spending might crowd out private investment **by arguing**[51] that it will take years **for the German economy to run, once more, at full capacity**[52].
He also claims that references to the 'openness' of the German economy **cannot be substantiated**[53] **as long as imports account for a mere third of the GDP**[54]. Nonetheless, **West European countries would be well-advised to adopt a joint approach**[55].

2.1 Notes on the translation

[1] *Konjunkturprogramm:* economic stimulation; economic stimulus package; pro-cyclical package/spending; spending aimed at economic stimulation

● ● ● ● ● ●

Depending on the context, there are multiple translations for *Konjunktur*. The German term usually denotes the repetitive pattern pursued by a nation's economic activities but it may also refer to the economy or the economic situation itself.

← Please note

'Business cycles', 'trade cycles' or 'economic cycles' usually experience periods of • 'expansion' *(Expansion, Aufschwung)* characterized by high levels of economic 'growth' *(Wachstum)*, 'consumer spending' *(Konsumausgaben)*, investment and employment. • A 'downturn', 'economic decline' *(Abschwung)*, 'slump' *(Talfahrt)* or 'recession' *(Rezession)* occurs after an expansion period ends. This period is also referred to as 'contraction' *(Kontraktion)*. Consequently, economic activity slows. Consequently, businesses often slash their 'inventories'

> (Lagerbestände), i.e. the amount of unsold goods they have stockpiled, thereby intensifying the economic decline.
> - When a contraction ends, the cycle reaches a 'turning point' *(Wendepunkt)*, also known as 'turnaround' *(Umschwung)* before it enters a phase of 'economic recovery' *(wirtschaftliche Erholung)*. When a new expansion phase begins, the business cycle repeats itself, although the upper turning point or 'peak' *(Konjunkturspitze)* and the lower turning point or 'low' *(Tiefpunkt/Talsohle)* tend to be higher each time.
> - Such an 'upturn' is also called 'upswing' *(Aufschwung)*.
> Factors that affect business cycles include fiscal and monetary policies, currency exchange rates, the prices of materials sold in world markets, military actions and political crises.

2. *muss der Staat helfen:* should the government lend a helping hand; should the state offer assistance
3. *unterstützende Eingriffe der Politik:* support policies; political support
4. *um die Wirtschaft wieder „auf Touren" zu bringen:* to rev up the economy; to speed up/accelerate economic growth
5. *Leiter des Forschungsbereichs „Öffentliche Finanzen":* Head of the 'Public Finance' Research Section; who heads the research section 'Public Finance'
6. *lehnt finanzpolitische Maßnahmen zur Anregung der Konjunktur rundweg ab:* rejects financial policies aimed at stimulating economic growth out of hand; totally opposes pro-cyclical financial policies; totally rejects financial policies intended to stimulate/encourage business activities
7. *wegen der kräftigen Leitzinssenkungen:* due to the substantial cuts in the key lending rates; owing to the slashing of the key reference rates/key (interest) rates
   Cf. also VIII.2.1 Notes on the translation, item [36].
8. *es sei anzunehmen, dass sich die Konjunktur ... erholen werde:* the economy can be expected to recover; the economy can be assumed to turn the corner
   Cf. also II.3.3 Expectations, recommendations and requests.
9. *es sei unsicher, ob:* it is doubtful whether; there are doubts if/as to whether
10. *tatsächlich positiv auf die Konjunktur wirken:* will effectively have a positive impact on business cycles; will really impact positively

on economic cycles; will really affect business cycles in a positive way
11 *denn die dafür erforderliche Aufnahme zusätzlicher Kredite durch den Staat:* as it necessitates additional borrowings on the part of the state; as it makes it necessary for the state to take out additional loans; as it requires the state to take out additional loans. For details on 'loans' and 'credits' cf. IX.2.1 Notes on the translation, items [9] and [30].
12 *die wiederum Privatinvestitionen verdrängen könnten:* which, in their turn, might crowd out private investment; which, for their part, might have a 'crowding out effect' on/might divert private investment

> 'Crowding out' *(Verdrängung)* occurs in the capital market when private borrowing is 'squeezed out' or marginalized by financially more robust governments which push up interest rates by taking out additional loans.
> In a broader sense, this term describes the effect of larger national spending in 'pre-empting' *(abziehen)* national resources leaving less for private consumption spending, private sector investment and exports. However, such real 'crowding out' would only occur to the effect that national resources are fixed and fully employed.

13 *die Nachfrage erhöhen würden:* were to boost demand; were to increase demand
For the relevant verb-noun collocations of 'demand' cf. IV.2.1 Notes on the translation, item [6].
14 *vorübergehend:* over the short term; in the short term; in the short run
15 *könnten sie eventuell erst „zur Unzeit" wirken:* their impact might be 'out of synch'; they might impact 'at the wrong time'

> The adverb 'eventually' is a false friend as it does not translate *eventuell* which in the above text is semantically covered by 'might'.

← Please note

16 *die Konjunktur erst dann ankurbeln, wenn sie wieder „angesprungen" sei:* they might not crank up the economy until recovery has actually 'kicked' in; they might not rev up the economy before it has already turned the corner

Please note →

> A 'crank' *(Kurbel)* is a mechanical device to transmit rotary motion. It can also be a handle which is applied to an engine in order to start it. This expression is the exact equivalent of *ankurbeln*.

Further examples
This machine cranks out lots of copies every day. *Diese Maschine produziert täglich massenweise Kopien.*
We have cranked up a successful advertising campaign. *Wir haben eine erfolgreiche Werbekampagne auf die Beine gestellt.*

17 *mit der Absicht der Konjunktursteuerung:* aimed at regulating economic cycles; that aims at controlling business cycles
18 *auf lange Sicht:* over the long term; in the long run
19 *die Erfahrungen der Vergangenheit lehrten:* the lessons to be learnt from the past are; past/previous experience has shown
20 *die Staatsausgaben:* government spending; national expenditure; public-sector spending; public spending

Please note →

> In the UK, the term 'government spending' and 'national spending' refer to the expenditure incurred by the central government in one year, whereas 'public spending' and 'public-sector spending' *(Ausgaben der öffentlichen Hand)* comprise the expenditure of the entire public sector.

21 *senken:* to cut; to lower; to decrease; to reduce
22 *während der Rezession:* during recessions; in periods of economic contraction/downturn; during economic slumps
23 *defizitbegrenzende Maßnahmen vorzunehmen:* to take measures to limit budget deficits; to take steps to contain/restrict budget deficits

> 'Budget deficit' *(Haushaltsdefizit)* is the excess of government spending' *(Staatsausgaben)* over government receipts *(Staatseinnahmen).*
> Related terms
> 'budget surplus' *(Haushaltsüberschuss):* the excess of government receipts over government spending

24 *im Aufschwung:* during economic upturns; during economic upswings
25 *den Nettokapitalzustrom:* inflows of net capital; inflows of funds; net capital inflows

> • • • • • •
> An open economy has a 'balance of payments' *(Zahlungsbilanz)* account which records the flows of money between one country and the rest of the world. Since 1998, it has consisted of three parts:
> - the 'current account balance of payments' *(Leistungsbilanz)* which includes a country's imports and exports plus its incomes and money transfers from abroad.
> - the 'capital account balance of payments' *(Kapitalbilanz)* which in the UK used to be identical with what is now known as as financial account. It credits the flows of funds into a country and debits those to countries abroad. These funds are largely associated with the acquisition or the disposal of assets.
> - In October 1998, the 'financial account balance of payments' was created. It lists inward and outward investments or deposits from and in foreign financial institutions.

[26] *und habe eine Aufwertung des Euro zur Folge:* thereby causing an appreciation of the euro; thus resulting in an appreciation of the euro

[27] *die wiederum die Ausweitung der Exporte bremsen würde:* which – for its part – would slow the expansion of exports; which would then hinder/impede export expansion

> Note that *Export und Import* has to be translated as 'exports and imports'.

← Please note

[28] *sei dieser letztere Effekt gering:* the latter effect would be negligible; this would be of minor/little significance

[29] *weil er sich auf alle Mitgliedsländer der EU verteile:* as it would be spread across all EU member states; as it would be shared by all EU members

[30] *Referatsleiter:* Section Head; Head of Department; Departmental Head

[31] *setzt sich... für ... ein:* argues in favour of; publicly promotes
For a detailed discussion of these and related terms see I.2.1 Notes on the translation, item [21], item [30] and item [54].

[32] *Fiskalpolitik:* fiscal policies

> 'Fiscal policy' primarily aims at
> - supporting demand during recessions and reducing it during economic booms

Business Cycles 93

- dampening the fluctuations associated with the business cycle.

'Expansionary fiscal policy' *(expansive Fiskalpolitik)* is intended to shorten prolonged recessions whereas 'deflationary measures' *(deflatorische Massnahmen)* are intended to soften the effects of rampant inflation.

This may involve increasing government expenditure and/or lowering taxes at the onset of recessions, or conversely, to raise taxes and reduce public spending when the economy is expanding. Such measures would be taken to prevent unhealthy economic growth.

Related terms
- fiscal stance *(Zustand des Haushalts)*: the degree of deflation or inflation affecting the budget
- fiscal drag *(fiskalpolitische Bremse)*: the tendency of automatic fiscal stabilizers to slow economic recovery
- discretionary fiscal policy *(diskretionäre/fallweise Fiskalpolitik)*: deliberate changes in tax rates or the level of government expenditure in order to influence the level of aggregate demand

[33] *Rezession sei die unmittelbare Gefahr:* he claims that it is recession ... which poses an immediate threat; he maintains that it is the economic downturn that constitutes/represents an immediate danger

[34] *zunächst:* as a first step; to start with

[35] *alleine:* on its own; alone; as a single measure

[36] *unwirksam:* ineffective

Please note →

Do not confuse 'effective' *(wirksam, wirkungsvoll, effektiv, in Kraft)* and efficient *(effizient; tüchtig)*.

'Effective' signifies 'having or producing an intended/desired/expected effect whereas 'efficient' means 'producing an effect with a minimum of energy input; waste, expense or unnecessary effort'.

Usage examples
He made an effective speech. *Er hielt eine wirkungsvolle Rede.*
This law is/becomes immediately effective. *Das Gesetz tritt sofort in Kraft.*
She is an efficient employee. *Sie ist eine tüchtige Mitarbeiterin.*

The transport system runs efficiently. *Das Verkehrssystem funktioniert reibungslos.*

37 *den entscheidenden Anstoß müsse der Staat ... geben:* it is the state that must provide the crucial stimulus; it is the state which has to provide the decisive/vital push

38 *durch eine vorübergehende Ausweitung der Neuverschuldung:* by temporarily expanding its short-term debt; by temporarily increasing its borrowings

39 *dabei sei ein Vorziehen der Steuerreform nur die zweitbeste Lösung:* bringing forward the tax reform has to take second place; speeding up the tax reform should be the second choice

40 *weil bei der Verlagerung der Ausgabenentscheidungen auf den privaten Sektor:* if the decisions on spending are left to the private sector; if the decisions on spending are shifted to/shift to private enterprise

41 *die vom Staat eingesetzte Konjunkturspritze:* the financial injections administered by the state; the financial aid injected by the state

42 *nicht in voller Höhe nachfragewirksam werde:* do not fully impact on demand; do not fully affect demand

43 *Ausweitung der öffentlichen Investitionstätigkeit:* extensive public investment; expanding public sector investment

44 *der Stabilitäts- und Wachstumspakt der EU:* the EU Stability and Growth Pact

> In 1997, the EU member states agreed at the European Council in Amsterdam that governments adopting the euro should seek to balance their budgets averaged over the course of a business cycle (i.e. to achieve a zero budget deficit), and that deficits should not exceed 3 per cent of GDP in any one year.

45 *für ein solches Konjunkturprogramm sei ... kein Hindernis:* does not constitute an impediment to such economic stimuli; does not present an obstacle to such an economic stimulus package/to such economic support policies/measures

46 *Bruttoinlandproduktes (BIP):* gross domestic product (GDP)

> The 'gross domestic product' is the total money value of all final goods and services produced in an economy over a one-year period.
> In 'macroeconomic accounting' *(volkswirtschaftliche Gesamtrechnung)* the GDP is assessed in terms of

● ● ● ● ● ●

- its 'origin' *(Entstehung)* by aggregating the sum of the 'gross value added' *(Bruttowertschöpfung)* by each industry in producing its output of services and commodities.
- its 'expenditure' *(Verwendung)* by examining as to how the goods and services produced were used by private consumers and the public sector.
- 'national income distribution' *(Verteilung des Volkseinkommens)* by measuring how the national income is distributed with regard to the factors of production.

⁴⁷ *noch eine zusätzliche Neuverschuldung von rund 20 Mrd. Euro zulasse:* would allow for additional borrowings of roughly €20bn; would make it possible (for the government) to take out new loans amounting to approximately/about €20bn

Please note →

- *Eine Milliarde* is 'one billion' or 'one thousand million': 1,000,000,000. In the US, Canada and France 'one billion' is the equivalent of *eine Milliarde*.
- *Eine Billion* is 'one trillion' or 'one million million': 1,000,000,000,000. This used to be the equivalent 'one billion' in the UK, but British economists and media have now more or less adopted the US usage.

Examples
7,8 Billionen US-Dollar: US $7.8 trillion or US $7,800 billion or US $7,800,000,000,000.

Please note →

In English, 'one thousand' is represented mathematically as 1,000. Decimal places such as 0.5 are separated from the major numeral by points (pronounced: 0 point five).

Please note →

When currencies are quoted in English, their national denominations such as 'pound/s' or 'euro/s' are placed behind the figure quoted whereas all symbols and abbreviations (e.g. DM) directly precede the accompanying sum. For pragmatic reasons, the traditional symbols for the dollar, the pound sterling, the yen and the euro are increasingly being replaced by 3-letter abbreviations such as USD ($) YEN (¥), GBP (£) and EUR (€).

Currencies can be expressed as follows:

pronunciation*	new abbreviations	traditional form
three million US dollars	USD 3m	US $ 3m
three thousand deutschmarks	DEM 3,000	DM 3,000
four pounds fifty	GBP 4.50	£ 4.50

The fully pronounced version is used when cheques are made out.
Example
Please pay the sum of three thousand dollars.
48 *Einwand:* objection; reservations
49 *anheizen:* stoking up; fuelling; firing; speeding up; accelerating

> 'To stoke (up)' means 'to tend to a fire' and 'to feed a fire'. *Anheizen* should not be confused with *anfeuern*: to spur on, to cheer.

← Please note

Examples
Scoring a goal might stoke up/stir up violence amongst the football fans.
50 *als nicht stichhaltig:* is unsound; is unconvincing; lacks force
51 *dem Argument ... hält er entgegen:* he counters the claim ... by arguing; he contradicts the statement ... by maintaining/claiming
52 *bis die Kapazitäten der deutschen Wirtschaft wieder ausgelastet seien:* for the German economy to run, once more, at full capacity; for the German economy to work/function, once more, at full capacity; for the German economy to utilize its capacities, once more, to the full
53 *nicht tragfähig:* cannot be substantiated; lack force; are unsound
54 *bei einer Importquote von einem Drittel des BIP:* as long as imports account for a mere third of the GDP; as long as imports only make up one third of the GDP

> The polysemous verb 'to account for' comprises such diverse meanings as 'to provide reckoning of something'; 'to hold somebody responsible for'; 'to give reasons for', 'to represent/ to make up one part of a total' as well as 'to destroy' or 'to put out of action'.

← Please note

Example
The treasurer of our badminton club has to account for *(Rechenschaft ablegen über)* the membership fees.
The rough sea accounted for the delayed delivery *(erklärte)*.
Her revenues from freelance journalism 'accounts for' *(machen aus)* thirty per cent of her monthly income.
Compare 'to account for' *(ausmachen; betragen)* with 'to amount to' *(sich belaufen auf; betragen)* in I.2.1 Notes on the translation, item [4].

[55] *sei eine konzertierte Aktion der westeuropäischen Länder wünschenswert:* the West European countries would be well-advised to adopt a joint approach; it would be advisable for the West European countries to co-ordinate their activities/to adopt a unified plan of action

V.3 Exercises

3.1 Economic cycles

Translate *Konjunktur/konjunkturell* in the following sentences. Use the appropriate expressions given below and in the Notes on the translation.

Economies can
- grow/boom/rocket/soar
- experience an upswing/upturn
- undergo a period of steady/continuous/progressive growth
- overheat
- slow/stagnate/cool off
- be in retreat/in a state of decline
- be ailing
- decrease/decline/slump/shrink
- experience a downturn/slowdown/slump
- slip into recession/slide into recession
- enter a phase of continuous/steady/progressive decline
- turn around/recover/turn the corner
- stabilize

Economies can be
- boosted
- revived/rejuvenated
- stimulated/encouraged
- cranked up
- revved up/accelerated

- stoked up/fuelled
- slowed/curbed/dampened
- depressed

Exercises

1. The German __ *(Konjunktur)* was off to a __/__ *(schleppend)* start into the year 2002.
2. Due to the __ __/__ __ *(Abkühlung)* of the international __ *(Wirtschaft)*, exports were markedly down on the previous year.
3. Since September 11th 2001, the US economy has been __ __ *(auf dem Rückzug)* and the general __ __ *(konjunkturelle Tendenz)* has remained negative.
4. Due to the __ __ __ *(rückläufigen Konjunktur)* private __ __ *(Konsum)* __ __ __ *(hat stagniert)*.
5. On the stock markets, uncertainty reigned with regard to the __ __ *(konjunkturelle Prognosen)*.
6. In February, the construction sector __ __ __ __ *([die Bau]konjunktur zog an)*.
7. Owing to __ __ *(konjunkturelle Erholung)*, the interest rates on borrowed capital are going to rise.
8. Further monetary __/__/__ *(Anreize)* are to __ __/__/__ *(ankurbeln)* the ailing economy.
9. __ __ __ __ __ __/__ __ __ *(Konjunkturprogramme)* are usually controversial.
10. A growing number of economists argue that __ __ *(Fiskalpolitik)* that seek to __ __ __ *(Konjunktur zu steuern)* will result in financial deficits for the state.

3.2 Citing statements

In contemporary English, 'reported speech' *(indirekte Rede)* is not as strictly governed by the sequence of tenses as grammar books sometimes seem to suggest. In German, too, there is usually more than one way of citing statements issued in the past. This can be advantageous for the translator, on the one hand, but can also create a fair amount of guesswork, on the other.

Quoting statements made in the past involves several snags.

Exercises

1 Reporting an activity which occurred previous to the speech

On reporting an activity which occurred before the statement about it was made, in a large number of cases, the past perfect (Translation A) and the simple past (Translation B) can be employed in modern English without changing the meaning of the message conveyed.

Example

Wir haben Euch gesagt, dass Frank an diesem Tag krank war/krank gewesen ist.

Translation A   We told you that Frank had been ill on that particular day.

Translation B   We told you that Frank was ill on that particular day.

Der Personalchef wollte wissen, warum der Betriebsrat am vergangenen Freitag nicht zur Gruppenbesprechung gekommen sei/wäre.

Translation A   The HR Manager wanted to know why the representative of the works council did not attend the team meeting last Friday.

Translation B   The HR Manager wanted to know why the representative of the works council had not attended the team meeting last Friday.

However, there are other situations (flag words) which clearly indicate that a past perfect is the only appropriate tense to use.

Example

Sie sagte mir, dass sie zuvor schon viele internationale Kongresse organisiert hätte.

Translation: She told me that she had organized international congresses many times before.

Now complete the following sentences by giving the verb in (brackets) its correct tense. Please consider that there may be more than one option.

a   Did our representative let us know why he __/__ __ to see this customer. (want)
b   We were informed that the foreign delegation __ already __. (arrive)
c   They asked the conductor when the train __ __. (leave)
d   Were you told that the profitability of this business unit __ __/__ __ __ (rise) before payroll cost was lowered.
e   The complaints manager was informed as to how the problem __ __ __ (solve)

2 Reporting a current activity or situation

Statements referring to a present situation can be reported in the simple past or – if we wish to stress that something is still true – in the present tense.

Examples

Er sagte uns, Paris sei/wäre noch immer seine Lieblingstadt./
Er sagte uns, dass Paris immer noch seine Lieblingsstadt ist.
Translation A   He told us that Paris was still his favourite city.
Translation B   He told us that Paris is still his favourite city.
Paul betonte immer wieder, dass sein neues Projekt (immer noch) sehr vielversprechend aussieht/aussehe/aussähe/aussehen würde.
Translation A   Paul insisted that his new project still looked highly promising.
Translation B   Paul insisted that his new project still looks highly promising.

Exercises

Fill in the gaps in the following sentences by giving the verb in (brackets) its correct tense. Please consider that there may be more than one option.

a   During the job interview, she was asked what she __ __ to achieve in life. (want)
b   They informed us that the service they __ __ was available now. (provide)
c   He let us know at 3 o' clock that he __ on his way and apparently he still __. (be; be)
d   The customer asked us where the company __ situated and how many people it __ /__. (be; employ)
e   Jim Casey, one of the founding fathers of UPS, is still quoted as saying that his business __ all about people and service. (be)

3 Reporting simultaneous activities

When simultaneous actions are reported (referring to something that is going on at that particular moment in time), the correct aspect of the tense has to be chosen; an aspect which is never explicitly expressed in the German sentence.

Examples

Wir haben uns gefragt, wer uns da gegenüber saß. We wondered what sort of/kind of person was sitting opposite us.
Die Kunden beklagten sich darüber, dass dieses Verfahren zu zeitintensiv war. The customers complained that this procedure was taking too long.

Exercises

Fill in the gaps below by giving the verb in (brackets) its correct tense and aspect. Please consider that there may be more than one option.
a   I wondered if Robert __ __ to the sales engineers there and then. (talk)
b   The Human Resources Manager enquired why so many accidents __ __ on the shopfloor. (occur)
c   We were informed that the foreign delegation __ __ at the gate at that precise moment. (arrive)
d   The complaints manager wanted to know if the customer __ still __. (wait)
e   She was pleased that we __ __ __ to crank up her old tractor. (try)

4   Present or future?

In reported statements which make reference to the present or the future, the speaker's intention is often hidden in the German subjunctive form which is more and more infrequently used – especially with certain verbs – and perceived by an increasing number of German native speakers as stilted. Sometimes the meaning is apparent from the context of the sentence but, more often than not, German subjunctive forms are far from being self-explanatory.

If the context of the sentence is not specific enough, translators have to guess what the speaker's underlying message is.

The following examples may therefore require two different translations.

Er sagte, die Regierung müsse die entscheidenden Impulse geben.
Translation A   He said the government had to provide the decisive stimulus.
Translation B   He said the government would have to provide the decisive stimulus.

Example A implies that the government has to provide the decisive stimulus because all governments must take this type of action during periods of economic recession. Example B makes reference to a measure designed by an individual government to counteract the current recession.

Er behauptete, dass er über Ostern in New York wäre.
Translation A   He claimed that he was (always) in New York over Easter.
Translation B   He claimed that he would be in New York this Easter.

Please complete the following sentences by putting the verb in (brackets) into the correct tense. Take a close look at the <u>contextual indicators</u> which may specify the meaning.

Exercises

a Wir haben uns gefragt, wie die Betroffene <u>auf diese schwierige Situation</u> reagieren würde. We wondered how the person involved __ __ to this difficult situation. (respond)
b Aber wir haben uns auch gefragt, wie man sich <u>normalerweise</u> in solchen Fällen verhalten würde/verhält. But we wondered as well, how people usually __/__ in such cases. (react)
c Wir machten deutlich, dass wir solche Vorschläge nicht für besonders hilfreich hielten/halten würden. We made it quite clear that we did not feel that sort of suggestion __/__ __ be very helpful. (be)
d Wir dachten, <u>diese Methode</u> brächte uns nicht weiter/würde uns nicht weiterbringen. We did not think that this proposal __ __ us anywhere. (take)
e Wir fragten, ob <u>schon</u> ein Komitee zusammengestellt werde/würde. We asked whether a committee __ __ set up. (be)

Business Cycles 103

Exercises

3.3 Combating recession

Translate the following sentences using the idiomatic expressions in (brackets) as well as your dictionaries and the terminology provided in the **Notes on the translation.**

1. Wenn die Regierung auf Dauer *(persistently)* ein Haushaltsdefizit hat *(runs a budget deficit)*, steigt die Staatsverschuldung.
2. Der Erfolg steuerpolitischer Massnahmen hängt weitgehend *(largely)* von der Genauigkeit *(accuracy)* der Wirtschaftsprognosen *(economic forecasting)* ab.
3. Einige Wirtschaftswissenschaftler bezweifeln, dass Konjunkturspritzen *(injecting money into the economy)* geeignet *(an appropriate means)* sind, Privatinvestitionen zu erhöhen.
4. Bei *(when facing)* einer Rezession dieser Größenordnung *(of this magnitude)* sollte man auf die Experten hören.
5. „Diskretionäre Fiskalpolitik" bedeutet dass die Regierung die Staatsausgaben bzw. die Steuereinnahmen gezielt *(deliberate)* verändert, um die gesamtwirtschaftliche Nachfrage *(aggregate demand)* zu beeinflussen.

VI   The European Union

VI.1   **Text: Der lange Weg zu einer gemeinsamen
europäischen Währung**   **106**

VI.2   **Sample translation**   **108**
VI.2.1   Notes on the translation

VI.3   **Exercises**   **114**
VI.3.1   Neologisms
VI.3.2   The Single Market
VI.3.3   The European Communities

VI.1 Text: Der lange Weg zu einer gemeinsamen europäischen Währung

VI The European Union

Im Europa der Nachkriegszeit entstand zwar schon bald die Idee einer wirtschaftlichen Annäherung, an deren Ende eine gemeinsame Währung stehen sollte, doch der Weg zum Euro war weit und mühselig.

(Photograph: Axel Seidemann/AP; in: The Guardian, August 31 2001)

Figure 1: *Abseilers unveil a replica euro banknote on the side of the European Central Bank in Frankfurt on 30 August 2001*

So verlief der Werner-Plan, der erste Anlauf zu einer Wirtschafts- und Währungsunion (WWU) in den siebziger Jahren, in Folge von Dollarkrise, Ölpreisschock und unüberbrückbaren Standpunkten zur Wirtschaftspolitik im Sande, und selbst das auf Initiative des französischen Staatspräsidenten Valéry Giscard d'Estaing und des deutschen Bundeskanzlers Helmut Schmidt gemeinsam vereinbarte Europäische Währungssystem (EWS) erlebte eine Reihe von Krisen.

Im Juni 1989 wurde von Jacques Delors, dem Präsidenten der Europäischen Kommission, ein neuer Plan zur Bildung der angestrebten Wirtschafts- und Währungsunion (WWU) vorgelegt, den der

Rat der Europäischen Union schließlich billigte. Die erste Stufe der WWU trat am 1. Juli 1990 in Kraft und führte zu einer vollständigen Liberalisierung des Geld- und Kapitalverkehrs zwischen den Mitgliedsstaaten und zu einer intensiveren Abstimmung ihrer Wirtschaftspolitik.
Nachdem 1991 im Vertrag von Maastricht sogenannte Konvergenzkriterien festgelegt worden waren, mit denen die Stabilität der gemeinsamen Währung gesichert werden sollte, begann 1994 die zweite Stufe der WWU mit der Einrichtung des Europäischen Währungsinstitutes (EWI), des Vorläufers der Europäischen Zentralbank (EZB), die die Geld- und Kreditpolitik der EU ausführt. Am 1. Januar 1999 wurde diese Entwicklung mit der dritten Stufe der WWU abgeschlossen: dem unwiderruflichen Übergang zum Euro als Einheitswährung. Allerdings beteiligten sich vier der 15 Mitglieder, und zwar Griechenland, das die Konvergenzkriterien für eine Teilnahme an der Einführung des Euro nicht erfüllen konnte, Großbritannien, Schweden und Dänemark, vorläufig nicht an der gemeinsamen Währung.
(R. Neubäumer, Zusammenfassung einer Übersicht in der *Frankfurter Allgemeinen Zeitung*, 2. Mai 1998)

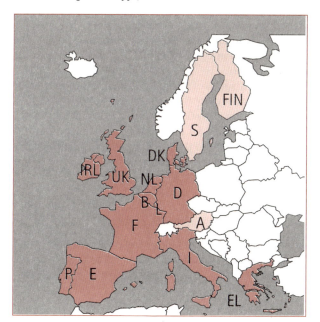

(Reproduction authorized, European Communities, 2000)

The European Union 107

VI.2 Sample translation

The long trek[1] to a single European currency[2]

Although **the idea of an economic rapprochement**[3], **which was to end in**[4] a single currency, **was not slow in forming itself**[5] in Europe after World War II[6], **the way that led to the euro**[7] was a long and **an arduous one**[8].

The Werner plan, **for instance**[9], which constituted the first attempt at an economic and monetary union in the 1970's, **floundered**[10] due to the dollar crisis, the **oil shock**[11] and irreconcilable positions on economic policy. Even the **European Monetary System (EMS)**[12], **which had been mutually agreed on at the initiative of the French President of State**[13] Valéry Giscard d'Estaing and the German Chancellor Helmut Schmidt **went through**[14] **a number of**[15] crises.

In June 1989, a new **scheme**[16] **to form**[17] the **desired**[18] **Economic and Monetary Union (EMU)**[19] **was submitted**[20] by Jacques Delors, the President of the **European Commission**[21], and **was finally approved**[22] by the **Council of the European Union**[23]. **Stage I**[24] of this union entered into force on July 1st, 1990, **resulting in the complete deregulation**[25] **of all movements of money and capital**[26] between the member states and in a closer alignment of their economic policies.

On having determined what are known as the **'convergence criteria'**[27] **in the Maastricht Treaty**[28], which **were to ensure**[29] the stability of the single currency, stage II of the EMU **commenced**[30] in 1994 with the establishment of the **European Monetary Institute (EMI)**[31], **the forerunner of the European Central Bank (ECB)**[32], **which executes the union's monetary policy**[33].

On January 1st, 1999, stage III of this development was completed **by irrevocably adopting**[34] the euro as a single currency. However, four of the fifteen EU members, namely Greece, which was unable to meet the required convergence criteria **for participating in the launch**[35] of the euro, Great Britain, Sweden and Denmark, are – **for the time being**[36] – not participating in the common currency.

2.1 Notes on the translation

[1] *der lange Weg:* the long trek; the long road to

> 'Trek' originates from South African English where it signifies 'journey'. Historically it implies 'a long and arduous' journey and thus seems to be the most suitable term in the above context.

Please note →

² *zu einer gemeinsamen europäischen Währung:* to a single European currency; to a common European currency

← Please note

> The term 'single currency' is derived from Single Market. Although 'common' currency' is a correct translation of *Gemeinschaftswährung*, too, 'single currency' is the received term.

³ *die Idee einer wirtschaftlichen Annäherung:* the idea of an economic rapprochement; the idea of a closer economic cooperation/ a greater economic integration was soon formed; was not slow in establishing itself

⁴ *an deren Ende ... stehen sollte:* which was to end in; which was to lead to
For the various translations of *sollte* see J. Bauer & M. Seidenspinner: *Betriebswirtschaft: Übersetzungsübungen, studium kompakt Fachsprache Englisch*, Cornelsen & Oxford, Berlin 2001, pp. 87-88.

⁵ *entstand zwar schon bald:* was not slow in forming itself; was not slow in manifesting itself/in emerging

← Please note

> The meaning of *schon bald* is included in the expression 'was not slow in'.

⁶ *im Europa der Nachkriegszeit:* in Europe after World War II; in post-World War II Europe

← Please note

> 'Post-war Europe' can be an option, too, as the context does not allow for any confusion with World War I.

⁷ *der Weg zum Euro:* the way that lay ahead for the euro; the way leading to the euro; the way to the euro; the way that led to the euro

⁸ *mühselig:* an arduous one; a laborious one
Alternative translation:
... the way ahead to the euro was long and arduous.
Further usage example
He enjoys his arduous *(anstrengend)* workouts in the gym. Weeding this overgrown garden will be a laborious job *(mühselige Arbeit)*.

⁹ *so:* for instance
For details on the usage of the English 'so' cf. I.2.1. Notes on the translation, item ¹⁴.

¹⁰ *verlief ... im Sande:* floundered; came to nothing; petered out

Please note →

[11] *Ölpreisschock:* oil shock; oil price shock

> Most English economics textbooks simply use the expression 'oil shock'.

[12] *Europäische Währungssystem (EWS):* European Monetary System (EMS)

> The EMS is an institutional arrangement which, after having come into force in spring 1979, has stabilized the currencies in the Eurozone. The participating countries set fixed exchange rates for their domestic currencies against the ECU (European Currency Unit). Bilateral currency fluctuations, e.g. that of the deutschmark against the Dutch guilder, were calculated on the basis of these central rates. However, under fixed exchange rates (which, up to 1993, were allowed a 'currency band' of ± 2.25 per cent), the central banks had to intervene when the actual currency rate risked 'exceeding' *(überschreiten)* or 'falling below' *(unterschreiten)* the fixed rate by more than 2.25 per cent.
> If there were 'fundamental disequilibria' *(fundamentale Ungleichgewichte)* in the 'current account balance of payments' *(Leistungsbilanz,* cf. V.2.1 Notes on the translation, item [29]) the central exchange rates were 'realigned' *(angepasst)* by 'appreciations' *(Aufwertungen)* or 'depreciations' *(Abwertungen).*

[13] *das auf Initiative des französischen Staatspräsidenten ... gemeinsam vereinbarte:* which had been mutually agreed on at the initiative of the French President of State; which had been mutually consented to at the initiative of the French President

[14] *erlebte:* went through; experienced; underwent

[15] *eine Reihe von:* a number of; a series of

[16] *Plan:* scheme
Cf. II.2.1 Notes on the translation, item [51].

[17] *zur Bildung:* to form; to establish; to set up

[18] *angestrebten:* desired; intended

[19] *Wirtschafts- und Währungsunion (WWU):* Economic and Monetary Union (EMU)

> The principal goals of the European Monetary Union are: high levels of employment and of convergence regarding 'economic outputs' *(Wirtschaftsleistungen)* and the standard of living while promoting non-inflationary and 'environmentally sustain-

able growth' *(umweltverträgliches Wachstum)* as well as social 'cohesion' *(Zusammenhalt)* between the member states.

● ● ● ● ● ●

The abbreviation EMU stands for 'European Monetary Union' *(Europäische Währungsunion)* and its common monetary system.

← Please note

[20] *wurde ... vorgelegt:* was submitted; was presented
[21] *Europäischen Kommission:* European Commission

The member states of the present-day European Union are, apart from the six signatories of 'the European Coal and Steel Community' agreement (cf. Exercise VI. 3.3 below), Greece, Portugal, Spain, Ireland, Denmark, the UK, Austria, Finland and Sweden.
The 'European Union' is administrated and supervised by the following bodies:
- The 'European Commission' is the central executive body responsible for the day-to-day administration and coordination of the Union's affairs, the control of the general budget and the implementation of EU policies. The 20 commissioners are appointed by their national governments and approved by the European Parliament. Their major task is to make policy proposals to the Council of Ministers, to administrate existing Union policy and to ensure its compliance with European Law. For this reason, the Commission is known as the 'Keeper of the Treaties'.
- The 'Council of Ministers' *(Ministerrat)* also known as 'Council of the European Unions' *(Rat der Europäischen Gemeinschaften)* has 'discretional power' *(Entscheidungsgewalt)* on all EU issues and reviews all legislative proposals from the Commission. It consists of 15 cabinet ministers (one from each member state) who are empowered to act on behalf of their governments in their specific area of competence. It is the agenda which decides which department (e.g. Finance) is represented at the individual meetings. The Council meets in Brussels or in the capital of the country that holds the union's presidency. Its chair rotates every six months to another member.
- The 'European Parliament' *(Europäisches Parlament)* is elected for five years in the local constituencies of the Union. It meets in Strasbourg where it debates the proposals of the

> Commission. The Maastricht Treaty has expanded the areas which require the Parliament's approval or 'codecision' *(Kodezision)*.
> - The 'European Court of Justice' *(Europäischer Gerichtshof)*. The ECJ meets in Luxembourg. It is the EU's Supreme Court which decides on the interpretation and application of EU law. The Court hears appeals made by governments, institutions and individuals. Its decisions are final and binding for all parties involved. Its judges are appointed by unanimous agreement of the member countries.
> - the 'European Court of Auditors' *(Europäischer Rechnungshof)* which, in the Maastricht Treaty, was given the status of official institution of the EU.

[22] *billigte:* was finally approved; was finally passed by

[23] *Rat der Europäischen Union:* Council of the European Union Cf. note [21] above.

[24] *die erste Stufe:* stage I; the first stage

[25] *und führte zu einer vollständigen Liberalisierung:* resulting in the complete deregulation; this led to the complete deregulation/liberalisation

[26] *des Geld- und Kapitalverkehrs:* of all movements of money and capital; of all monetary and capital transactions

[27] *Konvergenzkriterien:* convergence criteria

> The 'convergence criteria' were laid down for the European Monetary Union by the Maastricht Treaty of 1993. They limit divergences in exchange rates, inflation rates and interest rates and set maxima for budget deficits and the ratio of 'public debt' *(öffentliche Verschuldung*; cf. IX.2.1 Notes on the translation, item [38]) to GDP.
> Compliance with these criteria is decisive in determining whether a country qualifies for admission to the monetary union.
> - Applicants need to join the Exchange Rate Mechanism of the European Monetary System at least two years before their application is reviewed. Moreover, during this period, they must remain within the 'exchange rate band' *(Bandbreite des Wechselkurses)* without experiencing severe divergences or undertaking depreciations.
> - In the year before the review of their application, the average price increase in their country must not exceed the

> average inflation rate of those three member states who enjoy the lowest levels of price increases by more than 1.5 percentage points.
> - Long-term interest rates must not exceed the overall interest rates of the three member states which enjoy the highest level of price stability by more than two percentage points.
> - The maximum set for public debt is 3 per cent of the country's GDP; the maximum ratio of public debt to GDP is 60 per cent.

[28] *im Vertrag von Maastricht:* in the Maastricht Treaty; in the Treaty of the European Union
[29] *gesichert werden sollten:* which were to ensure; which were to safeguard; which were to warrant
[30] *begann:* commenced; was entered into
[31] *Europäischen Währungsinstitutes (EWI):* European Monetary Institute (EMI)

> The EMI existed from 1994 to 1998. It was founded to monitor the implementation of the European Monetary System (Cf. note [12] above).

[32] *des Vorläufers der Europäischen Zentralbank (EZB):* the forerunner of the European Central Bank (ECB); the predecessor of the European Central Bank

> The ECB, which is located in Frankfurt am Main, was set up in 1998 by the EU in the run-up to the EMU as an independent institution. It was given centralized powers to determine and coordinate monetary policy in the EMU countries. The ECB seeks to keep inflation low by a 'two-pillar-strategy' for monitoring the money supply in the Eurozone: it sets a reference rate for the growth in M3 and analyses the risk indicators with regard to price stability. It is managed by a six-member executive board – including its president – drawn from the EU countries.
> The ECB and the other twelve national banks of the Eurozone represent the 'eurosystem' which formulates the monetary policies which the national banks implement. The ECB is in charge of the money supply; the euro notes are issued by the national banks such as the Bundesbank and the Bank of France.

> The discretionary organ that sets the directives for the ECB's monetary policy is the ECB Council *(EZB-Rat)* which consists of the twelve presidents of the national central banks as well as four additional members who are nominated, by mutual consent, by the heads of the national governments.
> The 'board of directors of the ECB' *(Direktorium der EZB)* includes president, vice-president and the afore-mentioned four members.

33 *die Geld- und Kreditpolitik der EU ausführt:* which executes the union's monetary policy; which conducts/carries out/implements the union's monetary policy

34 *dem unwiderruflichen Übergang:* by irrevocably adopting; by irrevocably switching to
Alternative translation
... by irrevocably making the euro the EU's single currency.

35 *für eine Teilnahme an der Einführung:* for participating in the launch; for joining the launch; for taking part in the introduction

36 *vorläufig:* for the time being; for the present

VI.3 Exercises

3.1 Neologisms

In recent years, the prefix 'euro' has figured in a large variety of neologisms. In most – but not in all cases – those that are derived from 'Europe' are spelt with capital letters, those that refer to the new currency use lower case spelling. Match the expressions in the box with the explanations given in sentences 1 to 10.

Example
inclusive term for countries that use the euro as a currency: Eurozone

> Eurocrats • Eurocentric • eurocurrencies • eurodollars • Euroland • Euromarket • Europhile • Euro-sceptic • Eurozone • the United States of Europe

1 a person who ardently admires all things European or the EU: __
2 a person who is opposed to Britain's greater integration in the European Union: __.
3 senior members of the European administrative bodies (neologism derived from bureaucrats): __
4 an analogy inspired by 'Disneyland' which sums up the countries that have joined the EU: __

5 expression likening the united EU countries to the 'melting pot' USA; often used by those who fear a loss of national heritage and identity of the European people. __ __ __ __ __.
6 currencies held in a European country other than their country of origin __
7 the unimpeded movement of goods, services, labour and capital across national boundaries: __ __ __.
8 US dollars as part of a European holding: __
9 the European Union seen as one large market __
10 attitude which chiefly concentrates on European culture and Europe __

Exercises

(Reproduction authorized, European Communities, 2001)

Exercises

3.2 The Single Market
Fill in the gaps with the help of your dictionary and the Notes on the translation.
1. Since 1995, the EU has been an organization of 15 European countries which __/__/__ *(fördert)* the __ *(Wohlstand)* and the __ *(Wohlergehen)* of its members.
2. The Union is a major __ __ __ *(Freihandelszone)* and its __ __ *(Gesamtmenge)* of imports and exports is __ *(größer)* than that of any single country in the world.
3. It has succeeded in creating an __ __ /a __ __ *(Binnenmarkt)* and in __/__ *(beseitigen)* __ __ *(Zutrittsschranken)* and allows EU __ *(Bürgern)* to vote in the local and European __ *(Wahlen)* in the country of their __ *(Wohnsitzes)*.
4. The EU has established a __ __ *(Strukturfonds)* which supports regions that __ __ *(hinter ... herhinken)* the other EU states.

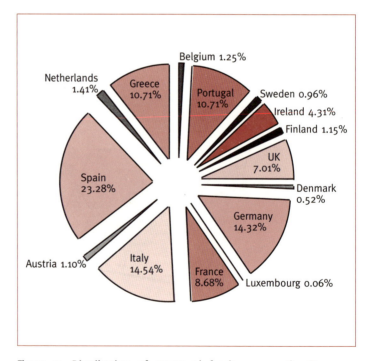

Figure 2: *Distribution of structural funds among the European countries, Agenda 2000 (Sloman, p. 655)*

5 Its most controversial platform, is its __ __ __ (gemeinsame Agrarpolitik) in line with which it __ (subventioniert) farming by __/__ (festsetzen) high prices for farm produce and by buying up the __ __ (Agrarüberschüsse).
6 The European Commission tries to __ (verhindern) the formation of monopolies by __ __ __ (Anti-Kartell-Maßnahmen) and __ __ (verbietet Absprachen) and coordinated business practices between companies as these would __ __ (sich nachteilig auswirken) competition.
7 In 1989, the Union adopted a __ __ (Sozial-Charta) which extends economic integration to the common development of a European __ __ (Sozialpolitik).
8 This charter warrants, amongst other things, each employee's rights to __ __/__ __ (auf anständige/angemessene Entlohnung) and working conditions as well as free __ __ (Berufsausbildung).
9 In addition, the Union seeks to protect the __ __ __ (ältere und behinderte Menschen), children and __/__/__ __ (Jugendliche) under the __ __ __ (Mindesterwerbsalter) of 16.
10 Last but not least, it __ (stimmt aufeinander ab) its policies in such matters as __ (Zuwanderung) and the control of illegal __ __ (Drogenhandel).

Exercises

3.3 The European Communities

Translate the following sentences using the English expressions given in (brackets) as well as your dictionaries and the terminology provided in the Notes on the translation to this chapter.
1 Jean Monnet, der 1979 im Alter von 91 Jahren starb, gilt allgemein *(is accredited with)* als Vater der Europäischen Gemeinschaften.
2 Er begann, sich für ein im Frieden vereintes demokratisches Europa zu engagieren *(commit himself to)*, als er erkannte *(realised)*, dass die wirtschaftliche Erholung Frankreichs eng an die seiner Nachbarn gebunden war.
3 Er war Gründungsmitglied *(one of the founding fathers)* der Montanunion, der EWG und von EURATOM.
4 Die Montanunion, die 1951 durch die Pariser Verträge ins Leben gerufen wurde, schuf einen Binnenmarkt *(internal market)* für die Kohle- und Stahlerzeugnisse ihrer sechs Mitgliedsstaaten.
5 Während Montanunion und EURATOM lediglich die Integration eng abgegrenzter Wirtschaftszweige in eine Zollunion *(customs union)* beabsichtigten, arbeitete die EWG auf eine schrittweise

Harmonisierung aller Bereiche der Wirtschaftspolitik hin, die für das Funktionieren des gemeinsamen Marktes ausschlaggebend *(instrumental in)* waren.

6 Deshalb werden die Römischen Verträge von 1957 gewöhnlich als ein Meilenstein *(landmark/milestone)* auf dem Weg zur EU bezeichnet.

7 1987 legte die Einheitliche Europäische Akte (EEA) mit der Verankerung der „vier Grundfreiheiten" den Grundstein *(cornerstone/ foundation)* für den Einheitlichen Europäischen Binnenmarkt.

8 Im Vertrag von Maastricht, der im Dezember 1991 unterzeichnet wurde, kommt der gemeinsamen Währung, die als „Vehikel" *(driving force)* einer verstärkten politischen Zusammenarbeit in Europa gesehen wird *(regarded as being)*, eine zentrale *(focal/ crucial)* Bedeutung zu.

VII The Dollar and the Euro

VII.1 Text: Technische Analysen   120

VII.2 **Sample translation**   123
VII.2.1 Notes on the translation

VII.3 **Exercises**   130
VII.3.1 But after September 11th all the bets were off ...
VII.3.2 The free fall of the euro
VII.3.3 Having a say!

VII.1 Text:
Technische Analysen

VII The Dollar and the Euro

(www.taprofessional.de/ ausgaben/ta990811.htm)

Figure 1: *A Technical Analysis of the Dollar Fluctuations*

Erläuterung

Die *T(echnische) A(nalyse)* in Abbildung 1 wurde von einem Chart-Analysten durchgeführt, der Aktienkursbewegungen ausschließlich auf der Grundlage der graphischen Darstellung des Kursverlaufs auswertet. Um Trends detailliert zu beschreiben und um Prognosen zu erstellen, arbeiten solche Investment-Analysten mit gleitenden Durchschnitten und bestimmten sich wiederholenden Formationen, wie z.B. symmetrischen Dreiecken (Abbildung 2), die sich aus den Diagrammen ergeben.

Diesem kontroversen Analyseverfahren, steht die *Fundamentalanalyse* gegenüber, die nur unternehmensbezogene Kurseinflussgrößen berücksichtigt. Sie geht von der These aus, dass der Börsenkurs um den „inneren" oder „objektiven Wert" einer Unternehmung schwingt. Zur Bestimmung dieses Wertes werden zum einen

quantitative Faktoren, wie Ertragslage und Organisationsform, herangezogen, zum anderen qualitative Faktoren, wie Kernkompetenzen und Innovationsfähigkeit.
Beide Verfahren lassen sich auf Wechselkurse anwenden. Die logarithmische Darstellung in Abbildung 1 ist eine „Technische Analyse" des Wechselkurses des US-Dollars gegenüber dem Euro. Die gezackte „Candlestick-Kurve" gibt die exakte Entwicklung des Dollarkurses wieder, bei der gepunkteten sowie der glatten Kurve handelt es sich um gleitende Durchschnitte.
(Renate Neubäumer)
Bitte sehen Sie sich Abbildung 1 genau an, bevor Sie den nachfolgenden Text übersetzen.

Lasst die Märkte entscheiden!

Das waren noch Zeiten! 1985, als der Euro für fast alle von uns noch eine fiktive Größe darstellte, erhielt man pro Dollar 3,00 DM, was heute etwas mehr als 1,50 € entspricht. Diesem Wert hatte sich die US-Währung seit 1980 langsam angenähert, ehe sie dann in den folgenden drei Jahren fast 50% ihres Wertes verlor und auf 0,90 € oder weniger als 2,00 DM abstürzte.

Figure 2: *Two symmetrical triangles used for trend analysis*

(www.taprofessional.de /ausgaben/ ta990811.htm)

Obwohl der „Greenback" sich mehrfach wieder vorübergehend erholte, setzte er seinen langfristigen Abwärtstrend, der durch den oberen rosa Balken verdeutlicht wird, bis 1992 fort, als er seinen bislang einmaligen Tiefstand von 1,38 DM erreichte. Gegenmaßnahmen wurden ergriffen, aber Finanzanalysten verlangten, *pari passu* zu intervenieren, um diese Entwicklung zu korrigieren. Der untere Balken zeigt allerdings deutlich, dass ihre pessimistische Einschätzung etwas voreilig war. Die Talfahrt des Dollars hatte sich nämlich seit Mitte 1994 (wo die beiden Balken sich überschneiden) erheblich verlangsamt. Trotzdem bewegte sich der Dollar auf eine weitere Talsohle zu, deren Tiefpunkt 1995 sogar noch geringfügig unter dem von 1992 lag.

(Thomson Financial Datastream; Bank of England; Goldman Sachs; Financial Times, August 2001, p. 16)

Im Jahre 1995, als die Europäische Wirtschafts- und Währungsunion Gestalt annahm, kehrte sich der primäre (d. h. der langfristige) Abwärtstrend endgültig um. Der Dollar zog stark an und mündete in eine ungewöhnlich steile Schubphase, in der er 40% oder 53 Pfennig an Wert gutmachte. 1997 wurde auch der sekundäre (d. h. der kurzfristige) Abwärtstrend endgültig gebrochen.

Nach Durchbrechen dieser Rückzugs- oder Widerstandslinie stand der Dollar Anfang 1997 bei 0,80 € und nach Vollendung der Schubphase im selben Jahr bei 0,95 €. Durch die Überschreitung selbst dieses Niveaus (angezeigt als waagrechte Gerade) im Frühjahr 1999 setzte der Dollar ein neues Kaufsignal. Es ist bezeichnend, dass die Deutsche Bundesbank damals erstmals seit Jahren wieder gegen den Dollar intervenierte, der trotz allem seinen Aufwärtstrend in Richtung Parität mit dem Euro fortsetzte.

In den letzten beiden Jahren lag die US-Währung deutlich über fast allen plausiblen Schätzungen ihres „echten Wertes" (Abbildung 3) sodass, als sie Mitte August schließlich dem Euro gegenüber fiel, Jim O'Neill, der Chefwährungsökonom der US-Investmentbank Goldman Sachs bemerkte, es sei zu hoffen, „dass ein wenig Vernunft in die Devisenmärkte zurückgekehrt sei"[1].

Außerdem, so O'Neill; deute einiges darauf hin, dass das US-Schatzministerium allmählich daran dächte, seine ausgeprägte Unterstützung für einen starken Dollars aufzugeben und dem Markt die Beurteilung des Werts der Währung zu überlassen. Inwieweit eine solche „Hände-weg-vom-Dollar-Politik" allerdings überleben würde, wenn es zum „freien Fall" des Dollars käme, bleibt offen.

(Margarete Seidenspinner)

An overvalued dollar?
Goldman Sachs estimates

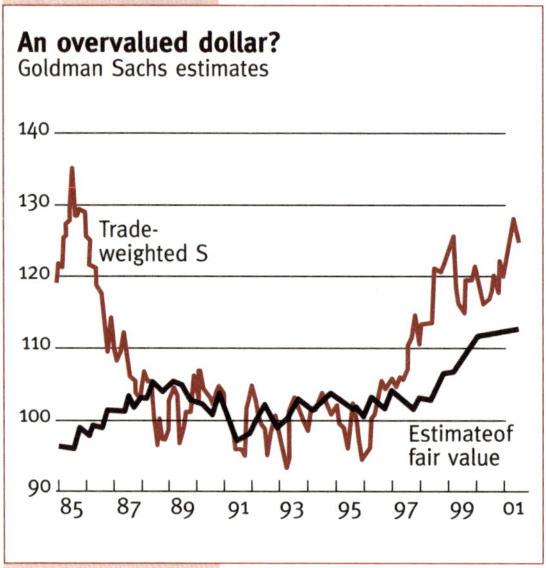

Figure 3: *An overvalued dollar?*

[1] quoted from Alan Beattie: 'Hands off the dollar', Financial Times, August 2001, p. 16

Technical analyses[1]
Explanation

The following T(echnical) A(nalysis) in Figure 1 was performed by a **chartist**[2] who **assesses**[3] **share price fluctuations**[4] exclusively on the basis **of their charted development**[5]. **In order to detail trends**[6], and **to make forecasts**[7] this type of investment analyst uses **moving averages**[8] and certain repeatedly occurring **patterns**[9], such as symmetrical triangles (Figure 2), **which emerge**[10] in the diagrams.

This controversial **analytical approach**[11] **is contrasted with**[12] the fundamental analysis which focuses exclusively on company-related factors affecting the development of equity charts. **This method is founded on**[13] the **assumption**[14] that stock exchange prices revolve around the 'intrinsic' or 'objective value' of a corporation. This value is determined, on the one hand, by quantitative factors, such as **actual revenues**[15] and the **company designation**[16], and by qualitative factors, such as **core competencies**[17] and innovation potential, on the other. Both methods can be applied to **currency trends**[18]. The **logarithmic chart'**[19] in Figure 1 represents a technical analysis of the exchange rate of the US dollar **against**[20] the euro. The **jagged**[21] 'candlestick curve' **records**[22] the actual development of the dollar, the smooth line and the dotted line represent sliding averages.

Please **examine**[23] Figure 1 before translating the following text.

Let the markets have their say[24]!

Those were the days! In 1985, when the euro still represented a **virtual**[25] quantity to most of us, one dollar **bought**[26] **three deutschmarks**[27] or its current equivalent of just over €1.50. The US currency **had been edging closer to this value**[28] since 1980, **before** losing nearly 50 per cent in the following three years and **nose-diving**[29] to €0.90, **which was equivalent to less than**[30] DEM 2.00 at that time.

Although the "greenback" **made several brief recoveries**[31], **it continued its long-term downward trend**[32] – **which is highlighted**[33] by the upper pink bar – until 1992, when it reached **its all-time low**[34] at DEM 1.38. **Countermeasures were taken**[35] but financial analysts were demanding **pari passu interventions**[36] in order to correct this development. However, the lower bar **clearly shows**[37] that their pessimistic **stance**[38] was somewhat premature as the **slump**[39] of the dollar had slowed considerably since 1994 where the two bars intersect. In spite of this, **the dollar went on to form a second trough**[40] whose 1995 minimum **was even marginally worse than the one reached in 1992**[41].

VII.2 Sample translation

In 1995, with the **European Economic and Monetary Union**[42] taking shape, the primary (i.e. long-term) downtrend was reversed **once and for all**[43]. The dollar **increased sharply**[44] and **moved into an unusually steep thrust phase**[45], in which it **gained**[46] nearly 40 per cent or 0.53 deutschmarks. In 1997, the secondary (i.e. short-term) downward trend was finally broken, too.

On breaking[47] this **fallback line or resistance line**[48] at the beginning of 1997, the dollar stood at €0.80 and **on completing**[49] its thrust phase in the same year at €0.95. By crossing this level (indicated by the horizontal bar) in spring 1999, the dollar **generated**[50] a new buying signal. It is of significance that, at that moment, **the Bundesbank**[51] intervened, for the first time in years, against the dollar which, **nonetheless**[52], continued its upward trend towards parity with the euro.

In the last two years, the US currency has been markedly higher than almost any plausible estimate of its 'fair value' (Figure 3) so that when it finally fell in mid-August 2001 against the euro, Jim O'Neill, the chief currency economist of the US **investment bank**[53] Goldman Sachs, commented that **it was to be hoped**[54] "that **some sanity**[55] had returned to the foreign exchange markets." Moreover, **O'Neill maintained**[56], **there were distinctive signs**[57] that the US Treasury **was slowly moving towards**[58] **abandoning**[59] its **deliberate**[60] support for a strong dollar and towards **letting the markets be the judge of the currency's value**[61]. However, to what extent such a "hands-off-the-dollar policy" would survive if the dollar were to go into free fall **is a moot point**[62].

Please note →

2.1 Notes on the translation

1 *Analysen:* analyses

> Words derived from ancient Greek and ending in '...is', such as 'analysis', 'thesis', 'hypothesis', 'crisis', have irregular plural forms, namely '...es' [pronounced: ...i:z].

2 *Chart-Analysten:* chartist; chart analyst

> 'Chartists' are investment analysts. Working on the assumption that history repeats itself, and that the movements of share prices conform to repetitive patterns, they record past movements of the share prices in order to forecast future developments. Chartists have been very popular in the United States.

3   *auswertet:* assesses; evaluates
4   *Aktienkursbewegungen:* share price fluctuations; stock/equity price fluctuations; fluctuations in the market prices of shares
5   *der graphischen Darstellung des Kursverlaufs:* of their charted development; of their development charts
    For the translation of *Verlauf* cf. III.2.1 Notes on the translation, item ¹.
6   *um Trends detailiert zu beschreiben:* in order to detail trends; in order to describe/outline trends in great detail
7   *um Prognosen zu erstellen:* to make forecasts; for forecasting purposes
8   *gleitenden Durchschnitten:* moving averages; sliding averages
9   *Formationen:* patterns; configurations; formations

> 'Pattern' *(Muster; Schema; Motiv)* denotes a recognizable arrangement or configuration of shapes, colours or structures that can be imitated and copied. 'Formation' *(Formation; Entstehung; Bildung; Formulierung)* refers to the act and/or process of forming or shaping something or to the matter that has been formed itself *(Gebilde)*.

← Please note

Examples
The patterns *(Motive)* of classical music are often copied by modern composers.
Individual patterns of thought *(Denkmuster)* are influenced by cultural heritage.
Heat causes the formation of steam *(Bildung)* from water.
The logical formation *(Struktur/Aufbau)* of his ideas made it easy for the students to follow his lectures.
Strategy formation *(Formulierung)* precedes implementation.
Clouds are formations *(Gebilde)* of tiny drops of water.

10 *die sich ... ergeben:* which emerge; which surface; which manifest themselves
11 *Analyseverfahren:* analytical approach; analytical method
12 *steht ... gegenüber:* is contrasted with; is juxtaposed with; is compared to
13 *sie geht von ... aus:* this method is founded on; this approach is based on; this analysis relies on
14 *These:* assumption; thesis

> 'Thesis' denotes a 'proposition' to be proved or to be maintained against objections or a preliminary 'assumption'. In

← Please note

addition, it refers to a long essay or dissertation submitted for the award of a university degree, e.g. 'doctoral thesis' *(Doktorarbeit)*.
For the pronunciation of 'theses' cf. note [1] above.

[15] *Ertragslage:* actual revenues; the revenues earned/achieved

Please note →

> 'Actual' is a 'false friend' as it does not translate *aktuell* (i.e. 'current' or 'present'). The adjective is synonymous with 'existing as a fact', 'real' and 'genuine'. In the above case, *Lage* refers to the 'actual figures' *(Ist-Stand)* as opposed to the 'targeted figures' *(Soll-Zahlen)*.

Example
Has this accident actually *(wirklich/tatsächlich)* happened?

[16] *Organisationsform:* company designation; type of company
[17] *Kernkompetenzen:* core competencies; core competences; core skills; key competencies

> 'Core competences' are the key resources and skills (e.g. specialist expertise, patents), processes or systems on which a company's 'core business' *(Kerngeschäft)*, 'strategic business areas' *(strategische Geschäftsfelder)* and 'competitive advantage' *(Wettbewerbsvorteil)* are founded.

[18] *Wechselkurse:* currency trends; exchange rates
[19] *logarithmische Darstellung:* logarithmic chart

> 'Logarithmic charts' plot data on a logarithmic scale, i.e. in a way which uses equally long distances for values which differ by the same percentage level. In Figure 1, for instance, the distance between 0.7 and 0.8 is significantly bigger than the distance between 1.55 and 1.65.

[20] *gegenüber:* against; compared to; in comparison to; versus
[21] *gezackte:* jagged; serrated; also: notched

Please note →

> 'Jagged' *(gezackt/zerklüftet)* signifies 'unevenly indented' or 'serrated' *(gezackt/gezahnt)*. The adjective characterises 'streaks of lightning' *(Blitze)* or 'rock formations' *(Gebirgsformationen)*. It is synonymous with 'serrated'.

Examples
a serrated leaf: *ein gezahntes Blatt*
a jagged rock: *ein zerklüfteter Fels*

a serrated knife: *ein Sägemesser*

> A 'notch' is a v-shaped cut, 'nick' (*Kerbe*) or 'tooth' *(Zahn)*, for instance in the 'serrated edge' of a saw or a knife. It can also be the valley formed between two mountains or an 'indentation' *(Einschnitt)* in a rising or curving surface. This type of 'notch' is used to keep a score or a record, and to measure.

← Please note

Examples
Notched poles *(gekerbte Pfosten)* facilitate climbing.
In winter, most people set their radiators several notches *(Stufen/ Einstellungen)* higher.

Figurative usage
The IT sector has notched (up) some impressive failures. *Die IT-Branche hat sich ein paar eindrucksvolle Misserfolge geleistet.*
Consumers are currently tightening their belts a notch. *Konsumenten schnallen zur Zeit ihre Gürtel ein Loch enger.*
This pupil has always been a notch above the others. *Dieser Schüler war immer einen Tick besser als die anderen.*
He needs to be taken down a notch or two. *Man muss ihn ein bisschen zurechtstutzen.*
She arrived in the very nick of time. *Sie kam in allerletzter Minute.*

[22] *gibt ... wieder:* records; charts; plots
[23] *sehen Sie sich ... genau an:* examine; take a close look at; study; scrutinize

> The meaning of the adverb *genau* may be implied in the English verb in which case it requires no translation.

← Please note

[24] *lasst die Märkte entscheiden:* let the markets have their say; let the markets be the judge
For further practice on the idiomatic usage of 'say' cf. VII3.3 Having a say!
[25] *fiktive:* virtual; fictitious
[26] *erhielt man:* bought; was worth
[27] *3,00 DM:* three deutschmarks; DEM 3.00; DM 3.00

> 'Deutschmark' can be spelt with a capital initial letter but lower case spelling is more frequent. For the spelling of currency denominations cf. V.2.1 Notes on the translation, item [47].

← Please note

[28] *diesem Wert hatte sich ... langsam angenähert:* had been edging closer to this value; had been nearing this value; had been approaching this value

29 *ehe sie ... abstürzte:* before nose-diving; before plunging; before plummeting
30 *weniger als:* which was equivalent to less than; which was worth less than
31 *sich mehrfach wieder vorübergehend erholte:* made several brief recoveries; made several short-term recoveries
32 *setzte er seinen langfristigen Abwärtstrend ... fort:* it continued its long-term downward trend; over the long term, it continued its downtrend
33 *der ... verdeutlicht wird:* which is highlighted; which is emphasized; which is marked
34 *seinen bislang einmaligen Tiefstand:* its all-time low; its hitherto lowest level; its lowest level ever
35 *Gegenmaßnahmen wurden ergriffen:* countermeasures were taken; counteraction was taken
36 *pari passu zu intervenieren: pari passu* interventions; equable interventions

> In academic contexts, *pari passu* (which is Latin for 'with equal step') signifies 'with equal speed' or 'with equal progress'. In economics, this meaning has been extended to 'of equal right', 'equal rank' or 'equably' *(in gleichem Maße).*
> Examples
> to proceed pari passu *(sich im gleichen Tempo fortbewegen),* i.e. to move in step with somebody
> pari passu measures: *Massnahmen gleichen Umfangs/gleichen Ranges*

37 *zeigt ... deutlich:* clearly shows: manifestly demonstrates/indicates
38 *Einschätzung:* stance; assessment
39 *Talfahrt:* slump; fall; steep decline
40 *bewegte sich der Dollar auf eine weitere Talsohle zu:* the dollar went on to form a second trough; the dollar continued its slump towards a second low
41 *sogar noch geringfügig unter dem von 1992 lag:* was even marginally worse than the one reached in 1992; was even slightly worse than the one in 1992
42 *Europäische Wirtschafts- und Währungsunion:* European Economic and Monetary Union
Cf. V.2.1 Notes on the translation, item [19].
43 *endgültig:* once and for all; finally

44 *zog stark an:* increased sharply; rose suddenly
45 *mündete in eine ungewöhnlich steile Schubphase:* moved into an unusually steep thrust phase; started an extraordinarily sharp upturn/upswing
46 *an Wert gutmachte:* gained; made good
47 *nach Durchbrechen:* on breaking; on exceeding; on crossing; on cutting
48 *Rückzugs- oder Widerstandslinie:* fallback line or resistance line

> Bear in mind that hyphenated noun compounds are usually translated as two full words.

← Please note

49 *nach Vollendung:* on completing; on the completion of; after/on finishing
50 *setzte:* generated; produced; sent out
51 *die Deutsche Bundesbank:* the Bundesbank

> *Deutsche Bundesbank* is not translated into English as such: Economic texts simply say 'the Bundesbank'. The reason for this may be that a direct rendering as 'Federal Bank' would invite confusion with the Federal Bank of the US.

← Please note

52 *trotz allem:* nonetheless; nevertheless; in spite of everything
53 *Investmentbank:* investment bank; merchant bank; wholesale bank
54 *es sei zu hoffen:* it was to be hoped

> Certain phrases formed with *da ist/es ist/es bleibt* are converted into English as passive voice forms of the infinitive (to be + past participle of the verb)

← Please note

Examples
Da war nichts zu machen. There was nothing to be done.
Das bleibt abzuwarten. This remains to be seen.
Das war zu erwarten. This was to be expected.
Das ist anders zu verstehen. This is meant/is to be interpreted differently.

55 *ein wenig Vernunft:* some sanity; a modicum of common sense
56 *so O'Neill:* O Neill maintained; O' Neill claimed
For further practice on the translation of 'indirect speech' cf. V.3.2.
57 *deute einiges darauf hin:* there were distinctive signs; there were definite/obvious signs; it was becoming more and more evident; it looked very much as if

⁵⁸ *allmählich daran dächte:* was slowly moving towards; was steadily moving towards; was beginning to think more often in terms of/about

⁵⁹ *aufzugeben:* abandoning; giving up; renouncing

⁶⁰ *ausgeprägte:* deliberate; obvious; distinct

⁶¹ *dem Markt die Beurteilung des Werts der Währung zu überlassen:* letting the markets be the judge of the currency's value; letting the markets have their say in determining the currency's value

⁶² *bleibt offen:* is a moot point; is an open question; remains to be seen

VII.3 Exercises

3.1 But after September 11th all the bets were off ...

This exercise has been designed to describe rate fluctuations. Look up the terms required for the exercise below in the Notes on the translation of this chapter and in Exercise VI.

1. When in August 2001, Alan Greenspan (cf. Figure 3), the __ *(Vorsitzende)* of the Federal Reserve, announced that interest rates had __/__/__ *(erreicht)* their __ __ *(tiefsten Stand)* since 1994, this was widely welcomed.

2. The Fed's latest attempt to __ __/__ *(abwehren)* recession by __ *(drastisch senken)* the borrowing costs for businesses was seen as a step towards __ __/__ __ *(ankurbeln)* the sluggish economy.

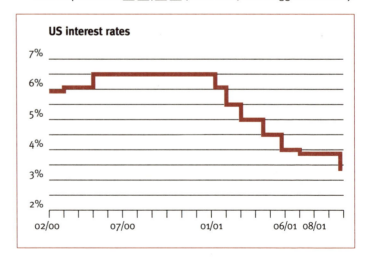

(The Editor magazine; the Guardian, August 25, 2001, p. 25)

Figure 4: *US interest rates*

3 However, the Dow Jones __/__ (stürzte) by more than 145 points as financial analysts failed to be impressed by the downbeat (i.e. pessimistic) tone of the Fed's accompanying statement warning of the possibility that the US economy might __ __/__ __ (abgleiten) a long-term __ (Talfahrt) with __/__/__ (deutlich) higher levels of unemployment.
4 In spite of all this, evidence that the economy was __ (sich stabilisierte) came from reports showing that consumer confidence had __ (sich verbessert).
5 But after the terrorist attack on the World Trade Center, business __ (Ausgaben) moved into __ (Rückwärtsgang) and all major world economies are currently in full __/__ (Rezession).
6 A number of economists still expect the __/__/__ (kränkelnde) economy to __ (sich erholen) but a long-term __/__ (Aufschwung) remains highly uncertain.
7 The major reason for expecting a quicker __ (Umschwung) is that for more than a year businesses have been running down their __ (Lagerbestände).
8 And with __ __ (Steuersenkungen) in the pipeline and lower __ __ (Hypothekenzinsen) included in a __ __ (Anreizpaket), there might be a __ (rasche Zunahme) in capital spending.

Exercises

Exercises

9 Other commentators are __ __ *(vorsichtiger)*, hoping that US consumers will continue to keep their country's economy __ *(über Wasser halten)*.

10 However, there is a broad consensus that with __/__ *(steigender)* unemployment, consumer spending will __/__ *(schrumpfen)*, and if job insecurity makes consumers __ __ __ *(den Gürtel enger schnallen)*, all the bets are off.

3.2 The free fall of the euro

Examine the graph below and fill in the gaps with the appropriate English equivalent of the German terms in (brackets). Use words and phrases from the **Sample translation**, the **Notes** and your dictionaries. This exercise was devised by R. Neubäumer. It is based on an article in the *Frankfurter Allgemeine Zeitung*, 2 May 1998.

(Deutsche Bundesbank)

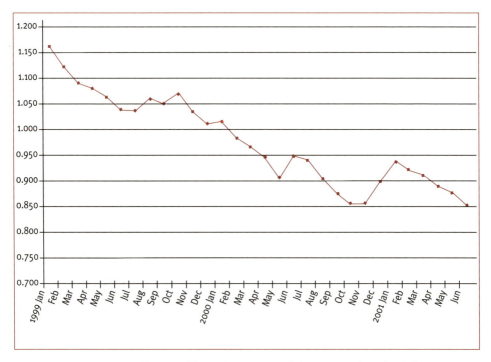

Figure 5: *The exchange rate of the euro against the dollar: 1999 to June 2001*

Exercises

1 As 1998 drew to its close, the value of the USD __ __ *(lag bei)* DEM 1.67, a figure to which it had gradually ___ *(kletterte)* from its midsummer __ *(Tiefpunkt)* of DEM 1.40 in 1995.
2 Upon the introduction of the euro on January 1, 1999, the value of this currency was __ __ *(festgesetzt auf)* DEM 1.9558.
3 Conversely, the deutschmark has since __ __ /__ *(war wert)* €0.511.
4 Unfortunately, this has meant that whenever the euro __ /__ *(schwächer wird)*, the value of the deutschmark against the dollar __ __ *(ist betroffen)*, too.
5 As a __ __ *(Folgewirkung)*, this has led to higher travel expenses on the part of those who need to fly to the US, for instance, and has __ /__ *(gemacht)* imports from the dollar countries a lot more expensive.
6 This is __ __ /__ __ *(nachteilig für)* car drivers who have had to __ /__ *(hinnehmen)* a 23 per cent rise in petrol prices between January 1988 and September 2001.
7 On the other hand, a stronger euro is good news for the Eurozone economies as it __ *(beseitigt)* the __ /__ *(Risiko)* of imported inflation and allows the ECB to reduce interest rates.
8 German companies who export their commodities to countries where invoices are __ __ /__ *(ausgestellt)* in USD, have welcomed the __ *(Verfall)* of the euro and have __ __ __ *(daraus Nutzen gezogen).*).
9 This has, on the whole, greatly improved the __ *(Wettbewerbsfähigkeit)* of German products and services in the world market.
10 But, at the same time, European __ *(Wirtschaftswissenschaftler)* call for caution for the following reasons.
11 Although the current state of the US economy is the biggest risk to world growth, in the last few months, some Eurozone economies have __ *(sich verschlechtert)* at an even faster rate than their US counterpart.
12 The repeated __ __ *(Korrekturen nach unten)* to productivity growth in the US have __ *(ausgehöhlt)* the illusion that, in the long term, a more expensive dollar would be __ *(gerechtfertigt)*.

Exercises

3.3 Having a say!

'Say' as a noun and a verb features in a fair number of idiomatic expressions.

Examples
You have had your say. Now let her have hers. *Du hast gesagt, was du zu sagen hattest, jetzt ist sie dran.*
You can say that again! *Das kannst du laut sagen!*
You don't say! *Wirklich! Ach was! Was, Sie nicht sagen!*

Please translate the following sentences which all explore the idiomatic usage of 'say'. Include these expressions.

let's say/say
not to say
to have a say in
to say nothing about
to say the least
when all is said and done

1 Die Bank möchte ein entscheidendes Wort bei der Gründung der Holding-Gesellschaft mitreden.
2 Die Mitgliedsbanken waren alle angehört worden, ehe die endgültige Entscheidung getroffen wurde.
3 Es war ein Fehler, das neue Produkt zu lancieren, um nicht zu sagen eine Katastrophe.
4 Das neue System spart viel Zeit und ist zudem noch kostengünstig.
5 Wenn man alles in Betracht zieht, sind die Mitarbeiter das höchste Gut eines Unternehmens.
6 Seine Manieren waren, milde ausgedrückt, ungeschliffen.
7 Angenommen wir erhöhen die Anzahl der produzierten Einheiten, z.B. um drei pro Minute, beseitigt dies unseren Lieferengpass?

VIII The Federal Reserve System

VIII.1 Text: Die Zentralbank der Vereinigten Staaten 136

VIII.2 Sample translation 138
VIII.2.1 Notes on the translation

VIII.3 Exercises 150
VIII.3.1 'Money is as money does'
VIII.3.2 Independent central banks
VIII.3.3 What if?

VIII.1 Text: Die Zentralbank der Vereinigten Staaten

VIII The Federal Reserve System

Das *Federal Reserve System (FRS)* dient den USA als Zentralbank. Sie wurde 1913 gegründet, um dem Land ein sichereres, flexibleres und stabileres Währungssystem zu geben und umfasst heute drei Organe: den Zentralbankvorstand der *FRS*, die zwölf regionalen Reservebanken und den Offenmarktausschuss.

1 Der siebenköpfige Zentralbankvorstand hat seinen Hauptsitz in Washington (D.C.). Seine Mitglieder werden gerne als „Tauben" betitelt, weil sie vom Präsidenten der Vereinigten Staaten nominiert und vom Senat bestätigt werden. Ihre einmalige Amtszeit dauert 14 Jahre. Nur ein Mitglied wird aus den Reihen der Präsidenten der Reservebanken gewählt, die anderen vertreten finanzielle, landwirtschaftliche, industrielle und kommerzielle Interessen auf einer breiten regionalen Basis. Der US-Präsident ernennt ein Mitglied des Vorstandes zum Vorsitzenden der *Fed* und ein weiteres zu dessen Stellvertreter. Beide Personen üben ihr Amt vier Jahre lang aus. Wiederholte Ernennungen sind möglich.

2 Die zwölf Reservebanken werden jeweils von einem Präsidenten geleitet, der häufig zur Gruppe der „Habichte" zählt, und ihnen ist ein Reservebankbezirk zugeordnet. Diese regionalen Zentralbanken bilden zusammen mit den nationalen Geschäftsbanken eine Genossenschaft. Alle nationalen Geschäftsbanken sind gesetzlich zur Mitgliedschaft verpflichtet, den Banken der einzelnen Bundesstaaten ist die Mitgliedschaft freigestellt. Jedoch unterliegen alle Geldinstitute, die Einlagen annehmen, den Mindestreservevorschriften der *Fed*.

3 Der Offenmarktausschuss und der Zentralbankvorstand des *FRS* treffen alle grundlegenden Entscheidungen über die Geldmenge, die Kreditversorgung der amerikanischen Wirtschaft sowie über den Handel mit Wertpapieren der öffentlichen Hand. Der Offenmarktausschuss setzt sich aus zwölf stimmberechtigten Mitgliedern zusammen, und zwar den sieben Vorstandsmitgliedern der *Fed*, deren Präsident den Vorsitz im FOMC führt, und fünf Präsidenten der Regionalbanken. Deren Mitgliedschaft rotiert jährlich, wobei der Präsident der New Yorker Regionalbank als stellvertretender Vorsitzender des Ausschusses diesem als ständiges Mitglied angehört.

Diese spezifische Struktur der Zentralbank soll ihre Unabhängigkeit gegenüber der amerikanischen Regierung gewährleisten. Ihr Vorsitzender ist zwar gesetzlich verpflichtet, zweimal jährlich dem Kongress über die Vorhaben der *Fed* zu berichten, sie trifft aber ihre geld- und kreditpolitischen Entscheidungen autonom. Auch finanziell ist sie unabhängig. Ihre Einnahmen stammen hauptsächlich aus dem Offenmarktgeschäft, dem Besitz ausländischer Währungen, Darlehen an Kreditinstitute und den Gebühren, die sie für erbrachte Dienstleistungen, z.B. für Beratung und für Wirtschaftsforschung erhebt. Für die Mindestreserven, die sie für ihre Mitgliedsbanken einlagert, zahlt sie keine Zinsen.

In erster Linie sind die Zentralbanken für die Ausgestaltung und die Umsetzung der nationalen Geldpolitik verantwortlich, die die Förderung von Preisstabilität und Wirtschaftswachstum anstrebt. Das wird vor allem dadurch bewirkt, dass die *Fed* Ziele für den Tagesgeldsatz festlegt, der durch die Durchführung von Offenmarktgeschäften, durch Diskontsatzänderungen und durch Veränderungen der Mindestreserven beeinflusst werden kann.

Wenn die *Fed* den Tagesgeldsatz senkt, indem sie zum Beispiel Offenmarktpapiere kauft und damit den Banken mehr Zentralbankgeld zur Verfügung stellt, wirkt dies auf die Wirtschaft wie eine Geldspritze. Die Banken folgen in der Regel diesem Beispiel und senken ihren Kreditzins für erste Adressen, d.h. den Referenzzins für Geschäftsleute und Verbraucher. Die daraus resultierenden geringeren Kreditkosten, z. B. für Hypotheken, erhöhen die Konsumausgaben und erleichtern den Unternehmen die Expansion. Darüber hinaus führen niedrigere Zinsen zu einer Abwertung des Dollars und senken damit die Preise für US-Exporte.

Zusätzlich zu ihrer geldpolitischen Verantwortung hat die Zentralbank zahlreiche Aufgaben im Zusammenhang mit der Abwicklung des Zahlungsverkehrs und der Überwachung des Bankensystems. Auch verwaltet sie die Ausgabe von US-Banknoten und erledigt das bundesstaatsübergreifende Scheck-Clearing für alle Geschäftsbanken.

(R. Neubäumer/M. Seidenspinner, Quellen:
- Deutsche Unesco-Kommission, www.us. market.de;
- www.federalreserve.gov/pubs/frseries/frseri.htm;
- us-market.de/archiv/investorwissen/federalreservebank.html;
- www.frbsf.org/publications/federalreserve/monetary/affect.html)

Corel Library

VIII.2 Sample translation

The 'Federal Reserve System' of the United States

The **Federal Reserve System**[1] (FRS) serves the United States as **its central bank**[2]. It was founded in 1913, in order to provide the country with a safer, more flexible and more stable monetary system and now **comprises**[3] three bodies: the **Board of Governors of the FRS**[4], the twelve **Federal Reserve Banks**[5] (FRBs) and the **Federal Open-Market Committee (FOMC)**[6].

1. The seven-member Board of Governors is based in Washington (D.C.). Its members **are often labelled 'doves'**[7] as they are nominated by the President of the United States and **approved**[8] by the Senate. **They each serve one 14-year term**[9]. Only one of the members is elected by and from the ranks of the presidents of the Federal Reserve Banks the others represent financial, agricultural, industrial and commercial interests **on a broad regional scale**[10]. The US President **appoints**[11] one board member as **chairperson**[12] of the 'Fed' and another for the vice-chair. Each person serves for four years and may be reappointed.

2. The twelve Federal Reserve Banks **are each governed by**[13] a president, who frequently represents the group of the **'hawks'**[14], and are allocated a **Federal Reserve District**[15]. These regional central banks and the **national commercial banks**[16] form a co-operative. All national commercial banks are required by law to become members, for the **state-chartered banks**[17] membership is **optional**[18]. However, all **deposit-taking banks**[19] are subject to the Fed's **minimum reserve requirements**[20].

3. The Federal Open-Market Committee and the Board of Governors make all key decisions on the **money supply**[21], the **availability of credit facilities**[22] in the US economy and on **the trading of government securities**[23]. It is made up of twelve voting members, **notably**[24] the seven governors of the Federal Reserve, whose president chairs the FOMC, as well as five FRB presidents. The membership of the latter rotates annually, with the President of New York Reserve Bank retaining a permanent seat as the committee's vice-chairman.

This specific structure of the central bank is intended to guarantee its independence from the US administration. **Although its chairperson is required by law**[25] to report twice a year to Congress about the Fed's planned undertakings, it decides on its **monetary policy**[26] autonomously. Financially, it is independent, too. **Its income derives, for the most part, from**[27] open market operations, holdings of foreign currencies, loans to credit institutions and from **the charges it raises**[28] for **services rendered**[29] e.g. for consultancy and for economic research. It pays no **interest**[30] on the minimum reserves it keeps for its member banks.

The primary responsibility of the central banks is the formation and implementation of their nation's monetary policy, which **aims**[31] at price stability and economic growth. This is **achieved**[32], above all, by setting **targets**[33] for the **federal funds rate**[34], which can be influenced by conducting **open-market operations**[35] and by changing the **discount rate**[36] and the minimum reserve requirements.

If the Fed lowers the funds rate by buying more open-market papers thereby making more central bank funds available to banks, this effectively injects money into the economy. **As a rule, banks follow the Fed's example**[37] by lowering their own **prime rate**[38], which is a reference rate for business people and consumers. Decreased borrowing costs, which result from this, strengthen consumer spending and facilitate corporate expansion. Moreover, low rates weaken the value of the dollar and reduce the price of US exports.

In addition to being responsible for monetary policies, the central bank has been assigned numerous tasks with respect to **the handling of payments**[39] and the supervision of the banking system. It also **administers**[40] the issuing of **US bank notes**[41] and **effects**[42] **interstate cheque clearings**[43] for all commercial banks.

2.1 Notes on the translation

1 Federal Reserve System

> The Federal Reserve System was founded by the 'Federal Reserve Act' in 1913 and substantially amended by the 'Bank Act' of 1935.

> Most people refer to the central bank of the United States as 'Federal Reserve' or 'the Fed'. 'FRS' is another label in use.

← Please note

2 *als Zentralbank:* as its central bank

> Central banks such as the Fed function as 'lenders of last resort' *(Refinanzierungsinstitute oder Kreditgeber der letzten Instanz)*, in other words, they are the bankers' bank and supply cash to the banking system in order to maintain liquidity and prevent bank failures.

● ● ● ● ● ●   Central bank money consists of bank notes and current accounts with the central bank.

Please note →   Please note that 'United States' can function as a singular or a plural noun.

³ *umfasst:* consists of; comprises
⁴ *Zentralbankvorstand:* Board of Governors of the FRS; also: the Federal Reserve Board of Governors

The name of this body is commonly abbreviated as 'Fed Board'. Until 1936, the Board's official title was: the 'Federal Reserve Board'. Since 1978, the Board of Governors has been required by law to report twice a year to Congress on its objectives and plans with regard to monetary policy.

Please note →   The translations *Zentralbankrat* and *Bundesbankrat* can also be found in German dictionaries.

⁵ *Reservebanken:* Federal Reserve Banks

Please note →   The translation *Regionalbanken* is equally common.

The twelve District FRBs are located in Boston, New York, Philadelphia, Cleveland, Richmond, Atlanta, Chicago, St Louis, Minneapolis, Kansas City, Dallas and San Francisco. Most of them have from one to five branches, which offer many of the services that the FRBs provide.

⁶ *Offenmarktausschuss:* Federal Open-Market Committee (FOMC)

The FOMC was established by the Bank Acts of 1933 and 1935 when it succeeded the 'Open-Market Investment Committee' (1923) which used to co-ordinate the Fed's investment policy through the Federal Reserve Bank in New York. Cf. note ³⁵. Its British counterpart is the Bank of England's Monetary Policy Committee (MPC).

⁷ *werden gerne als „Tauben" betitelt:* are often labelled 'doves'; are often termed 'doves'

'Doves' connotes the fact that this group tends to seek accommodation with governmental monetary policies. The 'doves' are committed to promoting growth. Their economic counterparts are the 'hawks' (cf. note ¹⁴).

> **Further usage examples**
> Alan Greenberg is a 'dove' and his gospel is 'growth, growth, growth'.
> In times of severe crises, the 'war hawks' tend to outnumber the 'peace doves'.

● ● ● ● ● ●

8 *bestätigt:* approved; confirmed
9 *ihre einmalige Amtszeit dauert 14 Jahre:* they each serve one 14-year term; they each hold one 14-year term of office; they each hold office for 14 years
Useful collocations
sein Amt antreten: to assume one's office/to take up one's office
für ein Amt kandidieren: to apply for a post/a position/an office; to run for an office/a post
in ein Amt eingesetzt werden: to be installed in office
seines Amtes walten: to execute one's authority
jemanden seines Amtes entheben: to discharge/dismiss somebody from office
10 *auf einer breiten regionalen Basis:* on a broad regional scale; on a broad regional basis
11 *ernennt:* appoints; nominates; designates
12 *Vorsitzenden:* chairperson; chair

> The 'chairperson' or 'chair' presides over a company's board of directors, a meeting or a debate *(Vorsitzende/r; Sitzungsleitung)*. Both terms refer to either a 'chairman' or a 'chairwoman' – terms which are no longer deemed politically correct.
> 'Chair' is a polysemous noun and verb that covers a variety of meanings. Amongst other things, it is short for 'electric chair', a 'professorship at a university' *(Lehrstuhl)* and the position of authority held by persons who preside over boards and chair meetings.

← Please note

For 'Board of Directors' and *Vorstand* cf. J. Bauer & M. Seidenspinner, *Betriebswirtschaft: Übersetzungsübungen*, Cornelsen & Oxford University Press, Berlin 2001, pp. 68-69.
Usage examples
The chair *(Sitzungsleiter/in)* called the meeting to order.
The speaker addressed his question on the agenda *(Tagesordnung)* to the chair *(an den Vorsitzenden/die Sitzungsleitung)*.

● ● ● ● ● ●   The new president chaired the Board *(war Vorstandsvorsitzender)* for four years.
Our principal will preside at/preside over/chair/will be in the chair at our meeting *(die Sitzung leiten).*
to take the chair: *den Vorsitz/die Sitzungsleitung übernehmen*

[13] *werden jeweils von … geleitet:* are each governed by; are each directed/chaired by

Please note →

> 'Presided over' would be the translation of choice here were it not for the fact that this would create a clash with the subject 'president'.
> 'To govern' and 'to direct' may connote slightly different meanings as shown in the following.

Usage example
The party who wins the presidential elections governs/rules *(regiert)* the US for four years.
When traffic lights fail, policemen direct *(regeln)* the traffic.
Can you direct *(den Weg weisen)* me to the labour exchange.
This is the second play he has directed *(in dem er Regie führt).*
The fireman directed *(zielte mit)* his hose at the burning tree.

[14] *Habichte:* hawks

> It usually falls to the 'hawks' to contain and to combat inflation. They have a history of opposing, at times aggressively, fiscal and monetary policies that stimulate growth at the price of inflation.

[15] *Reservebankbezirk:* Federal Reserve District

Please note →

> This is colloquially referred to as 'Fed District'.

[16] *nationalen Geschäftsbanken:* national commercial banks; national banks

> The 'national commercial banks' of the US are private credit institutions that conduct all general banking transactions such as accepting deposits and granting loans. Contrary to the 'state-chartered banks' (cf. note [19]), they are subject to national law only. The Fed provides a large number of services for the commercial banks. The most prominent sub-category in this group are the 'clearing banks' (cf. note [42]).
> In the UK, all banks, with the exception of the Bank of England, are commercial banks. The narrow specialisation between

banks and building societies has virtually disappeared with both types offering an overlapping range of services. Banks are broadly divided into:
- 'retail banks' or 'high-street banks' *(Banken für Privatkunden)* which are general purpose banks operating an extensive network of branches that transact business directly with the general public and publish their interest rates and service charges. Most retail banks operate a clearing system (cf. note [42]).
- 'investment banks', 'merchant banks' or 'wholesale banks' *(Unternehmerbanken; Merchant-Banken)*, which specialize in administrating large-scale deposits and loans for businesses and often act as 'brokers' *(Makler)* arranging loans from different sources. This category also includes finance houses and overseas banks.

[17] *Banken der einzelnen Bundesstaaten:* state-chartered banks; state banks

These are commercial banks which depend on the government of one of the US states for their concession.
Another translation for 'state-chartered banks' in the above context is *einzelstaatlich-konzessionierte Banken*.

[18] *freigestellt:* optional; non-compulsory; voluntary
[19] *Geldinstitute, die Einlagen annehmen:* deposit-taking banks; depository institutions

'Bank deposits' *(Bankeinlagen/Depositen)* are the money held by credit institutions and building societies. They may rise or fall on any particular day, but, over time, they have a tendency to rise. There are four major types of deposits:
- 'Sight deposits' *(Sichteinlagen)* paid out on demand without penalty whose most familiar form are 'current accounts' *(Girokonten)* that pay little or no interest.
- 'Time deposits' *(Termineinlagen)* which are held for longer periods of time and pay more interest but require a notice of withdrawal. They include the amounts deposited in 'savings accounts' *(Sparkonten)*.
- 'Certificates of deposit' *(Einlagenzertifikate)* which are large fixed-term deposits that are transferable from one holder to another.

- 'Repos' *(Pensionsgeschäfte)* which are sale and repurchase agreements between banks in which the seller agrees to repurchase these securities at a later date (e.g. at their time of maturity). Repos are issued when banks need to raise short-term funds. The assets banks offer as securities in such an agreement are mostly government bonds.

[20] *den Mindestreservevorschriften:* minimum reserve requirements

Since 1980, all depository institutions have been required by the 'Depository Institutions Deregulation and Monetary Control Act' to keep minimum reserves with their Fed district bank. They use their remaining deposits to grant loans. The minimum requirement can vary from 10 per cent for sight accounts to zero for savings accounts. High reserve requirements reduce the amount of funds member banks have available for loans. Low reserve requirements enable banks to lower their interest rates for both loans and deposits.
Changing the reserve requirement is a hard-hitting measure that is seldom used.

[21] *Geldmenge:* money supply

'Money supply' *(Geldmenge/Geldangebot)* is the total amount of money which is in circulation in an economy. A high percentage of the money supplies are deposits. Cheques, debit cards and credit cards, although they are used to pay for commodities and services, do not count as money.
Money supply is measured in 'monetary aggregates' *(Geldmengenaggregate)* which include narrow and broad definitions of money. In the Eurozone, three aggregates have been defined as
- M1: cash in circulation and private sector sight deposits
- M2: M1 plus short-term time deposits that mature within two years or require a notice of withdrawal of up to three months
- M3: M2 plus 'repos' (cf. note [19]) and 'fixed-interest securities' *(festverzinsliche Wertpapiere)* repayable after two years or later

In the UK, there are currently four basic distinctions, namely
- M0 or 'wide monetary base': notes and coins in circulation plus the 'till money' *(Kassenbestand)* of banks and building societies and their working deposits with the central bank

- M2 or 'narrow money' *(Geld im engeren Sinne):* all monetary items that can be spent directly plus private sector retail and building society deposits that can be readily converted into cash
- M4 or 'broad money' *(Geld im weiteren Sinne)*: M2 plus private sector wholesale deposits in banks and building societies plus 'certificates of deposit' (cf. note [19])
- M3H: M4 plus private and public corporations foreign currency deposits in banks and building societies

[22] *Kreditversorgung:* availability of credit facilities

For the usage of 'credit' and 'loan' cf. IX.2.1 Notes on the translation, item [9] and [30].

[23] *den Handel mit Wertpapieren der öffentlichen Hand:* the trading of government securities

'Government securities' are categorized according to the time of their 'maturity' *(Fristigkeit)*:
- 'Treasury bills' *(Schatzwechsel)* are short-term loans to the government. They are due for repayment after 90 days.
- 'Treasury notes' *(Schatzanweisungen)* are short-term or medium-term loans. The principal sum of these bonds is usually repayable in less than five years.
- 'Treasury bonds' *(öffentliche Schuldverschreibungen)* are long-term credit takings in domestic and foreign capital markets. They typically mature after ten years and yield a long-term fixed interest. Bonds are usually sold against loans.

[24] *und zwar:* notably, namely

← Please note

The English equivalents of the apposition *und zwar* are 'namely' and 'notably'. This should not be confused with *zwar ... (aber)* which is usually rendered as 'although' (cf. note [25]).

Examples
Excise duties are levied on certain commodities, most notably *(und zwar besonders)* on oil, tobacco products and alcoholic beverages.
There are two types of balances held by banks, namely *(und zwar)* 'active' and 'idle' ones.
Although the 'doves' are independent of the US administration, they avoid challenging official economic policies. *Zwar sind die*

●●●●●● *Tauben unabhängig von der US-Regierung, aber sie vermeiden es, offizielle wirtschaftspolitische Massnahmen in Frage zu stellen.*

²⁵ *ihr Vorsitzender ist zwar gesetzlich verpflichtet:* although its chairperson is required by law

> Regular reporting to Congress was enforced by the 'Humphrey-Hawkins Act' in 1978.

²⁶ *Geld- und Kreditpolitischen [Entscheidungen]:* monetary policy

> 'Monetary policy' is an inclusive term for all measures undertaken by monetary authorities such as the FRS to influence the availability and the cost of money and credit. Monetary policy is usually formulated in pursuit of broader goals such as improving general welfare and the standard of living.
> In the UK, the monetary authorities are the Treasury and the Bank of England.

²⁷ *ihre Einnahmen stammen hauptsächlich aus:* its income derives, for the most part, from; its income stems mainly from; it earns its income mainly from; it raises its income mostly from

> *Einnahmen* are the 'gross income' or 'receipts' of an individual, a group or a business over a period of time. They increase the private wealth of a person or group as well as the 'financial assets' *(Geldvermögen)* of a company.

²⁸ *Gebühren, die sie ... erhebt:* charges it raises; charges it imposes
²⁹ *erbrachte Dienstleistungen:* services rendered; services offered/supplied/provided
³⁰ *Zinsen:* interest

> 'Interest' is the charge paid by borrowers to lenders for the use of the loan sum granted. Interest is payable on a number of borrowings such as 'bank loans' *(Bankdarlehen)*, mortgages *(Hypotheken)*, 'instalment credits' *(Teilzahlungskredite/Ratenkredite)*, leasing, 'loan stocks' *(festverzinsliche Wertpapiere)*, 'debentures' *(ungesicherte Verbindlichkeiten)*, 'bonds' *(Obligationen)* 'Treasury bills' (cf. note ²³) and other 'bills of exchange'.
> Related terms
> *Darlehensbetrag:* principal; principal sum; capital borrowed

> *Nominalzins/Nominalverzinsung:* nominal interest/nominal interest rate
> *Effektivzins/Effektivverzinsung:* effective interest/effective interest rate
> *Zinseszins:* compound interest

[31] *Ziele:* aims

> *Ziele* can be translated by 'goals', 'aims', 'objectives' and 'targets' but all these terms have specific meanings.
> - 'Goals' and 'aims' are of a superordinate and general nature.
> - 'Objectives' are quantified or quantifiable aims.
> - Similarly, 'targets' are precisely defined, time-related objectives. In specific areas such as production, sales or finance the term 'target' is generally given preference.

← Please note

Examples
It is the goal/aim of our company to provide excellent service for our customers.
The company has reached its objective of increasing its market share by 20 per cent this year.
The actual sales are lagging behind the target figure.

[32] *erreicht:* achieves; attains; meets
[33] *Ziele:* targets
Cf. note [31].
[34] *Tagesgeldsatz:* federal funds rate

> Federal funds are money loaned by the national banks to the FRBs on a daily basis. The fund rate policy is an important instrument to turn long-term fixed interest investments into instantly available loans.

[35] *Offenmarktgeschäften:* open-market operations

> 'Open-market operations' were established as an instrument of public debt management but have evolved to become the principal monetary tool of the Fed. Their powerful effects on general credit conditions were discovered accidentally after World War I and this has contributed substantially to the bank's current status as an active financial policy-maker.
> Whenever the Fed purchases government securities (cf. note [23]) in the open market, it increases commercial bank reserves thereby easing credit availability and reducing interest rates. By contrast, when the Fed sells securities, it increases interest

rates. As the payments for the securities are drawn on banks, this leaves the banks less money to loan. To attract more funds, banks usually raise interest rates on deposits.

[36] *Diskontsatz:* discount rate; lending rate (UK)

'Bills of exchange' *(Wechsel)* are certificates that carry the promise of the borrower or 'drawee' *(Bezogener)* to repay to the lender or 'drawer' *(Aussteller)* a stated amount on a certain date, typically three months from their issue. These bills are either 'commercial bills' *(Handelswechsel)*, i.e. 'loans to com-panies', or 'Treasury bills' (cf. note [23]).
On buying bills of exchange from the lenders, commercial banks 'discount' *(abzinsen)* them. In other words, the drawer is charged a 'bill-discounting rate' or 'bill rate' *(Wechseldiskontsatz)* which depends on the current discount rate fixed by the monetary authorities. Commercial banks can sell bills of exchange to the central banks at the current discount rate.

[37] *die Banken folgen in der Regel diesem Beispiel:* as a rule, banks follow the Fed's example; banks generally follow suit

[38] *Kreditzins für erste Adressen:* prime rate

The 'prime rate' *(Kreditzins für erste Adressen; Prime Rate)* is the rate at which US banks lend money to first-class borrowers on a short-term basis. Its British equivalent is the 'base rate'.

[39] *Abwicklung des Zahlungsverkehrs:* the handling of payments; the payment procedures

[40] *verwaltet:* administers; oversees; monitors

[41] *US-Banknoten:* US-bank notes; Federal Reserve notes

The Federal Reserve notes make up nearly all the paper money issued in the United States. The notes are issued in seven denominations: $1, $2, $5, $10, $20, $50, and $100.
Each note has a letter, a number, and a seal that identify the issuing bank. In addition, each note bears the words Federal Reserve note and a green Treasury seal. Until 1969, Federal Reserve Banks also issued notes in four large denominations: $500, $1,000, $5,000, and $10,000.

[42] *erledigt:* effects; handles; takes care of; deals with; performs; carries out

⁴³ das bundesstaatsübergreifende Scheck-Clearing: interstate cheque clearing; cross-border check [US] clearing

> 'Clearing' *(Verrechnung/Clearing)* means the settling of interbank debts and, more precisely, the exchanging of cheques and bills between different banks.
> As a high number of cheques are paid into different commercial banks every day, a great many of them cancel each other out. For this reason, 'clearing houses' *(Verrechnungsstellen)* such as the FRBs or the London Clearing House collect the cheques on a daily basis, cross-cancel them and settle the difference between the commercial banks.

← Please note

> The expression 'the clearings' can adopt a specific meaning, namely, 'the total of the accounts settled in the process of clearing'.

Example
Commercial banks have recently experienced a rise in clearings.

VIII.3 Exercises

3.1 'Money is as money does'
Please translate the financial terms given in (brackets) to fill in the gaps below. Use your dictionary and the terminology provided in the Notes on the translation.

1. National __ *(Währungen)*, consist of __ *(Banknoten)* __ *(Münzen)* and __ *(Einlagen)*.
2. __ *(Darlehensgeber)* always demand a __ __ __ *(Nominalverzinsung)* from the __ *(Darlehensnehmer)* which is calculated as a percentage of the __ __/__ *(Darlehensbetrag)*.
3. The __ __ *(Kreditzins für erste Adressen)* is the interest rate that banks __ *(erheben von)* their best customers for __ *(kurzfristige)* loans.
4. A __ __ __ *(Wechsel)* is an unconditional __ *(Anweisung)* by a creditor to a debtor to __ __ *(auszuzahlen)* the amount stated on a certain day.
5. Banks __ *(abzinsen/diskontieren)* such bills, i.e. they purchase them before they are __/__ *(fällig; reif)* at less than their nominal value.
6. The main function of __ __ *(Geschäftsbanken)* is to accept deposits and to __ __/__ __ *(Kredite zu geben)*.

Exercises

7 Most of these banks operate a __ __ *(Verrechnungssystem)*, in other words, they __/__/__ *(austauschen)* cheques and bills at regular intervals and, subsequently, __ __ __ *(die Konten ausgleichen)* between themselves.

8 __ __ *(Offenmarktpolitik)*, __ __ *(Zinspolitik)* and the regulation of the __ __ *(Mindestreserven)* are the most efficient instruments used by the monetary authorities to control the __ __ *(Geldmenge)*.

3.2 Independent central banks

Please translate the terms given in (brackets) to fill in the gaps in the following exercise. they are all related to banks and their policies. Use your dictionary and the terminology provided in the Notes on the translation.

1 __ *(unabhängige)* central banks such as the Bundesbank and the ECB are free from governmental __ *(Einmischung)*.

2 They have a clear legal status and a precisely defined set of __ *(Aufgaben)* and __ *(Zuständigkeiten)*.

3 They can devote themselves to __/__/__ *(erreichen)* their long term economic goals.

4 Central banks which are not __ (*unterstellt*) to the government can __ (*schützen*) national currencies more efficiently.
5 Evidence suggests that the greater the independence of a country's central bank, the __ (*niedriger*) and __ __ (*stabiler*) is its __ __ __ (*Inflationsrate*).
6 So if __ __ (*Preisstabilität*) is the political __ / __ (*Ziel*), independence is certainly desirable.
7 The Chancellor of the Exchequer __ (*gewährte*) independence to the Bank of England in 1997 since the Labour government __ (*nahm an*) that an independent Bank of England would find it easier to __ (*sich anschließen*) the single European currency.
8 However, the opponents of total independence argue that this will make it more difficult for __ __ (*Geld- und Kreditpolitik*) to be integrated into wider __ __ __ (*wirtschaftspolitische Zielsetzung*).

Exercises

3.3 What if?

Not all present tense *if*-clauses are followed, in the superordinate sentence, by the future form of the verb. Especially in sentences, which describe recurring processes, the main clause employs the simple present. Instead of 'if', the related connectors 'whenever', 'each time' or 'when' can be used synonymously

Example
Wenn die Nachfrage für ein Produkt zurückgeht, sinkt gewöhnlich auch sein Marktpreis. If demand for a product slows, its market price usually falls, too.

Translate the sentences below: Pay attention to the flag words indicating 'regularity' and 'recurrence' of action.
1 Jedes Mal, wenn die Fed die Zinsen senkt, wirkt sich dies positiv auf das Kaufverhalten der Konsumenten aus.
2 Die Preise für amerikanische Exportgüter schnellen immer dann nach oben, wenn der Dollar an Wert gewinnt.
3 (Immer) wenn ich in die USA fahre, nehme ich meine Kreditkarte mit.
4 (Stets) wenn ein Scheck verrechnet ist, wird der Betrag ausgezahlt oder einem Bankkonto gutgeschrieben.
5 Die Fed kauft Wertpapiere der öffentlichen Hand (immer dann) zurück, wenn sie niedrigere Zinssätze will.
6 Wenn Banken ihre Hypothekenzinsen erhöhen, können es sich weniger Menschen leisten, einen Kredit aufzunehmen.

IX A New Economic World Order

IX.1	**Text: Die politische Aufgabe des IWF**	**154**
IX.2	**Sample translation**	**156**
IX.2.1	Notes on the translation	
IX.3	**Exercises**	**168**
IX.3.1	Who is the biggest? Comparing bar charts	
IX.3.2	Loans and credits	
IX.3.3	Current events	

I.1 Text: Die politische Aufgabe des IWF

IX A New Economic World Order

Der Internationale Währungsfonds (IWF) ändert sich. Die Lektion, die er aus der Finanzkrise Südostasiens von 1997 bis 1998 gelernt hat, heißt: „Der IWF und die Weltbank müssen politisch handeln. Auch muss der IWF seine Entscheidungsbasis derart erweitern, dass die Entwicklungsländer bei allen wichtigen Themen Gehör finden."[1]

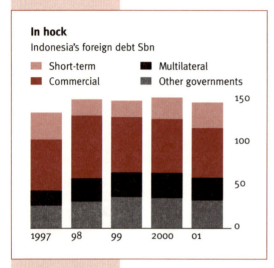

(*The Economist*, 8 December 2001, p. 58)

Figure 1: *In hock*[2]

Dieses Umdenken zeigt inzwischen erste Erfolge, wie z.B. die Anwesenheit von UN-Truppen in Osttimor, einem Gebiet, in dem indonesisches Militär brutal gegen Minderheiten vorgegangen war: Die UN-Soldaten durften das Land erst betreten, nachdem der IWF gedroht hatte, Darlehen in Höhe von 43 Milliarden US-Dollar zu kappen, die man Indonesien, dem größten Kunden der Weltbank (siehe Abbildung 1) und, gemessen an der Bevölkerung, fünftgrößten Land der Welt, gewährt hatte.

Es wird immer offensichtlicher, dass der Steuerungsmechanismus der globalen Wirtschaft aus den Fugen geraten ist. Die Europäer sind auf allen Entscheidungsebenen überrepräsentiert: Das gilt sowohl für die Fünfergruppe und ihre Nachfolger, die Kontrolle über die Weltbank und den IWF ausüben, als auch für den Interimsausschuss des IWF, den Wegbereiter seiner Modernisierung.

Im Jahre 1999, als die Gruppe X grünes Licht erhielt, wurde ein erster konkreter Schritt unternommen, um diese Unausgewogenheit auszugleichen. Dieser Wandel mag eines Tages dazu führen, dass ein diensterfahrener politischer Funktionsträger zum Geschäftsführer des IWF berufen wird, anstelle eines der Finanzbürokraten, die dazu neigen, über die Organisation wie absolutistische Monarchen zu herrschen.

---

[1] A. Brummer, „The new world economic order", in *The Guardian Weekly*, September 23 – 29, 1999, p. 12

[2] 'In hock' is a colloquial idiom which signifies 'in debt' or 'in prison'.

Auch von seiner Lieblingsvorstellung, dass seine finanziellen Transaktionen auf Regierungsebene gewöhnlichen Bankgeschäften ähneln, bei denen strengste Vertraulichkeit zu herrschen habe, musste sich der IWF verabschieden. Dies war eine unmittelbare Folge der Finanzkrise der südostasiatischen Länder, deren Schwachstellen zu spät erkannt worden waren und die zum Teil nur mit Hilfe kurzfristiger Darlehen, sozusagen auf Kredit, überlebt hatten.

Im Interesse einer stärkeren Transparenz, werden nun selbst vertraulichste Details der IWF-Gespräche mit Länderregierungen herausgegeben. Selbst die „Großen Acht" bleiben davon nicht verschont. Der IWF hat kürzlich einen Bericht über die US-Wirtschaft veröffentlicht, der noch vor wenigen Jahren in die Geheimablage der obersten Finanzbehörde gewandert wäre. Darin äußert er seine Besorgnis über die Überbewertung zahlreicher Aktien an den US-Börsen und rät, Haushaltsüberschüsse zum Abbau der Staatsverschuldung zu verwenden.

Unter den neuen IWF-Bestimmungen soll es keine Schlupflöcher mehr geben. IWF-Mitglieder, die sich nicht an die Regeln halten, werden öffentlich genannt und müssen mit einer Bestrafung rechnen. So hofft man, bestimmten Formen der Wirtschaftskriminalität, wie z.B. der Geldwäsche, schneller auf die Schliche zu kommen. Auch sollen Finanzanalysten und Geschäftsleute in die Lage versetzt werden, wirtschaftliche Entwicklungen wirksamer zu überwachen und ihre Strategien entsprechend auszurichten.

Und noch einem weiteren Übel will der IWF wehren: Nach volkswirtschaftlichen Grundsätzen hätte sich die Krise in Südostasien überhaupt nicht auf diejenigen Länder übertragen sollen, deren Wirtschaft auf festen Füßen stand. Diese konnten aber nicht schnell genug Mittel bereitstellen, um die Spekulanten in Schach zu halten und die Verkaufsflut auf den Aktienmärkten einzudämmen. Deshalb hat der IMF „Kredite für nicht vorhersehbare Ausgaben" geschaffen, die in solchen Fällen kurzfristig verfügbar sind. Ob diese allein ausreichen, das Problem in den Griff zu bekommen, sei einmal dahingestellt. Aber vielleicht können sie wenigstens den schlimmsten Fall, d.h. einen Börsenkrach in der Größenordnung von 1929, verhindern.

(M. Seidenspinner: Zusammenfassung von „The New World Economic Order", by Alex Brummer, in: *The Guardian Weekly*, September 23 – 29, 1999, p. 12)

IX.2 Sample translation

The political function of the IMF

The International Monetary Fund (IMF)[1] is changing[2]. The lesson it learnt from the crisis in southeast Asia between 1997 an 1998 is: 'the IMF and **the World Bank**[3] need to act politically. Moreover, the IMF has **to broaden its decision-making base**[4] **to such an extent that**[5] that **emerging countries**[6] **are allowed to have their say on all crucial issues**[7].'

In the meantime, this reorientation process has produced[8] its first results such as the presence of UN troops in East Timor, a region in which Indonesian military forces had committed atrocities against minorities. The UN soldiers were only allowed into the country after the IMF had threatened **to cut off the loans totalling US $43 billion**[9] that had been granted to Indonesia, the World Bank's **biggest client**[10] (cf. Figure 1) and the world's fifth largest country in terms of population.

It is becoming increasingly evident[11] that the steering mechanism for the global economy **has gone off track**[12]. Europeans are over-represented at almost every **decision-making level**[13]. This applies to **the Group of Five and its successors**[14] –- who supervise the World Bank and the IMF – as well as the IMF's interim committee, **which is at the forefront of the World Bank's modernisation**[15].

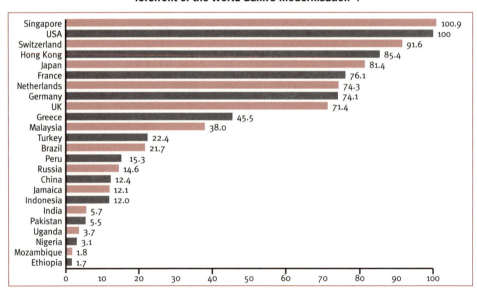

(World Development Report, World Bank)

Figure 2: *GNY per head in 1997 as % of US GNY per head (using purchasing-power parity exchange rates)*

In 1999, a first concrete step was taken **to redress this imbalance**[16] by giving **Group X**[17] the go ahead. This transformation may **eventually**[18] result in the appointment of **a senior political official**[19] as the IMF's **managing director**[20], instead of one of those financial bureaucrats who tend to **rule**[21] the organisation **like**[22] absolutist monarchs.

Moreover, the IMF **has been forced say farewell**[23] **to its favourite notion**[24] that its **financial undertakings**[25] at governmental level **are akin to**[26] ordinary banking transactions **where strict confidentiality has to prevail**[27]. This is a direct consequence of the financial crisis of the south-east Asian countries whose weaknesses had been **recognized**[28] **too late**[29] and who had, in some cases, been surviving exclusively on short-term borrowings, **on credit so to speak**[30].

In the interests of a greater degree of transparency, **even the most intimate**[31] details of the IMF's discussions with national governments **are now being released**[32]. **Not even the 'Big Eight' are exempt**[33]. The IMF has recently published a report on the US economy which, until a couple of years ago, **would have been filed as 'top secret' by the Treasury**[34]. **This report expresses the organisation's reservations**[35] about **the high number of overvalued shares**[36] **on the US stock exchanges**[37] and recommends that budget surpluses should be employed to reduce **national debt**[38].

Under the new IMF regulations, there are to be no more **loopholes**[39]. IMF members who **fail to adhere to**[40] the rules **will be publicly exposed**[41] and **are likely to face a penalty**[42]. **This, it is hoped**[43], will speed up the tracking down of certain economic crimes such as money laundering. Moreover, it will put financial analysts and business people in a position to oversee economic trends more efficiently and **to align**[44] their strategies accordingly.

And there is another evil that the IMF seeks to **ward off**[45]. According to fundamental economic principles, **the crisis** in southeast Asia **should, by no accounts, have contaminated**[46] countries **whose economies were sound**[47]. However, the latter were unable to provide funds quickly enough **to keep the speculators at bay**[48] and **to stem the tidal waves of selling on the stock markets**[49]. For this reason, the IMF has created **'contingency credit facilities'**[50] that can be made available on a short-term basis in such cases. Whether these will suffice in themselves **to come to grips with this problem**[51] **remains to be seen**[52], but they might be able to prevent the worst case, that is to say a stock market crash on a similar scale to that of 1929.

●●●●●● 2.1 **Notes on the translation**

[1] *der Internationale Währungsfonds (IWF):* the International Monetary Fund (IMF)

> The IMF was founded in 1945 in order to supervise the operation of a new international monetary regime. It seeks to ensure monetary stability and cooperation by establishing currency agreements between its member states and by promoting cross-border trade. Being a special agency of the United Nations, it provides additional international liquidity and lends money to poor countries. It is financed by quota subscriptions from member countries.
> The stringent conditions the IMF imposes on the borrower countries (e.g. deregulation of capital markets, downsizing of public welfare programs, privatisation of state companies) have often been criticised as too harsh. Some critics believe that the bank is overtly dominated by Wall Street and the US Treasury and responsible for exacerbating poverty rather than reducing it.

[2] *ändert sich:* is changing

Please note →

> *Ändert sich* describes a current development which, in German, can be semantically emphasized as: *Der IMF ist dabei sich zu ändern*. Such a context requires the present continuous form of the verb in the target language.

Cf. exercise IX.3.3 below.

[3] *die Weltbank:* the World Bank

> The World Bank, also known as 'International Bank for Reconstruction and Development' *(Internationale Bank für Wiederaufbau und Entwicklung)*, is based in Washington, DC. It was set up together with the IMF as a multinational, multilateral UN organisation that, almost exclusively, lends money for long-term development projects in emerging economies. It currently has 181 members. The bank's funds come mostly from the developed nations and from its own capital resources. Its name reflects its earlier involvement in the reconstruction of ruined economies after World War II.

[4] *seine Entscheidungsbasis ... erweitern:* to broaden its decision-making base; to expand/to extend its decisional platform

> 'To extend' and 'to expand' are not always synonymous. 'To extend' signifies 'to stretch (out)', 'to make longer', 'to prolong' as well as 'to widen' and also 'to enlarge'.

← Please note

Usage examples
extension cable: *Verlängerungskabel*
The bank extended *(erweiterte)* the client's credit line.
This contract is unlikely to be extended *(verlängert)* beyond the date originally agreed on.
The IMF extends help *(leistet Hilfe)* to poor countries.
They extended *(ausstrecken)* their hands in friendship.
The beach extends *(erstreckt sich)* for miles east and west.
Please extend *(bestellen)* my best wishes to Paul.

> 'To expand' means 'to broaden', 'to enlarge', 'to increase in size', 'to swell'.

← Please note

Examples
The company seeks to expand *(ausweiten)* its market.
We need to expand our production capacity *(erhöhen)*. It is necessary to expand *(ausweiten)* our market.
Balloons expand *(werden größer)* when they are blown up.

5 *derart:* to such an extent that; to an extent where
6 *Entwicklungsländer:* emerging countries; developing countries

> The term 'developing countries' was coined at the beginning of the 1950s for countries in need of economic and industrial development. It gradually replaced the synonymous expressions 'underdeveloped countries' or 'Third World Countries'. Both terms are now perceived as politically – and factually – incorrect.
> More recent synonyms are 'less developed countries' (LDCs), 'emerging countries' and 'emerging economies'. Taking a different focus, these countries may also be referred to as 'emerging markets'.

← Please note

> 'Emerging countries' are characterized by low levels of GDP ('gross domestic product': *Bruttoinlandsprodukt*) and 'per capita income' (i.e. 'GDP per head' or 'income per head': *Pro-Kopf-Einkommen*). LDCs are typically dominated by a large primary sector *(primärer Sektor)* and lack a middle-class urban population *(städtischer Mittelstand)*. The majority of their

• • • • • •

mostly rural population survive – after a fashion – on 'subsistence farming' *(Subsistenzwirtschaft)*.
This usually goes hand in hand with low 'life expectancy' *(Lebenserwartung)*, high rates of 'illiteracy' *(Analphabetismus)* and 'child mortality' *(Kindersterblichkeit)*. Related problems are 'rapid population growth' *(Bevölkerungsexplosion)*, rural depopulation *(Landflucht)*, also known as 'rural-urban migration', which swells urban unemployment and accelerates the formation of slums.
'Emerging economies' are additionally hampered by the overexploitation of their 'primaries' *(Rohstoffe)* and a bias towards inappropriate capital-intensive technology which is often unsuitable for the labour-abundant LDCs.
In order to measure development, 'gross national income per capita' (GNY) is widely used as an indicator (cf. Figure 2). In compliance with such indicators, LDCs are subdivided into:
LLDCs: Least developed countries: *am geringsten entwickelte Länder*
LICs: Low income countries: *Länder mit niedrigem Einkommen*
MICs: Middle income countries: *Länder mit mittlerem Einkommen*; they are subdivided into 'Lower MICs' and 'Upper MICs'
NICs: Newly industrializing countries: *Schwellenländer*
MSACs: Most seriously affected countries, i.e. those countries that were incapable of coping with the consequences of the 1973 oil shock themselves
For classification categories in terms of 'national debt' cf. X.2.1 Notes on the translation, item [26].

[7] *bei allen wichtigen Themen Gehör finden:* are allowed to have their say on all crucial issues; are heard on all essential matters

[8] *dieses Umdenken zeigt inzwischen:* in the meantime, this reorientation process has produced; this process of reorientation/ this reorientation has now/meanwhile engendered

Please note →

The present perfect (not the present simple!) is the correct tense here. *Inzwischen* and *erste Erfolge* are semantic indicators of the fact that the verb describes a process which started in the past but is not yet completed.

[9] *Darlehen in Höhe von 43 Milliarden US-Dollar zu kappen:* to cut off the loans totalling US $43 billion; to foreclose/cancel the loans amounting to US $43bn

'Loan' signifies 'property or money lent at interest/on credit over a period of time', whereas 'credit' has a much broader semantic scope which is dealt with in note [30] below.   ← Please note

Typical collocations
to apply for a loan: *ein Darlehen (einen Kredit) beantragen*
to negotiate a loan: *einen Kredit aushandeln*
to take out a loan: *ein Darlehen aufnehmen*
to approve a loan: *ein Darlehen genehmigen*
to grant a loan: *ein Darlehen gewähren*
to obtain/to be awarded a loan: *ein Darlehen erhalten*
to cancel a loan: *ein Darlehen kündigen*
to extend a loan: *ein Darlehen verlängern*
to foreclose a loan: *ein Darlehen vorzeitig zurückfordern*
to freeze a loan: *ein Darlehen einfrieren*
to pay back/to pay off : *ein Darlehen zurückzahlen/abzahlen*
to reschedule/restructure a loan: *ein Darlehen umschulden*
to write off a loan: *ein Darlehen (als Verlust) abschreiben*

Useful adverbial expressions
on a rental basis: *gegen Miete oder Pacht*
at interest: *gegen Zinsen*
größten Kunden: biggest client

To a large extent, 'customer and client' are interchangeable but there are subtle differences in the usage of these two terms:
'Customer' *(Kunde, Abnehmer)* is used for a person or business that purchases a commodity or a service from a seller or at a sales outlet.   ← Please note

In marketing and accounting, 'customers' are also seen as
income brackets: *Einkommensgruppen*
market segments: *Marktsegmente*
target groups: *Zielgruppen*
(key) accounts: *(Groß-)Konten*

'Client' also translates *Klient, Auftraggeber, Mandant*, i.e a person or business that uses the services of professional people such as accountants, bankers, consultants or lawyers. Certain trades and craftspeople have 'clients', too, (e.g. hairdressers, beauticians).

Please note →

[11] *es wird immer offensichtlicher:* it is becoming increasingly evident; it is becoming more and more obvious

> The appositive adverbs *immer* and *zunehmend* are flag words which state that an ongoing process is gaining momentum. In such situations, the present continuous form of the verb is generally required.

Cf. Exercise 3.3 below.

[12] *aus den Fugen geraten ist:* has gone off track; has spun/gone out of control; has become unbalanced; has gone off the rails

[13] *Entscheidungsebenen:* decision-making level; decisional level; decision level; level where decisions are taken

[14] *die Fünfergruppe und ihre Nachfolger:* the Group of Five and its successors

> - *G-5/Fünfergruppe:* the Group of Five (G5)
>   G5 were the US, Germany, France, the UK and Japan. These major industrial nations met regularly and informally to discuss common economic interests, mainly the stabilisation of economic conditions. The group consisted of the finance ministers and the central bank governors of each country.
> - *G-7/Siebenergruppe:* the Group of Seven (G7)
>   This group includes the US, Japan, Germany, France, the UK, Italy and Canada. Its members and the president of the European Commission have met annually since 1975 at the world economic summit in order to make a contribution to the solution of global economic problems, e.g. development aid, protection of the environment, drug dealing and organized international crime, terrorism or destructive conflicts.
> - *G-8/Achtergruppe:* the Group of Eight (G8)
>   These are the US, Japan, Germany, France, the UK, Italy, Canada and Russia. Russia is the only member that is not an OECD donor country. It was its strategic importance that 'tipped the balance' *(gab den Ausschlag)* in favour of its inclusion.
> - *G-10/die Zehnergruppe:* the Group of Ten (G10), namely the ten most powerful economies in terms of GDP, i.e. the US, Japan, Germany, France, the UK, Italy, Canada, the Netherlands, Sweden and Switzerland.
> - *G-X/die Gruppe X:* Group X/the G10 states plus China, India, Brazil, Mexico, South Korea, Saudi Arabia and South Africa

[15] *den Wegbereiter seiner Modernisierung:* which is at the forefront of the World Bank's modernisation; which is in the vanguard of this organisation's modernisation; which has put/placed itself at the leading edge of the World Bank's modernisation
[16] *diese Unausgewogenheit auszugleichen:* to redress this imbalance; to readjust its balance; to compensate for this imbalance

> 'To redress' means literally 'to put something (up)right' and metaphorically 'to make reparation for something' or 'to offer consolation'.

← Please note

[17] *Gruppe X:* Group X; GX; cf. note [14] above.
[18] *eines Tages:* eventually, one day

> The adverb 'eventually' is a false friend. It does not translate *eventuell* which is 'perhaps' in English.

← Please note

[19] *ein diensterfahrener politischer Funktionsträger:* a senior political official; a long-serving and experienced political official
[20] *Geschäftsführer:* Managing Director [GB]; Chief Executive; Chief Executive Officer [US]

> A *Geschäftsführer* in business organisations can also be a 'General Manager' (official title used especially in US-based stock corporations).

← Please note

For detailed explanations on *Geschäftsführer; Vorstand* etc. see J. Bauer & M. Seidenspinner, *Betriebswirtschaft: Übersetzungsübungen, studium kompakt Fachsprache Englisch*, Cornelsen & Oxford, Berlin, 2001; page 68.

[21] *herrschen:* rule; govern; dominate

> Note that 'dominate' is a less neutral expression as it implies *beherrschen* and *dominieren*. However, this squares well with the comparison of the IMF officials to absolutist monarchs.

← Please note

[22] *wie:* like; in the manner of
[23] *musste sich ... verabschieden:* has been forced to say farewell to; has been forced to abandon; has had to say goodbye to
[24] *von seiner Lieblingsvorstellung:* to its favourite notion; to its most cherished belief
[25] *finanziellen Transaktionen:* financial undertakings; financial dealings
[26] *ähneln:* are akin to; resemble; are similar/comparable to; can be compared to

●●●●●   [27] *bei denen strengste Vertraulichkeit zu herrschen habe:* where strict confidentiality has to prevail; which are subject to strict confidentiality
[28] *erkannt:* recognized; identified
[29] *zu spät:* too late; at too late a stage
[30] *sozusagen auf Kredit:* on credit so to speak; on credit as it were; virtually on credit

Please note →

> 'Loan' and 'credit' may be synonymous. However, 'on loan' *(leihweise/ausgeliehen)* and 'on credit' *(auf Kredit)* are not.

> In banking and accounting 'credit' (as a noun or compound noun) covers a large variety of meanings. Cf. note [9] above for the related term 'loan'.
> 'Credit' is a 'financial facility' *(Finanzierungsart)* which includes
> - borrowing money in general: *Geld aufnehmen*
> - the sum made available by a bank in excess of any deposit, i.e. overdraft: *Überziehungskredit*
> - having a positive balance in a bank account: *Guthaben*
> - acknowledging a capital item by entry on the right hand side of a bank account: *Gutschrift*
> - the time permitted for paying for such goods or services: credit period: *Kreditlaufzeit*
> - reputation for 'solvency' *(Zahlungsfähigkeit)* creditworthiness: *Bonität, Kreditwürdigkeit*
> - receiving goods or services before payment. This can take the form of a 'credit sale' *(Kauf auf Kredit)*, an 'instalment credit' *(Kauf auf Raten)* a 'credit account' *(Kreditkonto)* – also known as 'charge account' *(Kundenkonto)* – which grants trustworthy customers a credit period of usually one month, or – especially in larger-scale business transactions – an 'open account' which may include a credit period of up to 120 days.
> For 'Letter of credit' *(Akkreditiv)* and 'open account credits' *(Kontokorrentkredit)* cf. J. Bauer & M. Seidenspinner, *Betriebswirtschaft: Übersetzungsübungen, studium kompakt Fachsprache Englisch*, Cornelsen & Oxford, Berlin, 2001; p. 149.

Useful collocations
credit facility: *Kreditmöglichkeit/Kredit*
credit line/credit limit: *Kreditrahmen/Kredit(ober)grenze*

credit transfer/remittance: *Überweisung*
credit squeeze/credit crunch: *Kreditrestriktion/Kreditverknappung*
credit rating: *Bonität/Bonitätsstufe*
creditworthiness/creditability: *Kreditwürdigkeit/Glaubwürdigkeit/ Bonität*
credit rating agency: *(Kredit-)Auskunftei*
credit voucher: *Gutschrift*
credit note/credit slip: *Gutschrift*
Dispositionskredit: overdraft facility
Kreditnehmer: borrower
Kreditgeber: lender
zinsloses Darlehen: interest-free loan

[31] *selbst vertraulichste:* even the most intimate; even the most confidential

[32] *werden nun ... herausgegeben:* are now being released; are now being made public/revealed/disclosed/divulged

> 'To reveal', 'to disclose' and 'to divulge' connote *enthüllen*.   ← Please note

Example
They were promised that their personal data would never be revealed/divulged/disclosed.

[33] *selbst die ‚Großen Acht' bleiben davon nicht verschont:* not even the 'Big Eight' are exempt; no exception is made, not even for the 'Big Eight'

> In a military context, a more literal translation would be: 'no mercy is shown, not even to ...'.   ← Please note

[34] *in die Geheimablage der obersten Finanzbehörde gewandert wäre:* would have been filed as 'top secret' by the Treasury; would have disappeared/been buried in the 'top secret' files of the Treasury; would have been filed away as 'top secret' by the Treasury

> In the UK and the US, the 'Treasury' *(Schatzministerium)* is responsible for managing state funds, for authorizing the expenditure plans drawn up by the governmental departments, for supervising tax-gathering and advising the government on the budget and on all its financial activities.

[35] *darin äußert er seine Besorgnis:* this report expresses the organisation's reservations; in this report, the organisation voices its concerns

Please note →

> The pronouns *er* and *seine* have to be paraphrased in the English sentence in order to make it clear to which part of the previous sentence they refer.

³⁶ *die Überbewertung zahlreicher Aktien:* the high number of overvalued shares; the overvaluation of a great deal of stocks

³⁷ *an den US-Börsen:* on the US stock exchanges

> 'Overvaluation' means that the stock market fails to place a fair money value on a company's shares and permits an unhealthy level of speculation. In such a market, investors are likely to be overcharged when they purchase shares. When crisis hits such a market, share prices tend to collapse, putting companies out of business unnecessarily.

³⁸ *Staatsverschuldung:* national debt; government/public-sector debt; public debt

Please note →

> In the UK, the terms 'government debt' and 'national debt' refer to the budget deficit of the central government, whereas 'public debt' and 'public-sector debt' *(Schulden der öffentlichen Hand)* include the deficits of the central government, the regional and local governments and of public corporations.

³⁹ *Schlupflöcher:* loopholes; escape routes

⁴⁰ *sich nicht an die Regeln halten:* fail to adhere to the rules; fail to follow/comply with the rules

⁴¹ *werden öffentlich genannt:* will be publicly exposed; will be made known/divulged to the public

⁴² *müssen mit Bestrafung rechnen:* are likely to face a penalty; will probably be punished/fined

⁴³ *so hofft man:* this, it is hoped; this, one hopes

⁴⁴ *auszurichten:* to align; to adjust; to formulate

⁴⁵ *wehren:* to ward off; to keep at bay/to stave off/to avert

⁴⁶ *hätte sich die Krise überhaupt nicht ... übertragen sollen:* the crisis should, by no account, have contaminated
Alternative translation
... the crisis should not have spread to economically stable countries in the first place

⁴⁷ *deren Wirtschaft auf festen Füßen stand:* whose economies were sound; whose economies stood on sound foundations

⁴⁸ *um die Spekulanten in Schach zu halten:* to keep the speculators at bay; to keep the speculators in check

[49] *die Verkaufsflut auf den Aktienmärkten einzudämmen:* to stem the tidal waves of selling on the stock markets; to check/halt the sales floods on the stock exchanges
[50] *Kredite für nicht vorhersehbare Ausgaben:* contingency credit facilities; contingency funds

> These credit facilities are 'appropriations' *(Ausgabenbewilligungen)* reserved for contingencies. They take the form of preapproved loans that, in case of unforeseen incidents (i.e. contingencies), can by-pass the complex credit approval system.

> A contingency is an event whose occurrence is uncertain, incidental or accidental.

← Please note

Example
The company sought to build up reserves for every contingency *(alle nur erdenklichen [Not]fälle).*

> 'Contingency' is related to 'contingent' which can also signify 'a possible chance or occurrence' but mostly denotes 'a part of a military force' *(Truppenkontingent)* or 'a group distinguished by common origin or interest' *(Interessensgemeinschaft).*

← Please note

[51] *das Problem in den Griff zu bekommen:* to come to grips with this problem; to resolve this problem; to get on top of this problem
[52] *sei einmal dahingestellt:* remains to be seen; is an open question

Nova Development Corporation 1996

IX.3 Exercises

3.1 Who is biggest? Comparing bar charts

Compare the two bar charts which belong to the above translation. Find appropriate expressions for the gaps in the exercise below.

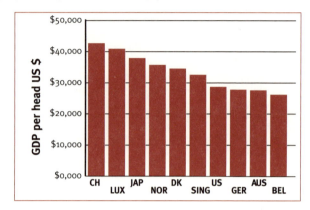

(Adapted from *The Guardian Weekly*, 23-29 September 1999, p.12)

Figure 3: *The ten richest countries*

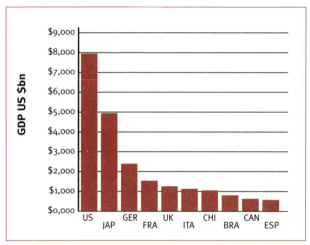

(Adapted from: *The Guardian Weekly*, 23-29 September 1999, p.129)

Figure 4: *Top ten economies*

1 I would like to start by __ __ __ *(Sie darauf aufmerksam zu machen)* to the fact that the above bar charts, which compare the world's ten biggest economies, in terms of their __ __ __ *(GDP)*, are not identical with the 'top ten' that enjoy the highest GDP __ __ __ /__ __ __ *(pro Kopf)*.

2 Moreover, it is essential to __ __ *(darauf hinzuweisen)* that the currently used economic indicators __ /__ *(unzureichend)* reflect the economic __ /__ *(Macht)* of the member states.

3 This means that Brazil, for instance, which ranks amongst the world's most powerful economic nations and whose GDP __ __ __ /__ __ *(etwa ... beträgt)* US $800 billion, has less say than the G10 member Sweden, with a GDP of only US $232 billion.

168

Exercises

4 The same __ __/__ __ __ *(trifft zu auf)* Spain which has __/__/__ *(erzielt)* a high level of sustainable growth by developing its agricultural as well as its IT sector.
5 Russia, the most recent addition to G8, does not __/__/__ *(tritt in Erscheinung)* in any of the charts __ __ *(behandelt)* here.
6 It was its strategic rather than its economic importance that __ __ __ *(den Ausschlag gab)* in favour of its inclusion.
7 The Group X will include all major __ __/__ __/__ *(Entwicklungsländer)* such as China, India, Brazil, Mexico and South Korea, all of which __/__ __ *(sich qualifizieren)* for membership on the grounds of the __ *(Größe)* of their economies.
8 South Africa, representing the entire African continent, will be __/__ __ __ *(aufgenommen)* too, as well as Saudi Arabia, which is the world's __/__ *(größter)* oil producer.

3.2 Loans and credits

Please fill in the gaps using your dictionary and the terminology provided in the Notes on the translation.

1 Economically speaking, __ __ *(sich etwas auzuleihen)* is a good deal for __ __ *(den, der sich etwas ausleiht)*.
2 S/He receives the items s/he requires __ __ *(leihweise)* but not __ __/__ __ *(gegen Zinsen)*.
3 This is very much like being __/__ *(einem ... gewährt wird)* an __ __ *(zinsloses Darlehen)*.
4 If we need a vehicle for temporary use, we __ *(leihen)* or __ *(mieten)* it.
5 Many people __ __ *(aufnehmen)* a __/__ *(Darlehen)* when they need a car and a __ *(Hypothek)* when they purchase a house.
6 Most debts are __ __/__ __ *(zurückgezahlt)* in __ *(Raten)* which include __ __ *(Bearbeitungsgebühren)* and __ *(Zinsen)*.
7 Credit institutes usually provide their giro customers with an __ __ *(Dispositionskredit)*.
8 Banks may refuse to __ __ *(Geld zu verleihen)* to __/__ *(Kunden)* who continuously __ *(überschreiten)* their __ __/__ __ *(Kreditrahmen)*.
9 __ *(Darlehensgeber)* are entiteld to __ *(vorzeitig zurückzufordern)* loans or __ *(kündigen)* them in certain cases.
10 Slack payment morale can damage a person's __/__ *(Kreditwürdigkeit)*.

Exercises

3.3 Current events

The following exercise will focus on the 'continuous aspect' of the present tense in the passive voice. This aspect is important when current developments are in the process of being completed.

In German, the current aspect of the present tense can be expressed semantically (by flag words: *jetzt, nun, derzeit, gerade*) or syntactically *(sie sind dabei etwas zu tun)*. Further semantic indicators are the connectors *während* or *als gerade* and the temporal adverb *immer* as an apposition to *größer, kleiner, besser* etc.

Some of the relevant English flag words in this context are: 'Look!' 'Listen!' 'Imagine!' and, obviously, 'at present', 'now' and 'currently'.

Examples

Listen! I think we are being followed! *Hör mal! Ich glaube, wir werden verfolgt.*

Even the most confidential details are now being released. *Selbst die vertraulichsten Einzelheiten werden jetzt herausgegeben.*

Translate the following sentences using the expressions provided in (brackets).

1 Werden Sie schon bedient *(served)*?
2 Unsere Kunden sind es nicht gewohnt, so behandelt zu werden *(used to being)*.
3 Alternative Kreditmöglichkeiten *(credit facilities)* werden zur Zeit überprüft.
4 Von Spekulanten übervorteilt *(cheated)* zu werden, ist keine angenehme Erfahrung für Kleinanleger *(small investors)*.
5 Stellen Sie sich vor, die Frankfurter Börse wäre an Sonntagen geöffnet *(being open)*.
6 Spekulanten werden heute zunehmend kritisch betrachtet *(viewed)*.
7 Ständig gefragt zu werden, ob der DAX endlich *(at long last)* gestiegen ist, ist eine nervtötende Erfahrung für Telefonberater.
8 Die Aktionäre werden gerade über die Gewinne des Unternehmens informiert.

X   The World Debt Crisis

X.1   Text: Schuldenerlass für die Ärmsten der Armen   172

X.2   **Sample translation**   175
X.2.1   Notes on the translation

X.3   **Exercises**   184
X.3.1   Poverty and underdevelopment
X.3.2   Mounting debts
X.3.3   Ecocide

X.1 Text: Schuldenerlass für die Ärmsten der Armen[1]

X The World Debt Crisis

UN-Generalsekretär Kofi Annan hat die reichsten und mächtigsten Länder der Welt aufgerufen, die Schulden der armen Länder zügiger zu erlassen und die digitale Kluft zwischen Industriestaaten und Entwicklungsländern zu überbrücken. Bis jetzt hätten sich im Rahmen der „Kölner Schuldeninitiative" erst acht Länder für einen Schuldenerlass qualifiziert, und nur 35% ihrer Schulden seien gestrichen worden. Afrikanische Länder zum Beispiel müssten bereits 40% ihres nationalen Einkommens zur Bedienung von Auslandsschulden aufwenden, die sich insgesamt auf 350 Milliarden Dollar beliefen.

Annan ersuchte die G-8-Länder, die Schulden aller hoch verschuldeten armen Länder zu erlassen, die nachweislich Anstrengungen zur Beseitigung der Armut unternommen hätten. Auch Ländern, die unter den Folgen von Krieg oder Naturkatastrophen litten, sollten sie die Schulden streichen.

Abbildung 1: *Die Weltbank*

(Global Policy Forum – Social and Economic Policy; www.globalpolicy.org/socecon/bwi-wto/bankind.htm)

Die Finanzierung des Schuldenerlasses[2]

Der größte Teil der aufgrund der HIPC-Initiative erlassenen Schulden konnte bei der Konferenz des IWF und der Weltbank in Washington, D.C., durch die Neubewertung der Goldreserven des IWF und den Rückgriff auf weitere Reserven von IWF und IDA verbindlich bereitgestellt werden. Aber vor allem beim Weltbank-Treuhandfonds, der auf die Zusagen mächtiger Regierungen angewiesen ist, gibt es noch Finanzierungslücken.

---

[1] Zusammenfassung eines Textes von T. Deen, „IPS-Bericht" vom 12. 7. 2000; www.ipsic.net/d_eu_ewipol/un_generalsekretär.htm
[2] frei gestaltet nach B. Unmüßig, „Aktionsgemeinschaft solidarische Welt", www.aswnet.de/swl168b.html

Die Abkommen von Köln und Washington werden gerne zu einem Durchbruch für die hochverschuldeten Länder hochstilisiert. Doch selbst wenn die „ungedeckten Schecks" der reichen Staaten bald vollständig eingelöst würden, bleibt zweifelhaft, ob der geplante Schuldenerlass den notwendigen finanziellen Spielraum für die Beseitigung der Armut schaffen wird. Denn die meisten der in Frage kommenden Länder wären ohnehin nicht in der Lage gewesen, ihre Schulden zu bedienen, sodass sie gar keine „Ersparnisse" haben, die sie für andere Zwecke ausgeben könnten.

Überhaupt nicht hinzunehmen ist jedoch, dass gleichzeitig mit dem Schuldenerlass die Entwicklungshilfe drastisch gekürzt werden soll, einschließlich der bisher für Armuts- oder Infrastrukturprogramme vorgesehenen Beträge. Dies ist der Hauptgrund, warum sich die allgemeine Lage der HIPC-Länder durch die Schuldenstreichungen kaum verbessern wird. Die „hoch verschuldeten Länder mit mittlerem Einkommen" befürchten zudem, dass die Entschuldung der Ärmsten auf ihrem Rücken ausgetragen wird. Sie bemängeln, dass die Niedrigzinskredite aus den Reserven der Weltbank, die bisher zur Armutsbekämpfung verwendet wurden, nun die Entschuldung der ärmsten Länder abdecken sollen.

Die HIPC- Initiative[3]

Zu Beginn des dritten Jahrtausends scheinen sich weltweit die makroökonomischen Bedingungen, die in den 80-er Jahren die Schuldenkrise auslösten, zu wiederholen. Die Weltwirtschaft wächst langsamer, die Preise für Handelsgüter haben ihren seit 150 Jahren tiefsten Stand erreicht, und der Ölpreis steigt. Da viele Entwicklungsländer auf Exporte angewiesen sind, um ihre Schulden abzuzahlen und um lebenswichtige Importe zu finanzieren, sind dies schlechte Bedingungen für die erhoffte nachhaltige Entwicklung, die allen Berechnungen zum Schuldenerlass zu Grunde liegt. Zusätzlich müssen diese Länder mit zunehmender Kapitalflucht und der Zerstörung ihrer natürlichen Umwelt fertig werden.

Alles in allem, ist die versprochene Streichung der „Dritte-Welt-Schulden" bisher ausgeblieben. Die Achtergruppe hat dieses Thema ad acta gelegt und stattdessen ihr Vertrauen in die HIPC-Initiative bekundet, aufgrund derer bisher nicht einmal 5% dieser Schulden gestrichen wurden. Obwohl 23 der hochverschuldeten armen Länder

---

[3] Zusammenfassung von „Vicious circle: The Genoa G8 Summit Briefing" in *Christian Aid*, July 2001, UK

inzwischen ein Teil ihrer Schulden erlassen wurde, beträgt der durchschnittliche Abbau der jährlichen Rückzahlungen weniger als 27 Prozent. Zusammen werden diese Länder, von denen viele schwer von HIV und Aids betroffen sind, im Jahr 2001 2,04 Milliarden US-Dollar für die Bedienung von Schulden ausgeben, die sie nie zurückzahlen können.

Aber während die Einzelheiten der 1999 gefassten Beschlüsse noch akribisch ausgearbeitet werden, formiert sich Widerstand gegen diese Pro-forma-Streichungen. Führende Hilfsorganisationen halten die Rückzahlungsforderungen der reichen Länder für moralisch illegitim. Im besonderen monieren sie

- den unzureichenden Umfang der gegenwärtigen Streichungen und die schleppende Umsetzung des Schuldenerlasses. Von den versprochenen 70 Milliarden US-Dollar wurden erst 13,2 Milliarden erlassen.
- die fehlerhafte Berechnung der Streichungshöhe, die auf unzuverlässigen ökonomischen Indikatoren und nicht auf dem tatsächlichen Verarmungsgrad dieser Länder basiert.
- einige der als zu streng empfundenen Bedingungen des IWF für einen Schuldenerlass und die Vergabe weiterer Kredite.

Der jüngste UN Entwicklungsbericht zeigt, dass trotz Schuldenerlass und einfallsreicher Vorschläge, die Schulden gegen vorteilhaftere Umschuldungsmassnahmen „einzutauschen", die internationalen Entwicklungsziele bis 2015 wohl nicht erreicht werden können. Diese sind

- die Zahl der Menschen, die in bitterster Armut leben, zu halbieren,
- jedem Menschen eine elementare Bildung und medizinische Grundversorgung zu garantieren,
- die Malaria- und Tuberkulosefälle auf die Hälfte zu senken sowie
- der Verbreitung von HIV Einhalt zu gebieten.

(Margarete Seidenspinner)

Debt forgiveness for[1] the poorest of the poor

UN General Secretary Kofi Annan **has appealed to**[2] the world's richest and most powerful nations to speed up the debt relief process for poor countries and **to close the digital divide**[3] between industrialized and developing countries. So far, only eight countries **had qualified**[4] for debt cancellation under the **'Cologne Debt Initiative'**[5] and a mere 35 per cent of their debt **had been waived**[6]. African countries, for instance, were already forced to spend as much as 40 per cent of their **national income**[7] on servicing foreign debts **which totalled US $350 billion**[8].

Anan **requested**[9] the G8-countries to cancel the debt of all those heavily indebted countries which had demonstrably made an effort **to eliminate**[10] poverty. Moreover, they should drop the debt of countries that **were suffering the aftermath of**[11] war or natural disasters.

Financing debt relief

At the IMF and World Bank conference in Washington, D.C., it was possible to secure the major part of the debt relief granted under the HIPC-Initiative by **revaluing**[12] the IMF's **gold holdings**[13] and **by tapping**[14] use of additional IMF and **IDA**[15] reserves. However, there are still financial gaps to be closed **especially with regard to**[16] the World Bank trust fund **which is sustained by**[17] the **pledges**[18] of powerful governments.

The Cologne and Washington agreements **are often served up as**[19] a breakthrough for the HIPCs. But even if all the **'bad cheques'**[20] of the rich countries were to be cashed in soon, **it is doubtful**[21] whether the planned debt relief would provide enough leeway regarding the elimination of poverty since most eligible countries would not have been capable of **servicing their debt**[22] **in the first place**[23] and therefore have no 'savings' which they could spend for other purposes.

However, **what is absolutely unacceptable**[24] is the fact that debt relief is to be accompanied by a drastic reduction of development aid including the sums that have so far been **earmarked**[25] for poverty elimination and infrastructure improvement programmes. This is the main reason why debt relief will do hardly anything to improve the general situation of the HIPCs. Furthermore, the **'Severely Indebted Middle Income Countries' (SIMICs)**[26] fear that debt cancellation for the poorest **will be at their expense**[27]. They complain that the **low-interest loans**[28] supplied from the World Bank reserves which have so far been employed for fighting poverty will be used to cover the debt relief for the poorest countries.

X.2 Sample translation

The HIPC-initiative

At the beginning of the third millennium, the conditions which first **precipitated**[29] the debt crisis in the 1980s **appear to be recurring**[30] on a global scale. Worldwide economic growth has slowed, commodity prices have reached a 150-year low and the oil price is rising. Since many LDCs rely on exports to pay off their debts and to purchase vital imports, these are poor conditions for the hoped-for **sustainable development**[31] on which all debt relief calculations are based. In addition, **these countries have to cope with mounting capital flight**[32] and **'ecocide'**[33].

All in all[34], **the pledged waiving of 'poor countries debt'**[35] **has so far failed to materialise**[36]. The Group of Eight **have shelved this issue**[37] **preferring to keep faith with the HIPC initiative**[38] under which not even five per cent of this debt has been cancelled up to now. Although twenty-three of the highly indebted poor countries have now been granted partial debt relief, the average reduction in annual repayments amounts to less than 27 per cent. **Collectively**[39], these countries, many of which are severely hit by HIV and AIDS, will spend US $2.04bn in 2001 on servicing debts they will never be able to pay back.

But **while the details** of the decisions taken in 1999 **are still being meticulously worked out**[40], **opposition to these 'token cancellations' is growing**[41]. Leading aid organisations **consider the rich countries' demands for debt repayment to be**[42] morally illegitimate. In particular, **they object to**[43]

- the **inadequate**[44] amount currently being cancelled and the **sluggish**[45] implementation of debt relief. Of the US $70bn promised only US $13.2bn **has been waived**[46].
- **the flawed calculation of the portions to be written off**[47] which is based on unreliable economic indicators rather than on **the actual levels of poverty**[48] in these countries.
- some of the conditions imposed by the IMF for debt cancellation and **further loans**[49] as being too **stringent**[50].

The latest UN development report shows that, in spite of debt forgiveness and **resourceful**[51] proposals **'to swap' the debt**[52] for more favourable debt rescheduling measures, the international **development targets**[53] are unlikely to be met by 2015. These targets are:

- **halving**[54] the **number**[55] of people **living in abject poverty**[56],
- **ensuring primary education and basic health care for everybody**[57],
- reducing the cases of malaria and tuberculosis by half, and
- **halting**[58] the spread of HIV.

2.1 Notes on the translation

[1] *Schuldenerlass für:* debt forgiveness for; cancelling/dropping/ waiving the debt of; debt cancellation/relief for

> 'Debt' – pronounced [dɛt] – is mostly used as a countable singular noun. Although the term 'debt forgiveness' may sound unusual, it is commonly used in economics.

← Please note

The most common verb-noun collocations with 'debt' are
to fall into/run into/get into debt: *sich verschulden*
to incur debt: *Schulden machen*
to be in debt to someone: *bei jemandem Schulden haben*

to repay/pay back the debt(s): *die Schulden zurückzahlen*
to settle the debt(s): *die Schulden begleichen*
to pay off the debt(s): *die Schulden abzahlen*
to service the debt: *die Schulden bedienen*

to cancel/wipe out/drop the debt: *die Schulden erlassen*
to write off the debt: *die Schulden abschreiben*
to waive the debt: *auf die Rückzahlung der Schulden verzichten*

to acknowledge/to honour the debt: *die Schuld(en) anerkennen*
'debt' as a compound
government debt/national debt: *Staatsverschuldung* (cf. IX.2.1 Notes on the translation, item [38])
bad debt: *uneinbringliche Forderung*
debt due: *fällige Rückzahlung*

debt crisis: *Schuldenkrise*
debt burden: *Schuldenlast*
debt relief/debt reduction: *(teilweiser) Erlass der Schulden*
debt counselling: *Schuldenberatung*
debt restructuring/debt rescheduling: *Umschuldung*
debt servicing: *Bedienung der Schulden*
debt redemption/debt amortization: *Tilgung der Schulden*
debt collector/commercial collection service: *Inkassobüro*

Further useful expressions
debtless/free of debt: *schuldenfrei*
to be deep in the red: *tief im Minus stehen*

[2] *hat ... aufgerufen:* has appealed to; has urged

³ *die digitale Kluft zu überbrücken:* to close the digital divide; to bridge the digital gap
⁴ *hätten sich ... qualifiziert:* had qualified; were eligible; had been designated
⁵ *Kölner Schuldeninitiative:* Cologne Debt Initiative; Initiative for Heavily Indebted Poor Countries; HIPC Initiative

> The HIPC-scheme seeks to reduce the debt burdens of the poorest countries to sustainable levels. It was launched in 1996 by the IMF and the World Bank in Cologne. Under this scheme, 41 countries have so far qualified for debt relief.

⁶ *seien gestrichen worden:* had been waived; had been dropped; had been cancelled
⁷ *nationalen Einkommens:* national income; net national product
⁸ *die sich insgesamt auf 350 Milliarden Dollar beliefen:* which totalled US $350 billion; which, all in all, amounted to US $350 billion; which added up to US $350 billion
⁹ *ersuchte:* requested; urged
¹⁰ *zur Beseitigung:* to eliminate; to eradicate
¹¹ *unter den Folgen von ... litten:* were suffering the consequences/ the aftermath of; were affected by the consequences
For details on 'aftermath' cf. II.2.1 Notes on the translation, item ².
¹² *Neubewertung:* revaluing; revaluating [US]
¹³ *Goldreserven:* gold holdings; gold reserves

> As the 'book value' *(Buchwert)* of the gold holdings was less than their 'actual value' *(tatsächlicher Wert)*, revaluing these reserves revealed hitherto 'undisclosed reserves' *(stille Reserven)*.

¹⁴ *den Rückgriff auf:* tapping; making use of; having recourse to; utilizing

Please note →

> 'To tap' *(anzapfen)* is an idiomatic expression employed whenever resources are made accessible. 'To make use of' *(nutzen)* also carries the meaning of 'take advantage of' or 'to exploit' *(ausnutzen)*. The synonymous verb 'to utilise' includes the more specific meaning of 'putting something to practical use' *(nutzbringend verwenden)*.
> 'To have recourse to' *(Zuflucht nehmen zu)* and 'to resort to' *(zurückgreifen auf)* connote an appeal for help or protection.

Examples
The production manager will utilize/make use of *(verwenden)* the unused factory space to install a coffee dispenser.
There was no need to resort to *(zurückzugreifen auf)* such drastic measures.
Students of foreign languages often have recourse to/resort to *(nehmen Zuflucht zu)* their bilingual dictionaries.
Politicians tend to resort to *(sich berufen auf)* blaming uncontrollable external factors when they are facing domestic problems.
The Head of Personnel believes in tapping the full potential of the staff.

15 IDA

> In 1960, the World Bank founded the 'International Development Agency' (IDA) which provides low-interest loans to its poorer members. A further World Bank affiliate is the International Finance Corporation which can invest directly in stocks and shares.

16 *vor allem beim:* especially with regard to; particularly as regards/ as far as ... is concerned
17 *der auf ... angewiesen ist:* which is sustained by; which lives on; which survives on/relies on
18 *Zusagen:* pledges; promises
19 *werden gerne zu ... hochstilisiert:* are often served up as; are often made out to be
20 *ungedeckten Schecks:* bad checks; uncovered cheques
21 *bleibt zweifelhaft:* it is doubtful; doubts remain as to
22 *ihre Schulden zu bedienen:* servicing their debt

> 'Debt servicing' includes interest payments as well as capital repayments.

23 *ohnehin:* in the first place; anyway
24 *überhaupt nicht hinzunehmen ist:* but what is absolutely unacceptable is; what is not acceptable at all is; what is completely objectionable is

> Note that negations and questions containing *überhaupt* are translated as:
> *Geht das überhaupt?* Will this work at all?

← Please note

● ● ● ● ● ● *Wir hatten überhaupt keine Informationen.* We had no information at all. We had no information whatsoever

[25] *vorgesehenen:* earmarked; reserved; allocated
[26] *hoch verschuldeten Länder mit mittlerem Einkommen:* Severely Indebted Middle Income Countries (SIMICc)

> The second group of developing countries in this category are the 'Severely Indebted Low Income Countries (SILICs).

[27] *auf ihrem Rücken ausgetragen wird:* will be at their expense; will be to their disadvantage
[28] *Niedrigzinskredite:* low-interest loans; cheap loans
[29] *auslösten:* precipitated; triggered; set off
[30] *scheinen sich ... zu wiederholen:* seem to be recurring; seem to be reproducing themselves
[31] *nachhaltige Entwicklung:* sustainable development

> 'Sustainable development' is an inclusive term for growth policies that limit the detrimental impact of economic activities on the natural environment (e.g. depletion of resources; pollution) and therefore safeguard the economic development of future generations.

[32] *müssen diese Länder mit zunehmender Kapitalflucht ... fertigwerden:* these countries have to cope with mounting capital flight; these countries have to tackle the problem of growing/increasing capital flight

> 'Capital flight' occurs when individuals or companies believe that they can achieve a better return for their investment abroad. Likewise in developing countries, some of the loans granted to finance the debt or to restructure the economy have been invested in foreign shares or deposits.

[33] *der Zerstörung ihrer natürlichen Umwelt:* ecocide; the destruction of their natural environment

> When faced with mounting debt, LDCs have often sought to increase their export earnings by 'deforestation' *(Abholzung)* of the rain forest, 'intensified farming' *(Intensivbewirtschaftung)* and the 'extraction' *(Abbau)* of minerals by means of 'open-cast mining' *(in Tagebau)* thereby causing irreversible 'environmental damage' *(Umweltschäden)* and destroying 'biodiver-

> sity' *(Artenvielfalt)*. The neologism 'ecocide' *(Mord an der Umwelt)* likens the destruction of the natural environment to 'genocide' *(Völkermord)*.

⁳⁴ *alles in allem:* all in all; when all is said and done; on the whole
³⁵ *die versprochene Streichung der Dritte-Welt-Schulden:* the pledged waiving of poor countries debt; the cancellation of Third-World debt that was promised
³⁶ *ist ... bisher ausgeblieben:* has so far failed to materialise; has so far failed them
³⁷ *hat dieses Thema ad acta gelegt:* have shelved this issue; have washed their hands of this issue
³⁸ *und stattdessen ihr Vertrauen in die HIPC-Initiative bekundet:* preferring to keep faith with the HIPC initiative; preferring to place their trust in the HIPC initiative
³⁹ *zusammen:* collectively; all in all; in total
⁴⁰ *während die Einzelheiten ... noch immer akribisch ausgearbeitet werden:* while the details ... are still being meticulously worked out; while the particulars ... are still being looked into
⁴¹ *formiert sich immer mehr Widerstand gegen diese Pro-forma-Streichungen:* opposition to these token cancellations is growing steadily; opposition against these bogus cancellations is gathering momentum

> 'Token' signifies 'having only the appearance of' *(scheinbar)* or 'nominal' *(nominal/nur dem Namen nach)*. 'Bogus' has stronger connotations, namely 'counterfeit' *(gefälscht)* and 'sham' *(geheuchelt/geschwindelt)*.

← Please note

Examples
a bogus company: *eine Scheinfirma*
a bogus dollar bill: *ein gefälschter Dollarschein*
a token woman: *eine Alibifrau*
a token payment: *eine pro forma Zahlung*
a token resistance: *ein nur scheinbarer Widerstand*

> Compare this to 'nominal value' *(Nominalwert)* versus 'real value' *(Realwert)*.

← Please note

⁴² *halten die Rückzahlungsforderungen der reichen Länder für:* consider the rich countries' demands for debt repayment to be; see the repayment demands of the rich countries as

The World Debt Crisis

⁴³ *monieren sie:* they object to; they take exception to; they have objections to

⁴⁴ *unzureichenden:* inadequate; insufficient

Please note →

> Although 'adequate' can signify 'satisfactory' *(zufriedenstellend)* it also implies 'barely sufficient' *(unzulänglich/unzureichend)*.

Examples
His wages were adequate *(reichten aus)* to support his family, not more.
He is adequate *(gut genug)* for the job.

Please note →

> In order to avoid contextual misinterpretations one can resort to 'appropriate' (i.e. right for this occasion; fitting) or 'suitable' *(angemessen)*.

Example
Heavy-duty wear is 'appropriate' *(genau richtig)* for construction workers.

⁴⁵ *schleppende:* sluggish; slow; cumbersome

> This makes reference to the fact that some donor countries actively sought to stall the implementation of the HIPC relief scheme. This problem was deepened when countries such as Japan were hard hit by recession themselves.

⁴⁶ *wurden erlassen:* has been waived

⁴⁷ *die fehlerhafte Berechnung der Streichungshöhe:* the flawed calculation of the portions to be written off; the faulty/incorrect calculation of the debts to be cancelled

⁴⁸ *dem tatsächlichen Verarmungsgrad:* the actual levels of poverty; the existing degree of poverty

⁴⁹ *die Vergabe weiterer Kredite:* further loans; future loans; further lendings

Please note →

> 'Further borrowings' *(Neuaufnahme von Krediten)* is also a possible translation in this context.

⁵⁰ *streng:* harsh; stringent; hard

> Under the HIPC scheme, countries must meet a set of economic criteria, and agree to a 'Poverty Reduction Strategy Paper' (PRSP).

Debt cancellation begins once the IMF and World Bank are satisfied that all the criteria have been met.

The IMF reform programmes usually demand the deregulation of capital markets, the downsizing of public welfare programs, and the privatisation of state companies. On the downside, this has caused 'capital flight' (cf. note [32]) and lower levels of health care and education. J. Sloman (p. 769) claims: 'Past experience has shown that two-thirds of the IMF programmes in the poorest countries break down within three years.'

[51] *einfallsreicher:* resourceful; ingenious
[52] *die Schulden ... einzutauschen:* to swap the debt

'Swap' is pronounced [swop].   ← Please note

'Swap the Debt' is the World Bank's response to the more militant political demand to 'Drop the Debt'. This scheme was jointly developed with representatives of the LDCs. According to J. Sloman, these proposals include
- 'debt for equity' *(Schulden gegen Firmenanteile)*. Banks sell the debt at a discount in the secondary market. The purchaser swaps it with the LDC's central bank for local currency which is invested in shares in local companies.
- 'debt for cash' *(Schulden gegen Bargeld)*. Rather than servicing the debt the debtor country sells it back to the donor at a discount.
- 'debt for bonds' *(Schulden gegen Obligationen)*. The debt is converted into low-interest bonds.
- 'debt for nature' *(Schulden gegen Umweltschutz)*. Debts are cancelled in return for projects that warrant environmental sustainability, i.e. the ability of the environment to survive economic exploitation.
- 'debt for exports' *(Schulden gegen Exporte)*. The debtor country sells its exports to donor countries provided that the revenues are used to pay off debt. This form of 'export protection' is controversial as it might support uncompetitive products.
- 'Debt to local debt' *(Schulden gegen Schulden in der Landeswährung)*: This scheme converts debt denominated in international currencies into local currency debt. The debt is sold to companies that require local currency for their business operations.

● ● ● ● ● ●   [53] *internationalen Entwicklungsziele:* international development targets
Cf. VIII.2.1 Notes on the translation, item [31].
[54] *zu halbieren:* halving; reducing by 50 per cent
[55] *Zahl:* number
Cf. I.2.1 Notes on the translation, item [3].
[56] *die in bitterster Armut leben:* living in abject poverty; living in wretched/abject destitution; living in miserable/degrading poverty

Please note →

> 'Abject' signifies 'so low as to be hopeless', 'wretched' *(elend)* and 'miserable' *(erbärmlich)* but also connotes 'contemptible' *(verachtenswert)*, 'demeaning' *(erniedrigend)* and 'servile' *(unterwürfig)*.
> 'Destitution' is synonymous with 'extreme poverty' and 'degradation' with 'debasement'.

Usage examples
Destitution *(Mittellosigkeit)* is the hallmark of the slums.
During the industrial revolution many workers, filthy and half-starved, lived in degradation *(Elend/Erniedrigung)*.

[57] *jedem Menschen eine elementare Bildung und medizinische Grundversorgung zu garantieren:* ensuring primary education and basic health care for everybody; providing elementary education and fundamental health care for everybody
[58] *Einhalt zu gebieten:* halting; checking; containing

X.3 Exercises

3.1 Poverty and underdevelopment

Use an appropriate English translation of the German terms or the acronyms in (brackets) in order to fill the gaps below. Use words and phrases from the **Sample translation** and the **Notes** in this chapter and the previous one. Remember that there may be more than one choice.

1 More than eighty per cent of the world's __ *(Bevölkerung)* __ *(lebt)* in LDCs – many of them in __ __ / __ __ *(bitterer Armut)*.
2 They __ *(verdienen)* only about 30 per cent of the world's __ *(Einkommen)*.
3 In 1997, the real __ __ __ *(GNY)* __ __ / __ __ *(pro Kopf)* of the 20 poorest countries __ *(betrug im Durchschnitt)* a mere US $220 whereas the richest countries __/__ *(erzielten)* US $26,950.
4 The majority of human beings are incapable of __ *(befriedigen)* their __ __ *(Grundbedürfnisse)* for __ *(Nahrung)*, __ *(Unterkunft)*, __ *(Wärme)* and __ *(Kleidung)*.

5 What's more, there is no __ (Zugang) to education and __/__ (ausreichender) __ __ (Gesundheitsversorgung).
6 People in LDCs frequently have to accept __/__ (erniedrigende) jobs and are paid extremely __ __ (Niedriglöhne).
7 Most development agencies use GNY as a __ (Massstab) for development because most countries __ (sammeln) GNY __/__ (Daten).
8 There is a close __/__ (Wechselbeziehung) between the GNY per head and other indicators such as __ (Sterblichkeits-) rates, __ (Analphabetismus-) rates and calorific or protein intake.
9 However, GNY only inadequately records __ __ __ (Bezahlung in Naturalien) – which are typical for __ __ (Subsistenzwirtschaften) – and the products which are made and __ (verbraucht) by the same households.
10 Moreover, this measurement __ __/__ __ (basiert) on market prices which may be __ (verzerrt) owing to monopolistic __ __ (Preispolitik) and lack of __ (Wettbewerb) in the local markets.

Exercises

Corel Library

Exercises

3.2 Mounting debts

Fill in the gaps by choosing the appropriate English equivalent of the German terms or the acronyms in (brackets). Use words and phrases from the **Sample translation** and the **Notes** in this chapter and the previous one. Note that there may be more than one option.

1. Severely indebted __ __ __ (LICs) and the __ __ __ (LMICs) in the same category are currently the major __ *(Empfänger)* of official loans.
2. The oil shock of 1973 presented the LDCs with a __ __ __ *(wachsender Schuldenlast)*.
3. Their attempts to __ *(bedienen)* these debts - in other words, to pay __ *(Zins)* at the same time as __ *(Raten)* on the __ __/__ __ *(Darlehenssumme)* put severe strains on their economies.
4. When the crude oil prices quadrupled and the world's economies went into recession in the mid-seventies, the __ __ __ __ (MSACs) were incapable of __ __ *(bewältigen)* the consequences such as high levels of inflation and __ __ *(Kapitalflucht)*.
5. In the early 1980's with the world's economies going into a deeper and longer recession and export prices falling, LDCs found it even more difficult to __ __/__ __ *(abzahlen)* their debts, and Mexico was the first country to __ /__ *(das ankündigte)* that it would have to __ *(aussetzen)* payments.
6. This engendered what is known as the __ __ *(Schuldenkrise)* which not only put the __ __ *(Schuldnerländer)* at risk but also the international banking system.
7. The crisis motivated the World Bank together with other monetary institutions to create efficient __ __ __ *(Umschuldungspläne)* and the __ __ __ *(Tauscht die Schulden ein!)* proposals with the developing countries.
8. Although these measures have been widely __ *(begrüsst)*, they fail to __/__ *(beseitigen)* the cause of the many evils befalling developing countries.
9. The IMF and the World Bank, in particular, have been criticized for their __ __ __ *(straffe Geld- und Kreditpolitik)* and the __/__ *(strenge)* implication of their reform programmes which have __ *(ausgesetzt)* the poor countries to the __/__ *(nachteiligen)* effects of market deregulation.
10. Moreover, some __ __ *(Industrienationen)* have tried to __ *(verzögern)* the __ *(Beitrag)* they __/__ *(versprochen haben)* to __ *(leisten)*.

3.3 Ecocide   Exercises

Translate the sentences below. They all deal with the damage wrought on the natural environment as a result of destructive exploitation. Use the English terms suggested in (brackets), the **Notes** in this chapter as well as your dictionaries.

1. Bereits *(as early as)* 1987 wurde im Bericht der Brundtland-Kommission die Bedeutung einer nachhaltigen Entwicklung für die Entwicklungsländer betont.
2. Der verstärkte (reinforced) Export ihrer Rohstoffe *(primaries)* hatte zur Folge *(have resulted in)*, dass die Umwelt in diesen Ländern schwer geschädigt wurde.
3. Leider sind die Umweltschäden *(damage wrought on the environment)* oft irreparabel.
4. Der wachsende Schuldenberg hat auch dazu beigetragen, die Situation zu verschlechtern *(the deterioration of)*.
5. Intensive Bewirtschaftung der Felder und rücksichtslose *(ruthless)* Ausbeutung der Bodenschätze haben die Artenvielfalt in einigen Regionen zerstört.
6. Seltene *(rare types of)* tropische Hölzer wurden in der Vergangenheit manchmal als billiges Nutzholz *(timber)* verkauft.
7. In Brasilien umfasst *(extends to)* die Abholzung des Regenwaldes inzwischen ein Gebiet, das größer ist als Frankreich und Belgien zusammen.
8. In Venezuela wurde durch die Gewinnung von Gold im Tagebau *(open-cast gold mining)* und durch die unsachgemäße *(negligent/improper)* Nutzung von Chemikalien das Amazonasbecken vergiftet und einzigartige Tier- und Pflanzenarten ausgerottet *(wiped out)*.
9. Der Neologismus „Ecocide" beschreibt zutreffend *(appropriately)* die Radikalität der Umweltzerstörer.
10. Selbst vor Einschüchterung und Ermordung ihrer Gegner schrecken *(shrink from/shy away from)* manche Konzerne nicht zurück.

Appendix

Key 190

Glossary 201

Reference Work & Further Reading 205

Index 207

Key

I Unemployment in Germany

Employment and pay

1	Arbeitgeber	employer/employers
2	Arbeitnehmer/innen	employee/s
3	Arbeitseinkommen	earned income; income from employment
4	arbeitslos	out of work; without work, unemployed
5	Aushilfskraft	temp; temporary (member of) staff
6	Beschäftigte/r	employee; person employed
7	Beschäftigung	employment
8	Beschäftigungspolitik	employment policy
9	Beschäftigungsverhältnis	employment contract; employment
10	Einstiegsgehalt	starting salary; initial salary; entry salary
11	erwerbsfähig	employable
12	erwerbslos	unemployed; without employment
13	Erwerbsquote	employment rate/rate of labour participation
14	Geldlohn	money wages; wages paid in cash
15	Leiharbeit	loan employment
16	Lohnarbeit	paid work
17	Lohnerhöhung	pay rise; pay hike (US); pay increase
18	Lohnpolitik	pay policy; compensation policy (US)
19	Lohnstruktur	pay/remuneration pattern; pay structure
20	Mindestlohn	minimum wages
21	Monatslohn	monthly pay-check (US); monthly pay; monthly compensation (US)
22	Naturallohn	compensation in kind; wages in kind
23	Nettoverdienst	take-home pay; net pay
24	Nominallohn	nominal wages; money wages
25	Spitzenlohn/-gehalt	top wages; top salaries
26	Tariflohn	basic wages; basic pay; basic compensation

Collective agreements and new forms of employment

1 Flexitime workers; core hours
2 removed/abolished; labour regulations/work regulations; business opportunities
3 pursue part-time employment
4 temporary staff; stand in for/deputise for
5 fringe benefits; perks; non-wage labour cost(s)/incidental labour cost(s)
6 service sectors; collective wage agreements
7 collective pay negotiations/collective bargaining; temporary employment
8 limited employment contracts; loan employment

1 Redundancies and the displacement of workers are always inevitable if the need for labour declines in a traditional industry. Making workers redundant and displacing them is always unavoidable if a traditional (branch of) industry finds itself in a state of decline.   Redundancies and dismissals
2 A great number of/a great many redundancies are brought about by productivity gains/growth in productivity.
3 The notice (of termination) was not served in time and is therefore invalid/void.
4 200 employees/people have been made redundant because there has been a continued slackening of demand in the company's core business.
5 This long-serving employee was dismissed two years before he reached the legally required retirement age.
6 After more than 40 years of service, he was entitled to a substantial redundancy payment/redundancy compensation.
7 Employment (protection) laws also regulate arbitration and mediation procedures between employers and employees.
8 It is customary to give at least a month's notice before resigning from a job/before tendering one's resignation.
9 The employer, too, may serve a notice of termination on an employee/may serve the employee with a termination notice.
10 The company refused to give reasons for the dismissal/for dismissing the two skilled workers.

II The East German Labour Market

1	angelernte Arbeiter	semi-skilled workers	Labour and work
2	Arbeiterschaft	labour	
3	Arbeitsangebot	manpower/labour supply; manpower/labour available	
4	Arbeitsmarkt	labour market/job market/employment market	
5	Arbeitsmarktpolitik	labour market policies/manpower policies	
6	Arbeitsnachfrage	demand for manpower/demand for labour/labour demand	
7	Arbeitsplatz	job (also: place of work/workplace)	
8	Arbeitsstunden	man hours; labour hours	
9	Arbeitszeit	working hours/hours of work/work hours	
10	Ausfallzeiten	downtimes/outage times/lost working hours	
11	Berufstätigkeit	the pursuit of/performing a job; pursuing an occupation	
12	Berufsunfähigkeit	occupational invalidity	
13	Erwerbsleben	working life	

	14 Erwerbstätigkeit	[pursuing] gainful/remunerative employment
	15 Facharbeiter	skilled/fully qualified worker/specially qualified worker
	16 Kurzarbeit	short-time work; working shorter hours
	17 Mindesterwerbsalter	minimum employment age
	18 offene Stellen	vacancies; positions/jobs to be filled; job openings
	19 Überstunden	overtime/overtime work
	20 ungelernte Arbeiter	unskilled workers

Employment and unemployment

1. cheap labour/low-wage labour
2. employable; seek; pursue; gainful employment
3. job creation; unemployment pay; short-term measure; job seekers
4. at facilitating; long-term unemployed; regular employment
5. back-to-work; lone parents/single parents
6. stop-gap measures; containing unemployment
7. employment rates/labour participation rates; displaced workers
8. structural unemployment; occupational retraining; redundant; incentives/inducements
9. cyclical unemployment; aggregate demand
10. workforce employed

Expectations, recommendations and requests

1. Our staff are expected to improve the operational processes/operative processes/the operations continuously.
2. Our skilled workers were requested/asked to attend the vocational retraining programmes.
3. Some employees were required to opt for early retirement/to take early retirement/to retire earlier.
4. at facilitating; long-term unemployed; regular employment
5. back-to-work; lone parents
6. We were recommended consulting a labour market specialist/expert.
7. Due to the expected economic recovery they were advised to refrain from making further employees redundant.
8. This procedure was not expected to succeed. This method was expected to fail.
9. He was assumed to be handing in his notice.
10. The new head of department is thought to/reputed to have a distinct employee focus.

III Supply and Demand

1. line diagrams; graphic presentation/ graph; flat; steep — Interpreting linear curves
2. positive slope; slope upward(s); a negative slope; slope downward(s)
3. straight line; incline/gradient
4. run in parallel; rotate; shift upwards; shift downwards, shift (to the) left (to the) right
5. cross/intersect/cut; x-axis/abscissa; y-axis/ordinate; point of origin/point o
6. lowest; minimum; low; maximum; peak
7. shape/slope
8. indicates/marks/plots; in relation to
9. measured; vertical; horizontal
10. positions; cuts
11. at; amounts to; value
12. equation; equals/is equal to
13. equilibrium; move; produces; commodities
14. decline in demand; concentration of demand
15. by; extension

1. graphic formula — Describing graphs, diagrams and charts
2. makes reference; diagram; relation; equation
3. drawing; sketches; outlines
4. geometrical; mechanical; cross-sections; longitudinal sections
5. graphic representation
6. plot; information; arranging; breakdowns; tables; diagrams

1. This curve represents/constitutes a supply curve./This curve plots the supply. — Prepositional objects
2. On drawing the curve/when the curve is plotted, make sure that all values are properly entered/indicated in the graph.
3. With this procedure, attention has to be paid/due consideration has to be given to the following.
4. The ceteris paribus condition assumes that all other factors remain equal. By applying/if one applies the ceteris paribus condition, one assumes that all other factors remain equal/constant.
5. If the price rises by 5 per cent, demand will probably decrease/fall.
6. Unfortunately, we came away empty-handed when we first attempted/tried to purchase the much-demanded model/the model that was very much in demand.

	IV Price Determinants
Depicting and explaining price trends	1 developed/fluctuated
	2 disproportionately high
	3 to determine/to specify
	4 contrasted/compared/juxtaposed
	5 the same/identical
	6 look at; dropped again/fell back
	7 rose steeply/increased sharply ; fluctuations; peaked/reached their all-time high; above
	8 slowing/slackening/weakening/falling off; tumbled; all-time low/absolute bottom
	9 climbed; downswing/downward trend; maintained
	10 compare; charts/plots
	11 trend set
	12 soaring; topped/exceeded
	13 underwent/experienced; decrease/decline
	14 buying up; produced/created; steadily widening; was being driven up/was being pushed
	15 rocket; approaching/moving towards
	16 runs parallel
	17 shoot up/soar; approach/move towards/edge closer to; merging; converged
A fair market price?	1 drives
	2 has ... built; were
	3 have looked/looked; have found/found; have bought/bought; have pushed/pushed
	4 were shipped
	5 were exported
	6 became/has become
	7 tumbled; was being paid; went
Putting on a price tag	1 The price of this computer totals/amounts to $1000.
	2 Stress at work is nearly always at the price of health.
	3 We paid a heavy/high price for increasing our market share in the middle/medium price ranges/medium price brackets.
	4 It would be difficult for me to put a price/price tag on this painting off the top of my head.
	5 The picture was priced at £50,000 by the gallery. The gallery priced the picture at £50,000.
	6 Do you want this information at any price/at any cost?

7 This model is absolutely priceless/beyond price.
8 This is a rather pric(e)y type of entertainment/hobby.
9 The term 'price fixing' refers to the illegal setting of sales prices by a price cartel.
10 Price cutters slash/drastically reduce their prices to undercut/to undersell their competitors.
11 The price level for MCs began to slide (downhill) when the first CDs were launched.
12 In order to assess your performance we will have to put a price tag on your contribution.
13 Not only are we able to compete with the market leader in terms of quality but also pricewise/with respect to the price.

V Business Cycles

1 economy; slow/sluggish   Economic cycles
2 cooling off/slow down; economies
3 in retreat; economic trend
4 negative economic growth; consumption; has been stagnating
5 economic forecasts
6 experienced an economic upturn
7 economic recovery
8 incentives/injections/stimuli; crank up/revive/rejuvenate
9 programmes aimed at stimulating economic growth/economic stimulus packages
10 fiscal policies; regulate the economy

1 a wanted/had wanted   Citing statements made
   b had; arrived   in the past
   c had left
   d was rising/had been rising
   e had been solved

2 a wanted/wants
   b provide/provided
   c was; is
   d is/was; employs/employed
   e is/was

3 a was talking
   b were occurring

    c   was arriving
    d   was; waiting
    e   were trying

4 a   would respond
    b   react/reacted
    c   was/would be
    d   would take
    e   was being

Combating recession

1 If the government persistently runs a budget deficit, national/public debt will rise/increase.
2 The success of fiscal policies largely depends on the accuracy of economic forecasting/forecasts.
3 Some economists doubt whether injecting money into the economy is an appropriate means to increase private investment.
4 When facing a recession of this magnitude, one ought to listen to the experts.
5 'Discretionary fiscal policy' means/signifies/that the government deliberately changes government/national expenditure/spending and government/national revenues/receipts in order to influence aggregate demand.

VI The European Union

Neologisms

1 Europhile
2 Euro-sceptic
3 Eurocrats
4 Euroland
5 the United States of Europe
6 eurocurrencies
7 eurodollars
8 Euromarket
9 Eurocentric

The Single Market

1 promotes/encourages/fosters; wealth; welfare
2 free trade area; total amount; greater
3 internal market/single market; removing/abolishing; entry barriers; citizens; elections; residence
4 structural fund; depressed; lag behind
5 Common Agricultural Policy; subsidises; setting/determining; agricultural surpluses

6 prevent; anti-trust measures; prohibits agreements; adversely affect
7 social charta; social policy
8 decent pay/decent wages; vocational training
9 elderly and disabled; adolescents/juveniles/young people; minimum employment age
10 aligns; immigration; drug trafficking

1 Jean Monnet, who died in 1979 aged 91/at the age of 91, is generally accredited with being the father of the European Communities.   The European Communities
2 He began to commit himself to a democratic Europe united in peace/a peacefully united democratic Europe when he realized that France's economic recovery was closely linked to that of its neighbours.
3 He was one of the founding fathers/founders of the European Coal and Steel Community (ECSC), of the EEC and of EURATOM
4 The ECSC, which came into existence through/as a result of the Paris Treaty of 1951, created an internal market for the coal and steel products of its member states
5 Whereas the ECSC and EURATOM merely sought to/intended to integrate closely defined economic sectors in a customs union, the EEC strove towards/aspired to a progressive harmonisation of all areas of economic policy which were crucial to/instrumental in the functioning of the common market.
6 It is, therefore, the Treaty of Rome of 1957 which is usually referred to as a landmark/milestone on the way towards the European Union.
7 In 1987, the 'Single European Act' (SEA) laid the foundation/cornerstone for the 'Single European Market' by providing for the 'four fundamental freedoms'.
8 The Maastricht Treaty, which was signed in December 1991, emphasizes the focal/crucial importance of the common currency which is regarded as being the/which is considered to be the driving force behind a strengthened/stronger political co-operation in Europe.

VII The Dollar and the Euro
1 chairman; reached/hit; touched lowest level   But after September 11th all the bets were off ...
2 stave off/avert; slashing; cranking up/reviving up
3 plunged/plummeted; slip into/slide into; slump; significantly/sharply/markedly
4 was stabilizing; improved
5 spending; reverse gear; retreat/recession
6 slumping/ailing/faltering; recover; upswing/upturn

	7 turnaround; inventories
	8 tax cuts; mortgage rates; stimulus package; surge
	9 more cautious; afloat
	10 rising/increasing; contract/shrink; tighten their belts
The free fall of the euro	1 stood at; climbed; low
	2 fixed at
	3 been worth/bought
	4 weakens/declines; is affected
	5 knock-on effect; rendered/made
	6 detrimental for/disadvantages for; suffer/bear
	7 removes; threat/risk
	8 made out/issued; decline; benefited from it
	9 competitiveness
	10 economists
	11 deteriorated
	12 downward revisions; undermined; justifiable
Having a say!	1 The bank would like to have a decisive say in the founding of the new holding.
	2 The member banks had all had their say before the final decision was taken.
	3 The launch of the new product was an error, not to say a disaster.
	4 The new system is much less time-consuming, to say nothing about its cost-efficiency.
	5 When all is said and done, people are a company's best asset.
	6 His manners were unrefined/unsophisticated, to say the least.
	7 If we increase the number of the units produced by, let's say/say, three per minute, will this remove our delivery bottleneck?

VIII The Federal Reserve System

'Money is as money does'
1 currencies; banknotes; coins; deposits
2 lenders; nominal interest rate; borrowers; principal sum
3 prime rate; charge; short-term
4 bill of exchange; order; pay out
5 discount; due/mature
6 commercial banks; make loans/grant loans
7 clearing system; exchange/swap/cross-cancel; settle the accounts
8 open-market policy; interest-rate policy; minimum reserves; money supply

1	independent; interference	**Independent central**
2	tasks; responsibilities	**banks**
3	attaining/meeting	
4	subordinate; protect	
5	lower; more stable; rate of inflation	
6	price stability; aim/goal	
7	granted; assumed; join	
8	monetary policy; economic policies	

What if?

1. Each time/whenever if the Fed reduces/lowers the rates, this has a positive impact/effect on the purchasing behaviour of the consumers. If the Fed reduces the rates, this affects/influences the purchasing behaviour of consumers positively.
2. The prices of US export goods/exports always soar when the dollar appreciates/when the value of the dollar increases.
3. Each time/if I go to the United States, I take my credit card.
4. If/As soon as the cheque is cleared, the amount is paid out or remitted to a bank account.
5. The Fed always buys back government securities if/when it wants lower (interest) rates.
6. If/when/each time banks raise their interest rates on mortgages, fewer people can afford to take out a loan.

IX A new Economic World Order

1	drawing your attention; gross domestic product; per head, per capita	**Who is biggest?**
2	point out; insufficiently/inadequately; power/clout	**Comparing bar charts**
3	amounts to roughly/totals approximately	
4	applies to/is true for; attained/achieved/reached	
5	feature/figure/appear; dealt with	
6	tipped the balance	
7	emerging countries/LDCs; qualify/are eligible; size	
8	admitted/taken on board; largest/biggest	

1	borrowing something; the borrower	**Loans and credits**
2	on loan; at interest/on credit	
3	granted/given; interest-free loan	
4	hire/rent	
5	take out ; loan/credit; mortgage	
6	paid back/paid off; instalments; handling fees; interest	
7	overdraft facility	

	8 lend money; clients/customers; exceed; credit line/credit limit
	9 lenders; foreclose; cancel
	10 creditability/creditworthiness
Current events	1 Are you being served?
	2 Our customers are not used/accustomed to being treated like this.
	3 Alternative credit facilities are being looked into/checked out/reviewed at the moment.
	4 Being cheated by speculators is not a pleasant experience for small investors.
	5 Imagine the Frankfurt Stock Exchange being open on Sundays.
	6 Speculators are being viewed more and more/increasingly critically these days.
	7 Being constantly asked whether the DAX has gone up at long last is a nerve-wracking experience for telephone consultants.
	8 The shareholders are currently being informed about the company's profits.

X The World Debt Crisis

Poverty and underdevelopment	1 population; live; abject poverty/extreme destitution
	2 earn; income
	3 gross national income; per head/per capita; averaged; achieved/attained
	4 satisfying; basic needs; food; shelter; warmth; clothing
	5 access; adequate/sufficient; health care
	6 demeaning/degrading; low wages
	7 measure compile; data/statistics
	8 correllation/relation(ship); mortality; illiteracy
	9 payments in kind; subsistence economies; consumed
	10 is based/is founded; distorted; price policies; competition
Mounting debts	1 low income countries; lower middle income countries; recipients
	2 mounting debt burden
	3 service; interest; instalments; principal borrowed/capital borrowed
	4 Most Seriously Affected Countries; coping with; capital flight
	5 pay back/pay off; announce/declare; suspend
	6 debt crisis; debtor countries
	7 debt rescheduling schemes; swap the debt
	8 welcomed; eliminate/eradicate

9 tight monetary policies; stringent/strict; exposed; adverse/disadvantageous
10 industrialised nations; delay; contribution(s); promised/pledged; make

Ecocide

1 As early as 1987, the report of the Brundtland Commission underlined/emphasized the importance of sustainable development for LDCs/emerging economies.
2 Reinforced exports of their primaries/primary products have resulted in/have caused great environmental damage in these countries.
3 Unfortunately, the damage wrought on the environment is often irreversible.
4 The mounting debt burden, too, has contributed to the deterioration of the situation.
5 Intensified farming and ruthless exploitation of natural resources have destroyed biodiversity in some areas.
6 In the past, rare types of tropical wood were sometimes sold as inexpensive timber.
7 In Brazil, the deforestation of the rain forest now extends to an area which is larger than France and Belgium together.
8 In Venezuela, open-cast gold mining and the improper usage of chemicals have poisoned the Amazon (river) basin and have wiped out unique species of plants and animals.
9 The neologism 'ecocide' appropriately describes the radical nature of those that destroy the environment.
10 Some large corporations do not even shrink from/shy away from intimidating and murdering their opponents.

Glossary

acronym: a pronounceable name formed from a series of initial letters, e.g. 'ASEAN' (Association of Southeast Asian Nations), 'NATO' (North Atlantic Treaty Organization) or 'NASA' (National Aeronautics and Space Administration). Strictly speaking, abbreviations, such a. 'NIC' or 'IMF', are not acronyms as they consist of independent phonemes.

adverb, adverbial phrase: a word or group of words that serves to modify a sentence, clause or phrase by specifying the context of the verb e.g. in terms of time, place, intensity, condition and other attributive features. Most adverbs are derived from adjectives or participles (e.g. an 'unjustifiably' harsh attitude).

analogy: an imitation of an existing linguistic pattern or model. 'Astronaut', for instance, is based on the model of 'Argonaut' and 'Euroland' on 'Disneyland'. In figurative speech, an analogy emphasizes the similarity between two things that are otherwise unlike. In economics, an 'analogy' is the inference that things, which are identical in certain respects, will be alike in at least one other.

ancillary construction (from 'ancilla' which is Latin for 'maid'): a supplementary, dependent or auxiliary structure *(Hilfskonstruktion)* such as *dabei*.

apposition: a grammatical construction in which a noun or noun phrase is pre- or post-posed to extend the meaning of the lexeme (see below) next to it. Appositive units may be nouns, adjectives, or adverbs. 'The Fed', (which is) the United States 'central bank...' is a noun apposite. 'The policies (which were) aimed at stimulating the economy' ... is a verb apposite. The company '(which was) anxious to pacify the customer' is an adjective appositive. Most apposite elements are non-restrictive. However, some such as 'Henry Ford III' are restrictive, in other words, an inseparable part of the expression to which they are joined.

attribute: in a general context, a characteristic feature associated with an object or a person (the dove is the attribute of peace). In linguistics, an attribute is the adjective or adjectival phrase that qualifies a noun, which in English can be pre-posed or post-posed. Pre-posed qualifiers in German, such as *die in diesem Fall getroffene Entscheidung* ('the decision taken in this matter') often have to be post-poned in English.

auxiliary verb: a verb used to indicate the tense (past, future), voice (active or passive) and mood (indicative, imperative, subjunctive) of another verb or to emphasise a statement made, e.g. 'but I did tell you'.

collective noun: a noun is singular in number but plural in meaning. Collective nouns usually refer to a group of items or persons such as 'crowd', 'people' 'labour'.

collocation: an arrangement of phonetic, semantic or grammatical components such as a word's consonants and vowels. As a figure of speech; collocation denotes a combination of semantic items whose meaning has been established by usage: e.g. 'on the other hand' *(andererseits)*.

compound word/composite word: a word that consists of two or more grammatical elements that – albeit joined – retain their semantic independence, e.g. 'business cycle', 'debt collector', 'horseshoe'. A compound sentence is made up of two or more main clauses.

conjugated forms: the inflection of a verb – apparent in the verb ending – which indicate the person (first, second, third), the number (singular or plural), the tense (present, future or past), the voice (active or passive) and the mood (imperative, subjunctive, indicative)

connector: a grammatical unit which joins the main sentence to a subordinate syntactical structure or to another main clause. Connectors are mostly conjunctions, i.e. words (other than relative pronouns) that connect sentences and other syntactical units, e.g. 'whether', 'although'.

connotation: an association or an implied/suggested meaning in addition to the simple or literal meaning of a semantic unit. Example: A merger does not necessarily connote power coercion or dominance.

declined forms/inflected forms: the inflected endings of nouns, pronouns or adjectives which reflect their grammatical case, number (singular and plural) and gender or their relation to other words in the sentence. German and English nouns have four declensions. The declension of 'who' in the possessive (genitive) case is 'whose', in the objective case (i.e. dative and/or accusative) 'whom'.

denote: indicate, designate, signify, to be a sign or symbol of something. Example: The character 'x' denotes multiplication.

derivative: a term which is based on another term in the same class or created by adding a prefix or suffix to a fundamental lexical structure (e.g. 'suitable'). Zero-derivations, for instance, are verbs that derive directly from nouns (e.g. 'impact' – 'to impact').

euphemism: an inoffensive or indirect expression which is substituted for one that is harsh or unpleasantly direct and thought to be ill-mannered or hurtful. 'Lay off' is generally used as euphemism for 'dismissal'.

false friend: an incorrect linguistic analogy. This expression was coined by the French linguists M. Koessler and J. Derocquigny in their 1928 publication *Les faux amis ou les trahisons du vocabulaire anglais*.

figure of speech/figurative usage: mode of expression which differs from the literal usage of words and phrases by using striking semantic combinations and connotations for the sake of ornament, emphasis or vividness and in order to add force to a message conveyed. Figures of speech are → metaphors, → similes, hyperboles, etc.

generic term/inclusive term: a term which is characteristic of a genus, kind or class of similar semantic units. 'Money' is a generic term, whereas 'coins' and 'notes' are specific terms.

grapheme: a written letter that represents a phoneme or morpheme. Example: The letter 'b' in the noun 'debt' is a silent grapheme: it is seen written but not pronounced.

homonym, homonymic: two or several distinctly different words that are homophone (i.e. have the same pronunciation such as 'died' and 'dyed'), homograph (i.e. have the same spelling, e.g. 'Mark' and 'mark') or a combination of both.

homonymic clash: misunderstanding or misconception due to homonymy.

idiom: a group of words or a phrase whose meaning cannot be derived, or not entirely be derived, from its individual constituents (e.g. a 'tall tale') which denotes a story that is hard to believe.

idiosyncrasy: an individuall peculiarity as of taste, behaviour or opinion. In the context of this volume, an highly idiomatic linguistic feature which usually defies translation.

impletive: a semantic filler such as 'actually' *(eigentlich)* or *denn* (in questions) that carries little or no meaning; impletives are mostly used for emphasis

intransitive verbs: verbs that are syntactically connected to the subject of a sentence which governs them. Some intransitive verbs cannot be followed by a direct object at all (e.g. 'this problem arose all of a sudden') others can switch from the intransitive ('he was standing at the window') to the transitive mode ('he never stood a chance').

inverted word order: a structure which changes the usual subject-verb-object order in a full sentence, e.g. when certain qualifiers such as 'little' (little did he know), 'hardly' (hardly had he entered) or 'not only' (not only did he expect us to ... but he ...).

lexeme: a minimal semantic unit, such as 'touch down' *(Landung)*, the meaning of which cannot be understood from its composite morphemes 'touch' and 'down'.

lexical item: a word listed in a dictionary, a canonized or well documented linguistic item

metaphor: a figure of speech in which a semantic unit is applied to an object (person, item, action, abstract) that it does not denote; thereby a similarity is implied without being mentioned verbatim, e.g. 'a tough cookie'. Metaphors are implied → similes.

metonym: a figure of speech in which an attribute is used to hint at a more complex and comprehensive concept or issue, e.g. 'he liked the bottle'.

modifier or qualifier: a semantic unit that qualifies the meaning of a word or phrase; e.g. this is highly unlikely. Modifier can be post-positive (i.e. placed after) or pre-positive (i.e. placed before the word they qualify).

neologism: a newly created word or term such as 'ecocide', 'green taxes' or 'electronic cottages'. Neologisms can be borrowed from other languages, such as *der Cashflow* in German and 'the Bundesbank' in English.

number: the form of a noun that indicates how many persons or objects are referred to.

phonemes: individual sound articulations that contribute to the significance of a word and which make it distinguishable from other word, e.g. 'd' in 'led' or the 't' in 'let'.

polysemous, polysemic: a semantic unit that shows polysemy; a word that has several easily distinguishable meanings, e.g. 'order'.

polysemy: the property of having many meanings or of showing a large semantic diversity. Words like 'head' show polysemy to a high degree.

prepositional object: an object that is preceded by one or two prepositions, e.g. (let's talk) 'to him', 'about him'; (let's get) 'down to business'.

qualifier: → modifier

quantifier: a word that indicates a certain level, degree of intensity, or quantity of something; e.g. 'much', 'many', 'a lot of'; 'as early as'

reflexive verbs: verbs which refer back to the subject of a sentence by means of a reflexive pronoun which in English is always post-positive in conjugated verbs. Example: The company distinguished itself by winning three awards.

semantic: relating to the meaning of a word; arising from the distinctions between different words

simile: figure of speech that directly associates a person with the quality of another being or thing. Example: He pretended to be as hard as nails but was as soft as a brush.

subject: grammatical entity (noun or pronoun) that governs all other parts of an independent sentence and thus decides on its semantic contents.

subordinate clause: a lesser-order clause whose meaning depends on the higher-order or superordinate sentence it supplements. Example: We would reconsider your proposal if we had time.

synonym: a word or an expression that has a similar or identical meaning as another one, e.g. 'hidden unemployment' and 'disguised unemployment'. Synonyms often cover distinguishing nuances of the same semantic item but hardly ever mean exactly the same. They contribute substantially to the intricacies and idiosyncrasies of natural languages.

syntax: the grammatical arrangement of words in a sentence or clause

term: a word or group of words used in connection with special purposes, subjects or fields of knowledge (e.g. a medical term: *ein medizinischer Fachbegriff*). Less specifically, 'term' can be any word or expression, e.g. an 'abstract term' *(abstrakter Begriff)*, a 'foreign term' *(Fremdwort)*.

transitive verbs: the largest group of verbs. They need to be governed by an object to specify their meaning: e.g. 'to raise one's hand' or to 'raise capital'.

uncountable noun: a noun, such as 'information' or 'data', that has no plural form and cannot be preceded by an indefinite article.

Reference Works & Further Reading

Bauer, J., Seidenspinner, M.: *Betriebswirtschaft: Übersetzungsübungen, studium kompakt Fachsprache Englisch,* Cornelsen & Oxford University Press, Berlin, 2001

Blum, U., et al.: *Grundlagen der Volkswirtschaftslehre*, Springer, Heidelberg, 1999

Collins *English Dictionary*, Harper Collins, Glasgow, 2001

Dictionary of American Business, ed. P. H. Collin, Peter Collin Publishing, Teddington, 1999

Dornbusch, R., et al.: *Macroeconomics*, McGraw-Hill, New York, 2000

Duden: Das große Wörterbuch der deutschen Sprache, 10 Bde., Bibliographisches Institut, Mannheim, 1999

Entering the 21st Century: World Bank Development Report 1999/2000, ed. S. Yusuf, Oxford University Press, Oxford 1999

Europäische Organisationen und Gremien im Bereich von Währung und Wirtschaft, Selbstverlag der Deutschen Bundesbank, Frankfurt am Main, 1997

Evaluation and Poverty Reduction, World Bank Series on Evaluation and Development, eds. O.N. Feinstein et al., Transaction Publishers, New Jersey,

Gallagher, J. D.: *Deutsch-englische Übersetzungsübungen*, Oldenbourg, München, 1996

Görgens, E., et al., *Europäische Geldpolitik. Theorie, Empirie, Praxis*, Werner, Düsseldorf 2001

Hadeler, T., Arentzen, U., *Gabler Wirtschaftslexikon*, Gabler, Wiesbaden, 2001

Hamblock, D., Wessels, D.: *Großwörterbuch Wirtschaftsenglisch*, Cornelsen & Oxford University Press, Berlin, 1999

Harrison, B., Nutter, R.: *GCSE Economics*, Addison Wesley, Longman UK, 1997

Homburg, S. *Efficient Economic Growth*, Springer, Heidelberg, 1992

Longman Business English Dictionary, Longman UK, Harlow, 2000

Longman Dictionary of Contemporary English, Longman UK, Harlow, 2001

LTP Dictionary of Selected Collocations, eds. J. Hill, M. Lewis, Language Teaching Publications, Hove, 1998

Mankiw, N.G.: *Grundzüge der Volkswirtschaftslehre*, Schäffer, Stuttgart, 2001

Oxford Advanced Learner's Dictionary of Current English, eds. A. S. Hornby; S. Wehmeier, Oxford University Press, Oxford, 2000

Oxford Dictionary of Business, eds. J. Pallister, A. Isaacs, Oxford University Press, Oxford, 1996

Oxford Dictionary of Economics, ed. J. Black, Oxford University Press, Oxford, 1997

Oxford Dictionary of Idioms, ed. J. Speake, Oxford University Press, Oxford, 2000

Pass, C., et al.: *Collins Dictionary of Economics*, Harper Collins, Glasgow, 2000

Pflugmann-Hohlstein, B., et al.: *Lexikon der Volkswirtschaft*, DTV, C.H. Beck, München, 2000

Powell, R.: *A Level Economics*, Letts Educational, London, 2000

Samuelson, P.A., Nordhaus, W.D.: *Economics*, McGraw-Hill, New York, 2001

Schäfer, W.: *Wirtschaftswörterbuch*, Band 1: Deutsch-Englisch, Vahlen, München, 1997

Schäfer, W.: *Wirtschaftswörterbuch*, Band 2: Englisch-Deutsch, Vahlen, München, 1998
Sloman, J.: *Economics*, Prentice Hall, Edinburgh 2000
Vahlens *Kompendium der Wirtschaftstheorie und Wirtschaftspolitik*, Hg. E. Dichtl, O. Issing, 2 Bde., Vahlen, Müchen 2000
Veth, K., Lister, R.: *Schlüsselbegriffe der Wirtschaft, studium kompakt Fachsprache Englisch,* Cornelsen & Oxford University Press, Berlin, 1999
Volkswirtschaftslehre. Grundlagen der Volkswirtschaftstheorie und Volkswirtschaftspolitik, Hg. R. Neubäumer, B. Hewel, Gabler, Wiesbaden, 2001
Webster's New World College Dictionary, ed. M. Agnes, MacMillan, Chicago, 2000
Weltweite Organisationen und Gremien im Bereich von Währung und Wirtschaft, Selbstverlag der Deutschen Bundesbank, Frankfurt am Main, 1997
Woll, A.: *Allgemeine Volkswirtschaftslehre*, Vahlen, München, 2000
Woll, A.: *Wirtschaftslexikon*, Oldenbourg, München, 2000

Index/Englisch

account for 15; 98
actual 18; 126
address 45
adequate 182
adhere to 157
administer 139
advocate 12
aftermath 38; 175
agreement 16
aim 147
align/alignment 108; 157; 166
amount to 15
appoint 138; 141
appreciation 88
appropriate 182
approve 108; 141
argue 88
assessment 128
assumption 123; 125
bad cheque 175
balance of payments 93
bank notes 139
benefit 37
billion 96
boost 88
borrowings 88; 91; 182
branch 22
budget 88
budget deficit 92
Bundesbank, the 124; 129
business administration 23
business cycle 88
buyer 54; 57
buying power 21
capital account balance of payments 93
capital flight 176; 180
ceteris paribus assumption 55; 63
(chair)person 138; 141
change to 36
charges 138
chart 59; 60; 123; 124
chartist 123; 124
cheque clearing 139; 149
child mortality 160
client 156; 161
collective bargaining 12; 19; 26
Cologne Debt Initiative 175

come to grips/come to terms *157;*
  167
commit *27; 156*
commitment *37; 48*
commodity *56*
common *28*
company designation *123; 126*
compensation *18*
competition *79*
confidentiality *157; 164*
consumer good *12; 21*
contain *184*
contingency *167*
continuing education *47*
convergence criteria *108; 112*
core competency *123; 126*
corrected for *18*
Council of Ministers *111*
countermeasures *123; 128*
crank up *88; 91*
credit (facilities) *138; 145; 157, 164*
crowd out *88; 91*
crucial *88*
currency *96; 97*
current account balance of
  payments *93*
curve *60; 64*
customer *161*
deal with *148*
debt forgiveness/debt relief ... *175*
debt servicing *179*
debt swap *183*
decision making *156*
defect/defective *36; 41*
deficiency *36; 41*
deliberate *124*
delivery *40*
demand *36; 42; 54; 76; 77*
deposits *143*
deregulation *23; 108*
destitution *184*

developing countries *159*
diagram *59*
digital divide *175*
direct *142*
discount rate *148*
discretionary fiscal policy *94*
disguised unemployment *36; 39*
dismissal *12; 23; 24*
distinct/distinctive *22*
dominate *163*
doves *138*
downturn *89*
downward trend *123*
duties *73; 78*
earmark *175*
earned income *12*
ecocide *176; 181; 187*
economic policy *18; 37*
economic stimulation *89*
upturn *90*
Economics; Economic Sciences *23*
effective *94*
efficient *94*
elastic; elasticity *54; 63*
elderly *43*
eliminate *175*
emerging countries *156; 159*
employment *24*
employment exchange *12*
employment protection *12; 25*
employment rate *36; 37; 42*
ensure *108*
equilibrium price *55; 62*
Eurocentric *114*
Eurocrats *114*
eurocurrencies *114*
eurodollars *114*
Euroland *114*
European Central Bank *108; 113*
European Commission *108; 111*
European Communities *117*

European Court of Auditors 112
European Court of Justice 112
European Economic and Monetary
   Union 108; 110; 111
European Parliament 111
European Union 111
Europhile 114
Euro-sceptic 114
Eurozone 114
even 157
eventually 91; 157
evident 156
exceed 129
Exchange Rate Mechanism 112
execute 108
exempt 157
expand/expansion 88; 159
extend/extension 159
external balance 18
fallback line 124; 129
fault 41
favourite notion 163
Federal Open-Market Committee
   140
Federal Reserve System 138; 139
figure 12; 14
final goods 56
financial account balance of
   payments 93
financial injection 89; 95
fiscal drag 94
fiscal policy 88; 94
fiscal stance 94
Five Wise Men 17
flexitime 26
flounder 108
for the time being 108
forefront 156
framework 36
fringe benefits 19
fundamental analysis 123

gain 12; 21; 129
gainful employment 37
generate 54; 124
goal 147
golden handshake 25
goods 56
govern 138; 142
government debt 166
government spending 88; 92
gradient 60; 62
graph 54; 58
gross domestic product (GDP) 89;
   95
Group of ... Eight 156; 157; 162; 163
halt 184
handle 139; 148
hence 17
higher education 43
histograms 60
holdings 175
IDA 179
illiteracy 160
impact 88
impediment 89; 95
import restrictions 73; 78
inadequate 182
incentive 37; 48
income 64; 138; 146
inducement 48
industrial sector 12
ineffective 88
inelastic 55
ingenious 183
interact 54; 62
interest 146
intermediate goods 56
International Monetary Fund 156
investment banks 143
involvement 48
irreconcilable 108
irrevocable 108; 114

Appendix/Index 209

issue *156*
jagged *123; 126*
job (opening) *12; 37*
job allocation *23*
job seeker *37; 48*
keep at bay *166*
labour *37; 38; 48*
labour market *36; 37*
labour participation *42*
LDCs *160*
leeway *12; 23*
lender *148*
lending rate *88*
lending *182*
levy *78*
line diagrams; linear curves *60; 64*
loan *161; 175*
loan employment *12; 24*
long term *88; 92*
loophole *157; 166*
Maastricht Treaty *108; 113*
managing director *157*
manpower *36*
marginal cost rule *73; 75*
Middle East *73*
minimum reserve requirements *138*
monetary policy *108; 114; 138; 146*
money laundering *157*
money price *74*
money supply *138; 144*
money wages *18*
moot point *124*
moving averages *123; 125*
national commercial banks *138; 142*
national debt *157*
national income *175*
national security contributions *19*
negligible *88*
NICs *160*
nominal prices *74*
nominate *141*

nonproducible asset *61*
nose-dive *123; 128*
notably *138*
notch *127*
notice *24*
number *13*
objection *89; 97*
objective *147*
occupational (re)training *37; 47*
off track *156*
official *157*
oil shock *108*
on credit *157*
open unemployment *37*
open-market operations *139; 147*
ordinary *28*
origin *65*
out of hand *88*
out of sync(h) *88*
outage time *36*
overtime (hours) *13*
pari passu *123*
part-time employment *12*
pattern *12; 125*
payload subsidy *47*
payment *139; 148*
penalty *157*
perk *19*
pledge *175*
plot *57*
plummet/plunge *128*
policy/politics *45*
politicking *45*
poverty *175; 184*
prepositional objects *69*
prevail *157*
price determinant *73*
price *54; 62; 74; 80*
primaries *160*
prime rate *139; 148*
procurement *73; 76*

producer good 56
production site 73
public (sector) 88; 92; 166
purchase 57
purchasing power 12; 21
rapprochement 108
real pay/real wages 12; 18
recession 89
recognize 164
record 123
recover/y 88; 90; 123
recur 176
redundancy pay 25
regular employment 46
release 157; 165
remuneration 18
repos 144
request 175
reservation 157
resistance line 124; 129
retail bank 143
retire/retirement 37
revalue 175
rule 163
salaried employee 13
sale 12
say 130; 156; 157
scatter diagrams 60
scheme 46; 108
secondary education 42
securities 145
seller 54
semi-skilled workers 28
senior 43
serrated 126
shape 55
share price 123; 125
shedding jobs 37; 45
short-time work 37
short-term 88
single currency 108; 109

Single Market 116
skilled worker 13; 28
slope 55
slump 123
so 17; 43
social security contribution 19
spending power 21
stance 123; 128
state-chartered banks 138
stock market 157
stoke up 97
stopgap measure 37
submit 108
subsistence farming 160
substanti-al/-ate 88; 97
supplier 60
supply 54; 77
sustain; sustainable 175; 176; 180
tackle 45
target 139; 147
temporary employment 24
term 138
therefore 17
thrust phase 124
thus 17
total 15; 156; 175
trade barriers 78
Treasury/Treasury bills 145; 157; 165
trillion 96
trough 123
unemployment 12; 40
unity 55; 63
university course 36
unskilled worker 28
unsound 89
utilization; utilize 12; 23; 73
vacancy 12
vacation replacement 25
vocational (re)training 47
wage 13; 18; 19; 27
waive 175

wake *38*
ward off *157; 166*
World Bank *156; 158*

x-axis/abscissa *54; 58*
y-axis/ordinate *54; 58*

Index/Deutsch

Abgaben *72; 78*
Abkommen *173*
Absatz *21; 41*
Abstimmung *107*
abstürzen *121; 128*
Abwärtstrend *121; 122; 128*
Abszisse *58*
Achsenkreuz *65*
Aktienkursbewegungen *120; 125*
älter *43*
Analphabetismus *160*
ändern *39*
Angebot *52; 77*
angelernte Arbeitskraft *28*
anheizen *87; 97*
ankurbeln *86; 92*
annähern; Annäherung *106; 109; 121*
Anreiz *48*
Arbeit/er *38*
Arbeitgeberleistungen *18*
Arbeitsamt *16*
Arbeitslosigkeit *40*
Arbeitsmarkt *38*
Arbeitsnachfrage *42*
Arbeitsplatz *15; 39*
Arbeitsschutz *26*
Arbeitssuchende/r *48*
Armut *172; 174; 184*
auf die Schliche kommen *155*
auf Kredit *155; 164*
Aufschwung *87; 90; 92*
Aufwärtstrend *122*
Aufwertung *93*
aus den Fugen geraten *154*
Ausgangspreis *52; 61*
auslasten *87; 97*

ausgeprägt *122; 130*
Ausgestaltung *137*
ausgleichen *154*
Aushilfe *25*
Auslandsschulden *172*
ausrichten *155; 166*
Ausschöpfung *87*
außenwirtschaftliches Gleichgewicht *18*
Bankeinlage; Sichteinlage; Termineinlage *143*
Bankgeschäft *155*
beanspruchen *72*
bedienen *173*
Bekämpfung *13*
bereinigt *18*
Bereitstellung *72; 76*
berichten *137*
beschaffen *76*
Beschaffung *77*
Beschäftigte *27*
Beschäftigung *46*
bestätigen *141*
Bestrafung *155*
Betriebswirtschaftslehre *23*
Bildung *42; 184*
Billion *96*
Bonität *165*
Börsenkrach *155*
Börsenkurs *120*
Branche *22*
Bruttoinlandsprodukt *87; 95*
Ceteris-paribus-Bedingung *53; 63*
Darlehen *161*
Defizit *87*
deutlich *77*

Deutsche Bundesbank *129*
Devisenmarkt *122*
diensterfahren *154; 163*
digitale Kluft *172*
Diskontsatz *137; 148*
diskretionäre Fiskalpolitik *94*
durchbrechen *129*
Effekt *87*
einfach *28*
einfallsreich *183*
Einflussgröße *53*
Eingriff *86*
Einhalt gebieten *174; 184*
Einheitswährung *107*
Einigung *16*
einlösen *173*
Einkommen; verfügbares *64*
Einnahmen *137; 146*
Eins *53; 63*
Einsatz *23*
Einschätzung *121; 128*
einschlägig *28*
Einwand *87; 97*
elastisch *53; 63*
Elastizitätswert *63*
Endprodukte *56*
Energienachfrage *72*
Engagement *48*
Entlohnung *18*
Entscheidungsbasis; -ebene *154; 158; 162*
entstehen *106; 109*
Entwicklungshilfe *173*
Entwicklungsländer *154; 159; 172*
Entwicklungsziele *174*
Erfahrungen *87*
erholen *90*
erlassen *172*
erleben *106*
erledigen *148*
ernennen; Ernennung *136; 141*

Ertragslage *121; 126*
Erwerbsquote; -beteiligung *42*
Erwerbstätige/r *46*
Europäische Kommission *106*
Europäisches Währungssystem *106; 110*
Europäische Zentralbank *107; 113*
Europäischer Gerichtshof *112*
Europäischer Rechnungshof *112*
Europäisches Parlament *111*
Europäisches Währungsinstitut *107; 113*
eventuell *91*
expansiv *87*
Facharbeitskraft *27*
Fehler *41*
fest *155*
Finanzbehörde *165*
Finanzbürokrat *154*
Finanzpolitik; finanzpolitisch *86; 87; 90*
Fiskalpolitik; fiskalpolitisch *86; 87; 94*
flexible Arbeitszeit *26*
Folge *172*
Förderung *72; 75*
Fortbildung und Umschulung *47*
freier Fall *122*
Fundamentalanalyse *120*
Funktionsträger *154*
Gebühren *137*
Gegenmaßnahme *121; 128*
Geheimablage *155*
Gehör finden *160*
Geld- und Kapitalverkehr *112*
Geld- und Kreditpolitik *87; 114; 146*
Geldinstitut *136*
Geldmenge; Geldangebot *136; 144*
Geldspritze *137*
Geldwäsche *155*
Gerade *65; 122*

Geschäftsbank 136; 142
Geschäftsführer 154; 163
gewähren 154
gewährleisten 137
gezackt 121; 126
Gleichgewichtspreis 53; 62
gleitender Durchschnitt 120; 121; 125
goldener Handschlag 26
graphische Darstellung 65; 125
Grenzkostenregel 72; 75
Grundsatz 155
Gruppe der Fünf ; Gruppe der Sieben ... 154; 162
Gruppe X; Zehnergruppe 163
Gut 52; 56
gut machen 122; 129
Handelsgut 57; 173
Haushaltsdefizit 92
herausgeben 165
herrschen 155; 163
Hindernis 96
HIPC-Initiative 172
hochstilisieren 173; 179
hoch verschuldete Länder 172; 173; 180
IDA 179
im Sande verlaufen 106
Importquote 87; 97
in den Griff bekommen 155; 166
in Schach halten 155; 167
Interimsausschuss 154
Internationaler Währungsfonds 154; 158
Investment-Analyst 120
jobben 25
Kapitalbilanz 93
Kapitalflucht 173; 180
Kaufkraft 21
Kernkompetenz 121; 126
Kindersterblichkeit 160

Klassenhäufigkeitstabelle; Histogramm 60
Kölner Schuldeninitiative 172
Konjunktur; konjunkturell 40; 86; 89; 99
Konjunkturspritze 87; 90; 95
Konjunktursteuerung 87; 92
Konkurrenz 73
Konsumgut 21
Kontrolle 154
Konvergenzkritierien 107
konzertierte Aktion 87
Korrektur nach unten 133
Kredit(aufnahme) 86; 87; 182
Kredite für nicht vorhersehbare Ausgaben 155; 167
Kreditversorgung 145
Kreditzins für erste Adressen 137; 149
Kunde/in 154; 161
kündigen; Kündigung 24;25
Kursverlauf 120
Kurve 121; 126
Leiharbeit 25
Leistungsbilanz 93
leiten 142
Leitzins 86; 90
Liberalisierung 107
Lieblingsvorstellung 155; 163
Lieferung 40
Lohn 18
Lohnkostenzuschuss 48
Lohnnebenkosten 19
Lohnpolitik 18
Maßnahme 46
Material 40
Milliarde 96
Mindestlohn 19
Mindestreserven 136; 137
Ministerrat 111
Mittlerer Osten 77

Motiv 125
mühselig 106
Muster 125
Nachfrage; nachfragen 52; 57; 76; 77
nachfragewirksam 87; 95
nachhaltige Entwicklung 173; 180
nachteilig 133
Nachwehen 38
Naher Osten 77
Nettokapitalzustrom 87; 92
Neubewertung 172
Neuverschuldung 87; 95
nicht vermehrbare Güter 61
Niedrigzinskredit 180
Nominallohn 18
Nominalpreis 74
Notfall 167
offene Stelle 15
Offenmarktausschuss 136; 140
Offenmarktgeschäft 147
öffentlich 87; 95; 145
Ordinate 58
Organisationsform 121; 126
pari passu 121; 128
Parität 122
Pensionsgeschäft 144
plädieren 87
Plan 46
Politik 45
preisbildender Faktor 72
Preis 74
Preiselastizität 52; 62
Privatinvestition 91
Problem 45
Produktionsgut 56
Produktivitätszunahme 20; 21
Pro-forma-Streichung 174; 181
prozyklisch 87
realer Preis 74
Reallohn 18; 20

Reservebank 136; 140
Rezession 87; 94
Rohstoffe 160
Rückzahlung 174
Rückzugs- oder Widerstandslinie 122; 129
Sachverständigenrat 18
schaffen 45
Schatzanweisung; -wechsel 145
Schätzung 122
Scheck-Clearing 137; 149
Schema 125
schleppend 174
Schlupfloch 155; 166
Schnittpunkt 52; 62
Schubphase 122; 129
Schulden 172; 173; 174
Schwachstelle 155
sich an etw. halten 155
sich einsetzen für 93
sich engagieren 27
sich erholen 121
sich verschieben 64
so; also 17; 43
sogenannt 107
Sozialversicherungsbeitrag 19
Spielraum 23; 173
staatlich 74; 87
Staatsausgaben 74; 87; 92
Staatsverschuldung 74; 166
Stabilität 107
ständiges Mitglied 136
Steigung 52; 60; 62; 65
Stelle 45
Stellvertreter 136
Steuerungsmechanismus 154
stichhaltig 87
stimmberechtigt 136
Streichung; streichen 172; 173; 181
Streuungsdiagramm 60
Subsistenzwirtschaft 160

Tagesgeldsatz 137
Talfahrt 121; 128
Talsohle 90; 121
Tariflohn 19
Tarifverhandlungen 19; 26
Tauben 136; 140
These 125
Tiefpunkt 121; 128
tragfähig 87; 97
Trend 125
Trennungsentschädigung 25
Überbewertung 155
Übereinkunft 16
überhaupt 179
übertragen 155
überwachen; Überwachung 155
umdenken 160
Umschuldung 174
Umschulung 47
Umwelt 173; 180
ungedeckter Scheck 173
ungelernte Arbeitskraft 28
Unternehmerbanken 143
unüberbrückbar 106
unwiderruflich 107; 114
unwirksam 87
unzureichend 182
Urlaubsvertretung 25
Verabschiedung 27
Verarmungsgrad 174; 182
Verbrauchsteuern 78
verdeckte Arbeitslosigkeit 39
Verdienst 18
verdrängen; Verdrängung 86; 91
vereinbaren; Vereinbarung 16; 106
verfügbares Einkommen 64
Vergütung 18
Verlauf; verlaufen 52; 55; 106
Verpflichtung 27
verschonen 155
Versorgung 72

Vertrag von Maastricht 113
Vertraulichkeit 155; 164
vertreten 136
Volkswirtschaftslehre 23
vorgehen 154
Vorhaben 137
vorläufig 107
Vorschlag 174
Vorsitzende/r 136; 141
Vorstand 136
Wachstumsimpulse 87
Währungssystem 136
Wechselkurs 121
wechseln 39
Wegbereiter 154
wehren 166
Weltbank 154
Wert 53; 120; 122
Wertpapiere 145
Wettbewerb; wettbewerblich 72; 73; 79
wirken 86; 91
Wirtschafts- und Währungsunion 106; 107; 110
Wirtschaftskriminalität 155
wirtschaftspolitisch 44
Wirtschaftswissenschaft 23
Zahlungsbilanz 93
Zahlungsverkehr 137; 149
Zeitarbeit 25
Zentralbank 139; 140
Zerstörung 173; 180
Ziel 137; 147
Zins 87; 147
Zölle 78
zurückgreifen auf 179
Zustimmung 16
Zwischenerzeugnis 56